praise for *good fish*

"Delicious recipes and spot-on advice for makin[...] [...]y seafood choices."

—**MONTEREY BAY AQUARIUM SEAFOOD WATCH**

....

"Whether you're a fish fanatic who owns a copper poaching pan and knows your fishmonger by name or a seafood scaredy-cat who hears the soundtrack from *Jaws* at the mere thought of buying—let alone cooking— a live Dungeness crab, *Good Fish* deserves a spot in your kitchen."

—*SEATTLE TIMES*

....

"*Good Fish* is a go-to book in my kitchen! Becky Selengut's recipes for the consciously minded piscivore strike a balance between chef-y and practical. Becky is an amiable stove-side companion who reveals the secrets of good fish cookery and will have you smoking sardines in no time."

—**LANGDON COOK**, author of *Upstream: Searching for Wild Salmon, from River to Table*

....

"Selengut has reaffirmed her commitment to both the ecosystems and the dining tables of the Pacific Northwest. *Good Fish* celebrates ethical seafood through delectable recipes that enshrine Selengut not only as a formidable culinary force, but as an indispensable guardian of our oceans. We need more chefs like this."

—**CASSON TRENOR**, author of *Sustainable Sushi* and *Time* magazine's "Hero of the Environment"

....

"I love Becky's wit almost as much as her great recipes! I can't think of a better kitchen guide to seafood, especially our Pacific Northwest favorites."

—**RANDY HARTNELL**, founder and president, Vital Choice Wild Seafood & Organics

....

"*Good Fish* is a good read! Becky Selengut is authentic, funny, and a great recipe writer! This clever book will help anyone learn about sustainable and seasonal fish. Her storytelling about these diverse dishes conjures up aromas and places I want to be in and makes me want to try these beautiful dishes at home."

—**ELIZABETH FALKNER**, chef, author, artist

good fish

100 Sustainable Seafood Recipes
from the Pacific Coast

BECKY SELENGUT

Photography by Clare Barboza
Beverage pairings by April Pogue

SASQUATCH BOOKS
SEATTLE

to dad

contents

1 Preface to the New Edition
3 Introduction
5 How to Use This Book
17 Sustainable Seafood Basics

25 *shellfish*
27 Clams
41 Mussels
53 Oysters
65 Dungeness Crab
79 Shrimp
91 Scallops
107 Squid

119 *finfish*
121 Wild Salmon
157 Pacific Halibut
177 Black Cod
189 Rainbow Trout
201 Albacore Tuna
217 Arctic Char
229 Lingcod
243 Pacific Cod
255 Mahi-Mahi
267 Wahoo (Ono)

279 *littlefish & eggs*
281 Sardines & Herring
297 Sustainable Caviar

309 Acknowledgments
311 Appendix A: A Note on Eating Raw Seafood
313 Appendix B: Sustainable Seafood Resources
314 Index

recipes

SHELLFISH

clams

31 Tamarind and Ginger Clams

33 Steamers with Beer

34 Razor Clam Chowder

35 Homemade Fettuccine with Clams and Marjoram

38 Geoduck Crudo with Shiso Oil

mussels

44 Mussels with Guinness Cream

45 Mussels with Apple Cider and Thyme Glaze

47 Mussels with Pancetta and Vermouth

48 Mussels with Bacon and Israeli Couscous

51 Mussels with Tomato-Espelette Butter

oysters

57 Oyster and Artichoke Soup

59 Hangtown Fry

60 Oysters on the Half Shell with Cucumber Sorbet

61 Oysters with Lemon-Thyme Sabayon

62 Jet's Oyster Succotash

dungeness crab

69 Dungeness Crab Panzanella with
     Charred-Tomato Vinaigrette

71 Newspaper Crab with Three Sauces

73 Chilled Cucumber-Coconut Soup with Dungeness Crab

75 Dungeness Crab Mac and Cheese

76 Dungeness Crab with Bacon-Cider Sauce

shrimp

83 Weeknight Linguine with Spot Prawns and Basil

84 Tom Yum Goong (Spicy Shrimp and Lemongrass Soup)

86 Pink Shrimp Salad with Grapefruit and Mint

88 Grilled Spot Prawns with "Crack" Salad

scallops

94 Scallop Crudo
97 Scallops, Grits, and Greens
99 Scallops with Carrot Cream and Marjoram
102 Summer Scallops with Corn Soup
104 Scallops with Tarragon Beurre Blanc

squid

110 Quick Squid with Red Chile Sauce and Herbs
112 Squid with Chickpeas, Potatoes, and Piquillo Peppers
113 Wok-Seared Squid with Lemongrass, Chile, and Basil
114 Chorizo-and-Apple-Stuffed Squid with Sherry Pepper Sauce
117 Grilled Squid with Tamarind and Orange

FINFISH

wild salmon

PINK AND KETA

128 Wild Salmon Chowder with Fire-Roasted Tomatoes
129 Hajime's Steamed Banana Leaf Salmon
131 Agedashi Salmon with Asparagus, Shiitakes, and Salmon Roe
132 The Easiest Recipe in This Book
133 Salmon in Spiced Tamarind Soup
135 Kerala Curry with Coconut Milk and Curry Leaves

COHO, SOCKEYE, AND KING

137 Jerk-Spiced Salmon with Coconut Pot Liquor and Sweet Potato Fries
140 Seared Salmon Tikka Masala
143 Grilled Salmon with Watercress Salad, Rye Croutons,
      and Buttermilk Dressing
144 Coriander-and-Lemon-Crusted Salmon with Poached Egg,
      Roasted Asparagus, and Hazelnuts
146 Grilled Sockeye Salmon with Fennel Two Ways
148 Roasted Salmon with Wild Mushrooms and Pinot Noir Sauce
151 Coffee-and-Spice-Rubbed Salmon Tacos with Charred Cabbage,
      Mango Salsa, and Avocado Cream
153 Fideos with Salmon, Clams, and Smoked Paprika
154 Seared Salmon, Morels, and Peas with Green Goddess Sauce

pacific halibut

159 Roasted Halibut with Radicchio-Pancetta Sauce, Peas, and Artichokes
161 Steamed Halibut with Sizzling Chile-Ginger Oil
162 Smoked Halibut with Stinging Nettle Sauce and Nettle Gnocchi
166 Halibut Escabèche with Anchovy-Almond Salsa Verde
169 Halibut Tacos with Tequila-Lime Marinade and Red Cabbage Slaw
171 Halibut Coconut Curry with Charred Chiles and Lime
174 Halibut with Vanilla, Kumquat, and Ginger

black cod

180 Roasted Black Cod with Bok Choy and Soy Caramel Sauce
183 Jerry's Black Cod with Shiso-Cucumber Salad and
　　Carrot Vinaigrette
184 Sake-Steamed Black Cod with Ginger and Sesame
186 Tataki's "Faux-Nagi"

rainbow trout

192 Cast-Iron Rainbow Trout
194 Pan-Fried Trout with Dilly Beans
197 Quinoa Cakes with Smoked Trout and Chive Sour Cream
198 Smoked Trout Mousse with Radish and Cucumber Quick Pickle

albacore tuna

204 Albacore Parcels with Mint-Pistachio Pesto
207 Albacore Niçoise
209 Olive Oil–Poached Albacore Steaks with Caper–Blood Orange Sauce
211 Seared Albacore with Ratatouille and Caramelized Figs
214 Gin-and-Tonic-Cured Albacore with Dandelion Crackers and
　　Lime Cream

arctic char

219 Pan-Fried Char with Crispy Mustard Crust
220 Char with Grilled Romaine, Grapes, and Balsamic Vinegar
223 Char with Roasted Cauliflower and Apple-Vanilla Vinaigrette
226 Char Katsu with Ponzu Sauce and Cucumber-Hijiki Salad

lingcod

233 Lingcod Bouillabaisse with Piquillo Peppers
235 Lingcod with Crispy Chickpeas and Quick-Pickled Apricots
238 Lingcod with Citrus and Arbequina Olives
240 Lingcod and Spot Prawn Paella with Charred Lemons

pacific cod	245	Cod and Squid Okonomiyaki
	248	Pacific Cod and Mussels with Crispy Potatoes and Warm Olive Oil and Bay Broth
	250	Thai Fish Cakes with Cucumber-Chile Sauce
	252	Jamaican Cod Run Down with Boiled Green Bananas
mahi-mahi	258	Mahi-Mahi Red Curry with Thai Basil and Lime Leaves
	260	Mahi-Mahi with Fried Basil, Avocado, and Tomato Salad
	263	Mahi-Mahi with South Indian Spiced Mango
	264	Mahi-Mahi with Tostones, Black Beans, and Tabasco Honey
wahoo (ono)	271	Wahoo with Orange-Chile Caramel and Blackened Broccolini
	272	Wahoo with Grilled Pineapple and Poblano Pepper Salsa
	274	Wahoo Torta with Pickled Jalapeños and Tomatoes
	276	Wahoo with Coriander-and-Cardamon-Spiced Coconut Sauce

LITTLEFISH & EGGS

sardines & herring	284	Dad's Sardines on Crackers with Caramelized Onions
	285	White Bean and Sardine Salad with Fried Eggs
	287	Skillet Herring with Fennel, Currant, and Pine Nut Salad
	288	Emmer Pasta con le Sarde
	291	Smoked Sardines with Piquillo Pepper Sauce
	294	Smoked Herring on Rye Bread with Radishes, Salted Butter, and Pickled Onions
sustainable caviar	299	Caviar Hash
	301	Four-Star Duck Eggs with Farmed White Sturgeon Caviar
	302	Potato and Beet Latkes with Horseradish Sour Cream and Caviar
	304	Caviar on Buttered Brioche with Crème Fraîche and Chives
	306	Celery Root Tart with Caramelized Leeks and Caviar

preface to the new edition

I'm thrilled to be able to dive back into the world of sustainable seafood and offer this fully updated and expanded edition of *Good Fish* to new and old readers alike. A lot has changed since the book first rolled out in 2011, and the good news is that Pacific Coast fisheries are being better managed and we're starting to see the results. Many fish populations have begun to come back due to good laws with teeth and collaboration between government, nonprofits, and fishermen. Several Pacific rockfish species, for example, are bouncing back from severe overfishing. Aquaculture (fish farming) has made great technological advances, such as reducing waste while helping to meet a greater demand for seafood.

There is still more work to be done, of course. Climate change is leading to warmer waters, which negatively affect habitat and species. Mislabeling of species continues to be rampant; bycatch is still a problem. But on the whole, the good news outweighs the bad, and I've been happy to see consumers asking more questions and looking critically at where their seafood is coming from. America is now—more than ever—a great country to source your seafood from. As I said back in 2011, the single best thing you can do to preserve our fish for the future is to source your seafood domestically. I'm happy to say that the fifteen species selected in the first edition are still good fish, thanks to the hard work, patience, and discipline of our ocean's stakeholders.

The original edition of this book focused on species common to markets in Alaska, British Columbia, Washington, Oregon, and California. With the addition of mahi-mahi and wahoo in this new one, I got to play around with two excellent Hawaiian fish staples as well. Herring, a fantastic littlefish harvested in Alaska and California, finds its way into a few recipes; razor clams, dug up on the coasts of Alaska, Washington, and Oregon, join the rest of its West Coast clam brethren (geoduck and manila clams). Pacific cod, or true cod, mostly known to the home cook in fish-and-chips form, gets run through its paces as an affordable and sustainable option. One of my favorite fish, lingcod, missed the boat in the first edition for space reasons, and I'm so happy to have more room to include it here. The wild salmon section has been much expanded, organized around species and best cooking methods: moist-heat cooking for the leaner pink and keta (chum) and dry-heat techniques for the richer coho, sockeye, and king. Finally, halibut also gets an expansion with a couple new recipes.

Regardless of which seafood covered in this new edition appeals to you most, I hope you enjoy cooking these recipes and sharing them around your table. Feel free to reach out to me anytime via my website: BeckySelengut .com. I love hearing from you.

—Becky, March 2018

REMEMBER THESE "GOOD FISH" RULES

F: Farmed can be OK (verify that it is done responsibly).

I: Investigate your source (ask questions; support good chefs, fishmongers, and markets).

S: Smaller is better (limit portion size; eat smaller fish, like sardines and young albacore).

H: Home (buy Pacific Coast fish because the United States has higher sustainability standards for fisheries, your money stays in the local economy, and you help the environment by not shipping seafood around the world).

introduction

I might as well have grown up with pickled herring in my baby bottle. I was weaned just as soon as I could drop my dime-store fishing pole in the big lake that was our backyard. My first real job was down the street at a seafood market in northwest New Jersey, on the shores of Lake Hopatcong. On weekends you'd find me selling crab-stuffed flounder rolls to bridge-and-tunnel businessmen and nice ladies from the neighborhood.

I eventually moved out west. While attending culinary school in Seattle, I stared in awe at a massive halibut's eyes, contemplating their migration from the sides of its head to the top. Two tours through Italian restaurants introduced me to the diversity of regional fish dishes. At one place, I worked with tuna roe (*bottarga*), and I soaked salt cod for fritters. Lots and lots of salt cod. At the other, I grilled little silver fish while the Italian owner waxed poetic about the best fish in the world (Grilled! From the Mediterranean! Salt! Olive oil! *Eccellente!*).

My most formative restaurant experience was cooking at the famous Herbfarm Restaurant in Woodinville, Washington. I was the fish girl there: I held still-quivering abalone in my hands, shucked the tiniest native Olympia oysters, faced more Dungeness crabs—antennae to eye—than I care to count, and scooped out luscious golden eggs from spiny sea urchins while wearing thick rubber gloves for self-defense. There I cradled in my arms, just barely, the stunning majesty of a forty-pound wild Alaska king salmon, as you would a precious baby, and I chuckled alongside my fellow line cooks at the phallic ridiculousness of a geoduck. I was miles and miles from the Atlantic Coast.

With the spirit of a local, I ran the galley of a boat headed up the Inside Passage to Alaska, peeling spot prawns and filleting salmon before climbing down the ladder to my quarters, each step pulling a bit more of the New Jersey out of the girl. A few winters ago I shed any remaining vestiges of my birthplace. I joined dozens of others on a traditional night dig for razor clams. There were cars lined up as far as the eye could see, their headlights like luminaria leading the way up the coast. When I got my limit and headed back to the cabin, I remember feeling that I had finally gone completely native.

The world of seafood is much more complicated now than it was when I pulled my first Jersey sunfish out of the lake; shortsighted economic gain, a morass of bureaucracy, and a universe of misinformation complicate it. It's clear that we have an insatiable appetite for far more than the oceans, rivers, and lakes can provide. Guilt and food are a terrible combination, certain to give you indigestion, or as my friend says, "Guilt makes for bad gravy." Denial or ignorance about the consequences of our food choices is far too widespread. Most insidious is the attitude that we might as well indulge in all types of fish while they are still around (because who knows when they might disappear).

My intention with this book is to help simplify some very complicated issues, thereby empowering you to make better, more sustainable seafood choices. The fish that appear in this book made the cut, and I leaned heavily on the highly regarded Monterey Bay Aquarium Seafood Watch Program, among other nonprofit organizations such as FishChoice, when conducting my research. Many factors are considered to determine which fisheries are sustainable, including, for example, the type of gear used to harvest the fish, the relative abundance of the species, the amount of accidental bycatch of non-target species, and the safety of the waters from which the fish are harvested.

This cookbook celebrates seafood from up and down the western coast of the United States, including Hawaii: seafood that is well managed, and fished or farmed in such a way as to protect the environment. I hope that the good management of these excellent choices and the hard work of those who educate us about making wise purchasing decisions will help keep all of these species around for a very long time.

There is a story evolving here, and the plot hinges on the health of our oceans and the sustainability of our fish. You, the consumer, are the protagonist. The most important thing you can do is ask questions. With each type of seafood I cover, I pose questions you might ask your fishmongers in order to be sure you are purchasing seafood that is healthy for you and your family as well as for our oceans. If you are satisfied with the answers, support those fishmongers. Tell your friends about them. Encourage them to continue doing the right thing by giving them your business.

Forgive me the double negative, but this book isn't about what you *shouldn't* do. It's a celebration of what you *can* do. Eat these fish with joy, share these recipes with your favorite people, and know that you are actively doing your part to ensure that seafood survives—and perhaps someday soon, thrives again.

how to use this book

This book is divided into sections based on three broad categories of seafood: shellfish (clams, mussels, oysters, Dungeness crab, shrimp, scallops, and squid), finfish (wild salmon, Pacific halibut, black cod, rainbow trout, albacore tuna, arctic char, lingcod, Pacific cod, mahi-mahi, and wahoo), and littlefish and eggs (sardines, herring, and caviar).

My goal is to help you feel comfortable and confident purchasing these twenty types of sustainable seafood from your local fishmonger, fisherman, or seafood counter. Look for the following information at the beginning of each chapter:

WHAT MAKES THIS A GOOD FISH

Before asking you to wield your very influential buying power, I want to make sure I've given you the most current information about why I've included these particular species.

BY ANY OTHER NAME

Seafood naming can be very confusing: one person's black cod is another person's sablefish. This is the section where I list all the names you might see for the type of seafood you are purchasing. Keep in mind that the best way to identify a fish is to ask what the exact species is, which is why I have included Latin names.

SEASON

Just like produce, most types of seafood have a season; it is worth knowing so you can get the freshest quality at the right time of year. That said, well-handled frozen seafood can often be of equal or better quality than fresh. For more information, see Fresh Versus Frozen on page 17.

BUYING TIPS

Here is where you'll find out all the things chefs do to scope out freshness and quality in seafood.

QUESTIONS TO ASK BEFORE YOU PULL OUT YOUR WALLET

There is only so much you can see with your eyes, smell with your nose, and touch with your fingertips (before getting caught). To get all the information you want, you should have a conversation with your fishmonger or fisherman. This is a great way to find out how much or how little the person selling the seafood knows about the product. This is also the time to inquire about its origin—there is a big difference between domestic farmed shrimp and imported shrimp, for example. The more you know, the easier it will be to decide if this is the seafood you want to purchase.

CARING FOR YOUR GOOD FISH

After reading all about how to select the freshest seafood, you'll want to know how best to store it. Shellfish, finfish, littlefish, and fish eggs all have different needs. This is the section where you'll learn how to keep your seafood as fresh as possible.

HOW THIS TYPE OF SEAFOOD IS RAISED OR HARVESTED

It's incredible how often we eat things without having any idea of how they came to be. This is especially true for farmed seafood. Look to this section to learn, for example, how a mussel can be farmed or how sustainable albacore is caught.

SUSTAINABLE SUBSTITUTES

There will be times when you head out shopping with a recipe in hand looking for a specific type of seafood. It's helpful to know ahead of time what some good substitutes are in case you can't find what you're looking for, or if the quality doesn't pass muster.

RECIPES

The recipes in this book are coded based on their difficulty: ▸◆▸◆▸◆ for the simplest, with easy-to-find ingredients and a 30- to 60-minute preparation time. ▸◆▸◆▸◆ for recipes that are more intermediate, take an hour or so to make, and may require a trip to a specialty market. ▸◆▸◆▸◆ for advanced recipes that might take multiple hours to prepare, contain subrecipes, and call for ingredients that could be more of a challenge to track down. Here's a little more about what you can expect from the different difficulty levels:

▸◆▸◆▸◆

EASY RECIPES

These recipes are designed for a beginner who is eager to learn how to cook with seafood but may be intimidated by it, or the home cook who wants a recipe that can be prepared in thirty minutes or so on a weeknight. I love helping novice cooks (especially intimidated novice cooks) learn how to work with seafood. In these recipes, I will gently hold your hand throughout the cooking process and hopefully anticipate any questions you might have. I tell this to all my students, but it's especially important for inexperienced cooks: make sure to read the recipe through at least twice before starting. Pay special attention to the Ingredients and Terms Defined (page 9), Tools of the Trade (page 13), and Fresh Versus Frozen (page 17) sections as well as the Anatomy of a Flake (page 126). Also be sure to check out the links for online cooking videos (see How-To Videos, page 8), especially if you are a visual learner like I am. Buy a digital thermometer or two—and use them!

▸◆▸◆▸◆

INTERMEDIATE RECIPES

These recipes are written for a more experienced home cook and can be prepared in about an hour. Intermediate-level recipes also expose you to less familiar species (geoduck) and ingredients (shiso, kombu, hijiki), and they may require some special equipment (a wok or ice cream machine) and advanced prep time (presalting or marinating fish).

▸◆▸◆▸◆

ADVANCED RECIPES

These recipes are designed for the adventurous and involved cook, perhaps a self-described "weekend warrior"—someone who is happy spending several hours in the kitchen and likes a challenge. They are also meant to appeal to my fellow chefs out there who want to flip directly to recipes that involve more advanced techniques such as fish smoking, pasta making, curing, or working with multiple steps, components, and/or garnishes.

Wine pairings are selected by my partner in life, work, and sometimes crime, the lovely (no bias here) and talented sommelier April Pogue. April has worked at some of the finest restaurants on the West Coast: Fifth Floor in San Francisco, Spago Beverly Hills, and in Seattle at Earth & Ocean, Yarrow Bay Grill, and Wild Ginger. April is currently the general manager of Loulay Kitchen and Bar in downtown Seattle. April first gives you her ideal pairing—a varietal she hopes you'll be able to find at your local wine shop. If you aren't able to get her first choice, she offers a secondary option as a good alternative. From time to time I stick my nose in and suggest a booze or beer pairing.

HOW-TO VIDEOS

Scattered throughout the book are links to short, fun how-to videos (denoted with the symbol ‡) in which I show you how to perform some techniques that are hard to capture in words. Check out GoodFishBook .com, where you'll see the following:

- How to select quality seafood
- How to clean a geoduck
- How to debeard, clean, and store mussels
- How to shuck an oyster
- How to cook and clean a Dungeness crab
- How to devein shrimp
- How to sear a scallop
- How to clean and cut up a whole squid
- How to remove the skin from a fish fillet
- How to remove pin bones from salmon, trout, or char
- How to fillet a fish
- How to wok-smoke fish
- How to butterfly and debone a sardine
- How to make a quenelle with caviar
- How to season a cast-iron skillet
- How to cook bacon in the oven without the mess
- How to scramble an egg

INGREDIENTS AND TERMS DEFINED

CLAM JUICE

If you don't have extra seafood stock stored in your freezer, bottled or canned clam juice makes a flavorful stock. Be sure to season your recipe cautiously as different brands can vary in saltiness.

DICING

Small dice: Technically—as in "culinary school instructor walking around class with a ruler"—this is defined as ¼ inch cubed, but just use that as a very rough guide. *Medium dice:* ½ inch cubed. *Large dice:* ¾ inch cubed.

DRY WHITE VERMOUTH

We're mostly red wine drinkers in my house, and I used to feel guilty cooking with white wine and then later realizing it had gone bad before we remembered to drink it. Dry white vermouth has a long shelf life and tastes delicious when used as a cooking wine—after all, it's a fortified white wine infused with herbs and spices. (I thank my friend Susan for teaching me this handy tip.)

FISH SAUCE

Fish sauce can be found in the Asian foods aisle of large supermarkets. It's made from fermented anchovies and is one of those very special ingredients that adds an incredible salty-savory umami taste to foods. One wonders who the first person was to taste the fermented juices of rotting anchovies and declare it a delicious seasoning, but incredibly, they were right. Fish sauce on its own is pungent; in a dish it is magical. I've used many brands throughout the years with good results, but Red Boat is my favorite by far. There's no need to refrigerate fish sauce: it's already rotten!

HIGH-HEAT VEGETABLE OIL

A lot of folks don't know that each type of oil has a different point at which it will start smoking/burning (called the smoke point) and that smoking oils can be carcinogenic. I like to teach people to use the right oil for the job. When I specify using a high-heat vegetable oil for sautéing, pan-frying, or stir-frying, use any of the following oils: peanut, safflower, sunflower, coconut, or grapeseed. You can also fry with clarified butter (ghee). Look for expeller-pressed oils that are mechanically, not chemically, refined.

JERSEY GIRL See Introduction (page 3). Exit 28, in case you're wondering.

....

LEMON JUICE Always fresh squeezed, pretty please.

....

MIRIN Mirin is a sweet rice wine that can be found in the Asian foods aisle of most large supermarkets. Think of mirin as the Japanese version of an off-dry Riesling.

....

PACIFIC COAST For the purposes of this book, I've selected seafood that is either farmed or native to the US West Coast, British Columbia, Alaska, and Hawaii.

....

PANKO Panko is a flaked Japanese bread crumb that is becoming more and more popular as a substitute for old-fashioned bread crumbs. I really like the texture it lends to pan-fried foods, especially oysters or fried fillets—it seems to give the food an extra lightness and crunchiness. I know it has hit the mainstream because out on Washington's Long Beach Peninsula—which is razor-clamming territory—I saw it being sold in a large bulk bin at the local supermarket/hardware store.

....

SAKE Sake can now be found at most large supermarkets where wine is sold; you can substitute with Chinese rice wine in a pinch.

....

SALT For the purposes of this book, unless otherwise specified, assume fine sea salt. My favorite brand is Eden French Celtic. If you prefer to use kosher salt, I strongly recommend Diamond Crystal brand. You should use 1¾ teaspoons Diamond Crystal kosher salt for every 1 teaspoon fine sea salt called for in a recipe, as kosher salt takes up more volume with its larger crystals, but as always, check the seasoning as you cook and adjust to taste. Morton's brand kosher salt is really dense, so that substitution would be more like 1¼ teaspoons for every 1 teaspoon fine sea salt.

SEASONED RICE WINE VINEGAR

I use this ingredient a lot throughout the book. This is a convenience product made of rice vinegar that has some salt and sugar in it. You can make your own by heating ¼ cup plain rice vinegar with 4 teaspoons sugar and ½ teaspoon kosher salt. Stir until the sugar and salt melt. Cool before using. Seasoned rice wine vinegar makes the simplest dressing ever: just toss it with cucumbers, carrots, sesame seeds, etcetera—no oil necessary, though a drop or two of toasted sesame oil is magnificent.

SHISO

Shiso (also known as *perilla*) is sometimes called Japanese mint. You can find it at Japanese or Asian markets. Substitute with spearmint.

TAMARIND

Tamarind is sold in several forms: dried in the pod (in the produce section of some stores, especially Mexican markets); as a paste, with or without seeds; and as a thin concentrate. To remove seeds and sticky pulp, rehydrate the paste or pod innards in a small amount of hot water, then push the tamarind through a sieve. For convenience, I recommend buying the seedless paste. For use in recipes, 1 teaspoon paste is the equivalent of 1 tablespoon concentrate. Tamarind—in one form or another—is becoming very easy to find these days, but if you're having difficulty, lemon juice works fine in a pinch.

OYSTER SHUCKER

FILLETING KNIFE (SCIMITAR)

FISH SCALER

FISH SPATULA

CRAB CRACKER

FISH TWEEZERS

THERMOWORKS THERMOPOP
THERMOMETER

CHEF KNIFE

TOOLS OF THE TRADE

CAST-IRON SKILLET

I love cast iron so much, I wrote a dorky poem about it.

ODE TO A CAST-IRON SKILLET

Carry that weight and think of your foremothers
who never needed gym memberships—if they
could even imagine them.

Heave that iron and fight osteoporosis;
your skillet is a healer, a weapon, a tool.

Only in modern times could we cast aside cast iron
in favor of flimsy fry pans with deeply etched scars.
Heft that pan! Sear that scallop! Bake that cornbread!

Carry that weight and think of your foremothers
who never had those little flaps of skin under their arms.

You can watch a video I made about how to season a cast-iron skillet at GoodFishBook.com.

DIGITAL THERMOMETER
(see opposite page)

The surefire way to know if your fish is perfectly done is to use a digital thermometer. Sure, you look cool touching the fish to determine doneness (and I explain how to do that on page 126) but that takes time and experience. Fish you want to cook through (lingcod, halibut, etcetera) should be pulled off the heat at 130 to 135°F. I cook salmon to 120 to 125° for medium-rare, scallops to 125 to 130°. Seared rare albacore tuna should be pulled off the heat anytime before it hits 115°. My favorite thermometers are made by ThermoWorks.

DOG

Nothing is more effective at cleaning a kitchen floor than a dog. For the first edition of *Good Fish*, our Labrador retriever, Bubba, was a canine Zamboni, efficiently wet-mopping our floor with her tongue just as soon as we said the word. Our mutts Izzy and Pippin have followed in Bubba's footsteps and haven't skipped a lick.

FILLETING KNIFE
(see page 12)

Your knife need not be expensive or fancy, but it should be ever so slightly flexible to help you maneuver around delicate, curved rib bones. I think one in the range of seven inches is good for working with both small and larger fish. I like to use a larger knife, sometimes called a scimitar knife, to fillet whole salmon or albacore.

....

FISH SCALER
(see page 12)

Like pin boning, fish scaling is a job that fishmongers are happy to do for you, and for many reasons, you should be happy they are happy to do it. It's a messy job, and I know from experience that despite submerging the fish in a sink of cold water (highly encouraged), those scales tend to go everywhere, including onto your skin, where they become one with you. However, you might find yourself needing to scale a fish that was caught by someone you know, in which case this nifty tool will come in handy. Place the fish in a sink of cold water, wear an apron, and then run this tool from tail to head, grabbing and pulling off the scales. You can use a spoon if you don't have a fish scaler handy (not as effective, but still workable).

....

FISH SPATULA
(see page 12)

Sometimes it all comes down to the right tool—and a fish spatula, with its thin, metal, slightly upturned edge, really helps gently flip or transfer a delicate fillet or whole fish.

....

FISH TWEEZERS
(see page 12)

Fishmongers are usually happy to remove pin bones from salmon, trout, or char if you ask nicely, but sometimes they don't take enough care and can snap them in half or tear the flesh. The pin bones that run through a salmon or trout fillet can be brittle, and it takes some finesse to remove them (go to GoodFishBook.com to watch me demonstrate the technique). If you decide you want to try it yourself, you'll need a pair of fish tweezers. In a pinch, I've used clean needle-nose pliers or even kitchen tongs to remove pin bones.

OYSTER SHUCKER
(see page 12)

I've seen cooks and deckhands, fishermen and drunks open oysters with all manner of things: knives, screwdrivers, a hammer and nail, and keys. Just because it can be done doesn't mean it *should* be done, especially if you are a beginner. Whether your shucker is blunt or sharp is a personal choice, though I recommend blunt if you are a novice. Go to GoodFishBook.com for a demonstration of how to shuck oysters.

....

SCRUB BRUSH

A solid, stiff brush will come in handy when I suggest scrubbing off the little barnacle bits that have jumped on board your oyster shell, or the fibrous strands of algae and whatnot on your mussels. Wild clams, too, can use a good scrubbing.

....

SPICE GRINDER

I find a spice grinder to be an indispensable kitchen tool. You know those fancy, expensive spice blends that all the chefs are marketing these days? Some fresh spices plus a spice grinder and two minutes is all that keeps you from creating your own fresh blends with which to dress that gorgeous piece of fish before throwing it on the grill. I provide several recipes for spice blends that will get you started. I recommend a Krups F203.

sustainable seafood basics

FRESH VERSUS FROZEN

Ah, that age-old question for which too many have a knee-jerk answer: "Oh," they say, "I only buy my fish fresh, never frozen!"

Not all fresh fish are the same, and you may be shocked to know that "fresh" does not have any legally defined meaning. A fish that has never been frozen but is eleven days past harvest, was poorly handled, and is in questionable condition can still be marketed and sold as fresh. Alternatively, a well-handled fresh fish (and by "well-handled" I mean landed gently, bled, and quickly chilled) has a longer shelf life, and its quality can be maintained for many days out of the water. A quality fresh fish will have its scales intact and will smell good; its flesh will be firm enough that a touch to its skin will not leave an impression. (Go to GoodFishBook.com for a demonstration of how to select quality seafood.)

Not all frozen fish are the same. Again, it comes down to the handling. A well-handled fish prior to freezing makes all the difference in the world. Many fish are frozen right at sea and can be extremely high quality. Alternatively, if a fish is banged around and not chilled down quickly enough, the frozen product will suffer: the telltale signs will be water loss, gaping, and tearing. Home freezers are not designed to freeze fish well, but, that said, I've had success with really good, well-handled albacore tuna loins. I've vacuum-sealed them, frozen them, and then used them within two months.

If you don't live near a local source of fish, there is a carbon-footprint benefit to purchasing your fish frozen. Fresh fish needs to be flown all over the world, consuming huge quantities of jet fuel in order to get to you, whereas frozen fish can be delivered via more fuel-efficient means, such as ship, rail, or truck.

HOW TO SAFELY THAW FROZEN FISH

The best way to thaw a frozen piece of fish is to leave it overnight in the fridge. If you are in a pinch and need it quickly, put the fillet in a ziplock bag inside a large metal bowl filled with cold water. Replace the water with fresh cold water every half hour until the fillet is thawed. Why not use warm water to speed up the process? Two reasons: 1. Warm water—depending on how warm—could actually start to cook the delicate fillet. 2. Thawing is safest out of the "danger zone," which is 40 to 140°F. Thawing with warm water would put the fish in perfect bacterial heaven: great for the bacteria, not so much for you. Keep it cold.

A PROPERLY FROZEN FISH

Sustainable seafood educator Amy Grondin (also a commercial fisherman) helped simplify for me the commercial freezing process that brings high-quality frozen fish to our markets. I'll let her explain in her own words:

"To maintain the quality of fish as a frozen product, fish must be frozen to below 0°F (−18°C) as quickly as possible. Fish tissue can contain up to 80 percent water and has little connective tissue to hold the cells together. When water freezes, it expands. If the freezing happens quickly, the ice crystals formed in the fish are small and cause minimal change to the cell structure of the flesh. When the fish is slowly defrosted in a refrigerator in a drip pan, the result is a firm piece of fish.

"Freezing fish slowly makes big ice crystals that break the connective tissue and cell walls of the fish. The fish will be mushy when it is defrosted. Think of the bottle you accidentally left in the freezer when attempting a quick chill. The same thing happens to the fish flesh when you try to freeze it at home.

"The freezers used on fishing boats and by processors are not the same as a domestic freezer, which is designed to hold frozen products, not create them. Industrial freezers use blast units and other techniques that freeze fish quickly, bringing the fish through the critical temperature zone between 32°F (0°C) and 0°F (−18°C) where cell damage can occur."

FARMED VERSUS WILD

Which is better? I'd like to tell you that there is a very simple answer to this question, but the fact remains that the answer is: it depends. Half the people I talk to assume that farmed fish is bad and wild is good. The other half think we need to stop eating all wild fish to give them a break and eat only farmed fish. My goal here is to simplify the issue as much as humanly possible without glossing over some important points. Remember, there are always exceptions to rules, and this is where knowing your fisherman or fishmonger will help. Have a conversation when there is time for them to consider your questions.

wild fish

Many species of wild fish caught in the United States are doing quite well. Their fisheries are well managed, which means that the catch is highly regulated, preserving fish for future generations. Furthermore, the environment is not destroyed in the process of catching these fish. Pacific Coast albacore and the five species of Alaska wild salmon come to mind. Pacific Coast squid don't seem to be threatened. Ditto for halibut.

What's important to keep in mind when purchasing wild fish is how they were caught. The most environmentally sound way to catch fish is in small, focused quantities. Examples include "trolling"—also known as "hook and line"—which is essentially the commercial version of dipping a fishing pole into the ocean; catching shrimp or crabs in a pot; and small-scale purse seining (using a net to enclose a school of fish).

Other methods are not as ocean- and fish-friendly. Two big ones I try to avoid are fish caught by dredging/bottom trawling (which, unfortunately, sounds very similar to "trolling") and certain kinds of longlining. Bottom trawling scrapes the ocean floor by dragging heavy weighted nets, which is especially bad if they are fishing over sensitive habitat (very often the case). Bottom trawling also produces a lot of "bycatch." Bycatch consists of non-targeted, accidentally caught species, which are unintentionally killed in the fishing process. Not only is this a complete waste of protein, if the bycatch includes juvenile fish killed before they can spawn, it upsets the life cycle of the species. Bycatch is bad all around, and it's crucial that commercial fisheries limit it as much as possible.

Longlining involves setting a single main line, armed with many hooks that drop down at regular intervals, often for miles on end. There are two types of longlines: pelagic or midwater longlines that fish near the ocean surface, and demersal or bottom longlines that are set on the sea floor. Pelagic longlines have a sordid history of being indiscriminate and hooking all sorts of unintended species (such as turtles, seabirds, and sharks). These animals are most often dead when the line is drawn in. Luckily, not all longlining is the same, and there are major exceptions: demersal longlining is done on the sea floor—for example, in Alaska's sustainable halibut and black cod fisheries—and has a much better track record of catching only intended species.

The important questions to ask when buying wild fish are: what is the species, where was it caught, and how was it caught? If you want Pacific Coast wild seafood, you can feel good picking the types I specify in this book, though keep in mind that this is a constantly evolving story—which makes the information found in the Sustainable Seafood Resources section on page 313 indispensable.

farmed fish

Let's clear up a common misconception: while there can be some issues with shellfish farming (obstructed access to beaches, complaints of unsightliness, litter), in general it is extremely sustainable for two very important reasons. First, farmed shellfish are not fed using wild fish feed, so there is no negative drawing of species (protein loss) from the oceans to convert to feed. Farmed shellfish, just like wild shellfish, filter feed, thus contributing to better water quality. Second, unlike farmed salmon that are raised in net pens near shore and destroy the habitat around them, farmed shellfish are grown in the same area that wild shellfish would naturally occur. This allows farmed shellfish to exist in harmony with their intertidal zone neighbors rather than wiping them out. There are few simple decisions when it comes to eating seafood ethically, but here is one: shellfish such as oysters, clams, and mussels make the oceans cleaner. Three cheers for these little pumping filter feeders!

Let's move on to fish farming. On the Pacific Coast we're mainly talking about salmon farms that are floating in the ocean right next to the shore (versus on land in tank-based recirculating aquaculture systems, known as RAS). This method of farming carries with it huge problems. Studies are finding that ocean farming hurts wild fish. Think of it this way: if there were an outbreak of disease on an island where there were no ferries or bridges, the disease would be self-limiting. Compare this to a disease breaking out in the middle of New York City—pretty limitless how far that disease could spread, right? It just seems like a bad idea to mix and mingle high-density fish farms right in the middle of wild-fish ocean migration routes. The ocean is an extremely efficient distribution medium; we need to be very careful about what we introduce into this vast open system. Tank-based recirculating aquaculture systems make a lot more sense.

Other issues worth considering when thinking about fish farming are feed ratio and quality of feed. Carnivorous fish at the top of the food chain require a lot of wild fish feed to convert to usable protein. (For example, farmed bluefin tuna—depending on which study you're looking at—are said to have a feed ratio of anywhere from 5:1 all the way up to 20:1. The first number of the ratio refers to the pounds of wild feed necessary to produce 1 pound of farmed fish flesh.) If you are purchasing farmed fish, it is much more sustainable to choose a species that has been fed a vegetarian diet or required a smaller amount of wild fish protein in their diets. Another issue worth exploring is the quality of the feed given to farmed fish. I'm interested in the sustainability of our oceans but also in the health of the fish for those who consume it. Farmed fish may be a renewable resource, but if that fish is fed genetically modified grains treated with chemicals, I can't, in good conscience, get behind it. This is an area that needs more investigation; consumer pressure will help get to the bottom of these issues.

LESS IS MORE

We humans eat too much fish.

We humans eat too much of the same kinds of fish.

We have forgotten that fish and shellfish have seasons, just like fruit and vegetables. We have forgotten that there is a cost associated with getting what we want whenever we want it. Generally speaking, industrial fishing operations that drive out small boats have become too damn good at catching wild fish, and some operations are greedy and shortsighted when it comes to farming fish. If we stay on this track, will we eat all the wild fish and destroy the environment by farming fish and shrimp? The industrial models of fishing and fish farming, just like big agriculture and meat production, are incredibly efficient on the one hand and incredibly destructive on the other. So what are seafood eaters to do?

I am asking that you reconsider your relationship with seafood.

We need to think about fish and fishermen the way we have started to think about produce and farmers: the closer you are to your food source, the better your ability to know what you are eating and how it was harvested or raised. We need to consider consuming seafood (and all animal proteins, especially beef) in smaller portions. We can broaden our menu horizons by trying new species of fish for dinner. Sources of seafood that can feed us while being environmentally responsible include land-based recirculating aquaculture systems; farmed clams, mussels, and oysters; and community-based fisheries.

Am I suggesting you stop eating fish? Not at all, but think about serving smaller 4- to 6-ounce portions and try some new species. Popular favorites like salmon, shrimp, and tuna come from sustainable and unsustainable sources, meaning we need to pay attention when purchasing them.

Yes, it can be confusing, but I'm here to help. When you write a shopping list to prepare a dish from this book, take a few seconds to review the advice offered in the "Questions to Ask" and "Sustainable Substitutes" sections at the beginning of the chapters. You'll be prepared to confidently choose good fish or pick a sustainable substitute should your first choice not be available or you want to try something new.

FOUR THINGS CAN MAKE A WORLD OF DIFFERENCE

DIVERSIFY THE KINDS OF FISH YOU EAT. There are five species of salmon, not just king and sockeye. Little silver fish such as herring, sardines, mackerel, smelt, and anchovies are delicious, nutritious, versatile, and affordable.

BUY LOCAL, AND IF NOT LOCAL, DOMESTIC. When buying seafood, look for US wild-caught seafood, US finfish raised in land-based closed containment systems (versus at-sea open-net pen farms), and US farmed shellfish. Although these systems are not perfect, they are regulated, and efforts are being made to improve them. At this point, though, perfect should not be the enemy of the good. We have a lot of power as consumers. Pull out your wallet only when you are comfortable that the fish you have selected is both healthy for you and for the planet. You deserve to eat good fish.

LIMIT THE AMOUNT OF SEAFOOD ON YOUR PLATE. I've written these recipes to reflect my desire to rearrange the priorities on our plates. Generally speaking, ¼ pound (4 ounces) of seafood per person is affordable and reasonable; for shellfish I recommend about ½ pound (8 ounces) per person to account for the weight of the shells. Most of these recipes are based on a meal for four, so I recommend buying 1 pound of quality sustainable seafood. It's budget- and planet-friendly. We're all supposed to be eating more vegetables anyway, so let this cookbook give you a gentle push in that direction. Less is more.

TRY FROZEN SEAFOOD. Quality frozen seafood is a win for the environment and for your dinner plate. If you don't live in a coastal community, finding fresh seafood can be challenging. Fresh seafood often needs to be put on a plane to make it to the market while it is still fresh, delivering with it a big carbon footprint and a ticking bomb as the fish gets older day by day. Frozen seafood can be shipped by boat, truck, or rail with much less impact on the environment. Frozen-at-sea (FAS) methods and other quality freezing systems offer fishermen a chance to "extend the season" for seafood. The seafood is basically held in time from the moment it is frozen to the time it is defrosted. This doesn't mean frozen seafood is good indefinitely, but it allows for more time in transportation from boat to plate. When correctly processed, frozen seafood cannot be discerned from fresh seafood once defrosted. Besides that, you can have frozen seafood on standby in your freezer for a quick defrost that will result in dinner in less time than going to the store for something else.

SHELLFISH

clams

New Jersey: August 1978. I can still smell the scent of hundreds of clams splitting themselves open in our speckled and spigoted black-and-white steamer pot. Our family lived in three houses on the lake, separated by one mile and the time it took for short legs to traverse the distance. Each house presented a different snack opportunity, with my aunt and uncle's place being the dinnertime final destination. On late-summer days we would gather there, sun-burned and boat-weary, and circle a large pot, filled to the rim with more clams than we believed the pot should hold.

These clams were my very first taste of shellfish, and it's true what they say: you always remember your first. Their bounce-back brininess—their sweetness and salinity—formed the centerpiece of so many of our summers. Clams, shared with my boisterous and loving family, etched themselves firmly onto my culinary map. They were my proverbial first dip of the toe into the ocean. I was hooked early, at the age of eight, and my familial clan of shellfish worshippers could only clutch helplessly at their wallets because lobster was just around the next corner.

WHAT MAKES THIS A GOOD FISH	Clams are an especially sustainable choice because, whether they are wild or farmed, they act as filter feeders, improving ocean water quality. Nutritionally, clams are high in vitamin B_{12} and iron. Clams can be found everywhere!

BY ANY OTHER NAME	Manila clams (*Venerupis philippinarum*), accidentally brought over from Japan in oyster spat (young oysters), are easily available and widely cultivated. Manilas have a long shelf life.

Geoduck (*Panopea abrupta*), pronounced "gooey-duck," are quite expensive these days, with much of the harvest exported to China. Every once in a while, though, geoduck is a special treat, and I couldn't help but include a recipe for it, as it is one of my favorite types of clam.

Other clams you might find on the Pacific Coast are our native littleneck (*Leukoma staminea*), the Pacific razor clam (*Siliqua patula*), California's pismo clam (*Tivela stultorum*), and the butter clam (*Saxidona giganteus*). A warning: Butter clams can hold toxins in their flesh for several years—check the beaches for reports of PSP (paralytic shellfish poisoning, commonly referred to as "red tide") if you plan to harvest them yourself. In Washington, call the Shellfish Safety Hotline at 1-800-562-5632. |

SEASON	Wild clams can be harvested year-round but are easiest to gather in spring and early summer when the lowest tides occur during the daylight hours. (Follow all state regulations for licensing, limits, and harvest method, paying close attention to water-quality reports and closed beaches to keep you safe.) Farmed clams are pretty great year-round, though I tend to avoid clams altogether in mid- to late summer when they spawn and their shelf life is shortened.

BUYING TIPS	Look for unbroken clams that smell neutral or pleasant. If a clam is open, close it with your fingers; if it springs back open and doesn't gently close itself, it is probably dead. Pitch it. If the clam is mostly closed but you can see a bit of the foot sticking out, don't be shy about touching it to check for movement—the foot should retreat back into the shell. Extremely cold clams may be a bit sluggish but will still react. After cooking clams, you may notice that a few don't open. You may have heard that eating these clams will make you sick, but the truth is that they may be full of mud or just haven't been cooked long enough. Try cooking the closed ones a little longer, and if they still don't open, pitch them.

Sometimes you'll see live razor clams, which are a special treat. I've also seen them cleaned and vacuum-packed on ice.

QUESTIONS TO ASK BEFORE YOU PULL OUT YOUR WALLET

Where are these clams from? Clams are an abundant worldwide resource, making it unnecessary to ship them from far-off places. Consider reducing your carbon footprint by buying clams sourced as close to your home as possible. Are they wild or farmed? (This will give you a sense of how dirty or gritty the mussels might be—farmed tend to be a lot cleaner). The majority of commercially sold clams are farmed. Also ask, when were they harvested? I look for clams harvested within five days of purchase.

CARING FOR YOUR GOOD FISH

If your clams were wild, they are likely to be sandy or muddy. Scrub them really well under cold running water. If caught recreationally, I'd also consider purging them, as I've had one or two sandy clams ruin a whole pot. To purge clams, place them in clean seawater after harvest and let them sit for twenty minutes. (Soaking clams in fresh water will kill them, and, as a wise person once said, a dead clam is not a tasty clam.) Then switch out the seawater and let them sit for another twenty minutes—this will usually clean the clams of any sand. I've never had to purge commercially farmed clams, since they are purged prior to sale. I still give farmed clams a quick scrubbing though.

Store clams in a bowl in a cold corner of your refrigerator. Place a damp towel directly on top of the clams (refrigerators are very dry places, and the towel protects against dehydrating your live shellfish). Good fishmongers store them live in saltwater or on ice that can drain easily. If a supermarket stores them on plastic trays, there should be perforations in the packaging so the clams don't suffocate. Ideally, use clams the day you buy them for best quality, but during the colder months they can last up to seven days after the harvest date, depending on how well they've been handled. In the warmer summer months, use clams within three days of the harvest date. Special geoduck care: Geoducks will "die within thirty seconds of being submerged in fresh water," says Peter Downey, who grows geoducks for a living just outside Port Townsend, Washington. Store them in a bowl in the refrigerator, covered with a damp towel, and use within five days of harvest.

HOW THIS TYPE OF SEAFOOD IS RAISED OR HARVESTED

In commercial clam farming, clam "seed" is produced in hatcheries, then grown out to harvestable size. Clams are placed either directly on the sea-floor or in nets, bags, or trays. Most Pacific Coast clams are harvested with hand rakes. Farmed geoducks can be harvested either by divers when the water is deep or from the beach at low tide when the clams are exposed. Both wild and farmed geoducks are harvested with the use of pressurized high-volume water nozzles. Divers gather wild geoducks in areas specified by shellfish managers. Razor clams are harvested by hand, using either a shovel or a "clam gun."

....

SUSTAINABLE SUBSTITUTES

In most recipes, it is fairly easy to substitute one type of shellfish for another. If fresh clams are not available, look for mussels. Another option would be to use fresh or frozen razor clams in place of manila clams, or vice versa. Geoduck is a unique ingredient with a texture and flavor all its own, so if you can't find geoduck, make a different recipe!

All commercial shellfish come with harvest tags that list the date and location from which the shellfish were taken. If you ask someone to produce this tag and they can't, turn on your heel and make a dramatic exit (with lots of flair) because they have not earned your business. Shellfish of dubious origin is not to be trusted.

tamarind and ginger clams

SERVES 4

2 stalks lemongrass
1 tablespoon high-heat
    vegetable oil
1 tablespoon grated fresh
    peeled ginger
1 serrano chile, cut into
    thin rings
1 red bell pepper, cut into
    small dice
1 teaspoon tamarind paste
½ cup dry white wine
2 pounds clams, scrubbed
1 (5.6-ounce) can full-fat
    coconut milk, refrigerated for
    a few hours
½ cup roughly chopped Thai or
    regular basil, for garnish

PAIRING: First choice is Alsatian
Riesling; second, Alsatian
gewürztraminer.

My first taste of tamarind was eye opening. Pleasantly tart with an almost caramel berry flavor, it's a great option when you want to move beyond pairing seafood with the ubiquitous lemon wedge. Not that there is anything wrong with lemon. But, you know—push yourself to try something new. I like serving this dish with crusty bread for dipping into the juices, or with a bowl of fragrant jasmine rice.

Prepare the lemongrass by cutting off the top half of each stalk (where it is thinner and darker); discard this. (The bottom half is where all the flavor is.) Trim the very bottom of each stalk and discard, then cut the stalks into 1-inch pieces. Smack each piece several times with the back edge of a chef's knife to help release its flavor.

In a large saucepan or pot over medium-high heat, add the oil. When the oil is hot, add the lemongrass, ginger, serrano, and bell pepper. Sauté for 2 to 3 minutes, then add the tamarind, wine, and clams. Cook, covered, for 3 to 5 minutes, or until the clams open. (Any clams that do not open can be cooked longer or discarded.)

Pour the clams and vegetables, along with the "pot liquor," into a large serving bowl. Scoop the thick cream layer from the top of the coconut milk into a bowl, and stir well, reserving the rest of the milk for another use. Drizzle the coconut cream over the top of the clams and garnish with the basil. Instruct your guests to chew on—but not swallow—the flavorful lemongrass pieces.

steamers with beer

SERVES A ROWDY FAMILY
OF 6 TO 8

2 cans pilsner or other
   light lager
2 onions, cut into medium dice
3 ribs celery, sliced ¼ inch thick
1 tablespoon Old Bay seasoning
5 pounds clams, scrubbed
1 cup (2 sticks) unsalted
   butter, melted, for serving
1 cup cocktail sauce (make your
   own by combining ½ cup
   ketchup and ½ cup prepared
   horseradish with lemon juice
   and salt to taste), for serving
4 lemons, cut into wedges,
   for serving

PAIRING: First, last, and
ONLY choice—beer! And
make it cheap.

Back in the day, my family would get wild clams from Asbury Park on the Jersey shore. We preferred littlenecks or cherrystones and believed the smallest clams were the most desirable (which gave us something to fight over). Here on the Pacific Coast, it's manila and native littleneck country. If you have someone in your family who is a bivalve-a-phobe, this is the perfect gateway recipe. For the beer, we always used St. Pauli Girl, but any pilsner or light lager will do.

In a large steamer pot (or you could use a pasta pot and steam the clams in two batches), combine the beer, onions, celery, and Old Bay seasoning. Let the liquid come to a boil over high heat and then reduce the heat and simmer for 5 minutes before adding the clams (in the steaming basket) on top. Cover the pot. As the clams start to open (check after 3 to 4 minutes), start removing them with tongs to a heated bowl. (Any clams that do not open can be cooked longer or discarded.)

Serve the clams with bowls of melted butter, cocktail sauce, lemon wedges, and tiny cocktail forks. You can also dip the clams into the steaming brew. If you're really fond of salt, beer, and clams, you'll want to do what my grandfather did: use the spigot on the bottom of the steamer pot and pour yourself a mug of the infused brew. "Papa" wasn't a drinking man, but he sure liked his salty clam brew.

razor clam chowder

SERVES 4

2 tablespoons unsalted butter
   or extra-virgin olive oil

4 strips (about 3 ounces) bacon,
   cut into small dice

1 large leek, white and light-
   green parts only, halved
   lengthwise and cleaned, cut
   into small dice

2 ribs celery, cut into small dice,
   ¼ cup tender leaves reserved
   for garnish

2 bay leaves

1 tablespoon roughly chopped
   fresh thyme leaves

⅛ teaspoon cayenne

1 pound unpeeled Yukon
   Gold potatoes, cut into
   medium dice

¼ cup dry white vermouth

1 (8-ounce) bottle clam juice

1 cup water

1½ cups heavy cream or
   cashew cream*

2 teaspoons fish sauce

¾ pound cleaned razor clam
   meat, cut into small dice

Buttery crackers (such as Ritz),
   broken up, for garnish

Tabasco or other hot sauce

PAIRING: First choice is California chardonnay; second, viognier.

The original edition of *Good Fish* did not contain a recipe for a cream-based clam chowder in the New England style. Apparently that was an oversight, because over the last six years many readers have requested my take on this classic dish. While sticking pretty close to the classic, I have chosen buttery leeks in place of onions, and substituted razor clams in place of the more commonly used manila clams (though you should feel free to use manilas if you have any difficulty finding razors). I opt for no flour as a thickener and less cream than most recipes to keep it lighter.

....

In a medium pot over medium heat, add the butter and bacon. Cook the bacon until its fat is rendered and it crisps up, 7 to 10 minutes. Remove half of the bacon with a slotted spoon to a paper-towel-lined plate and reserve for garnish; leave the rest in the pot. Add the leek and cook for 3 minutes, or until tender. Add the celery, bay leaves, thyme, and cayenne and cook for another minute. Add the potatoes and increase the heat to medium-high. Cook the potatoes for 2 to 3 minutes, stirring occasionally. Add the vermouth to deglaze the pan, scraping up all the brown bits. Add the clam juice and water to cover the potatoes. Bring to a boil over high heat, then reduce to a simmer and cook the chowder uncovered until the potatoes are tender, 8 to 12 minutes more. Add the cream and fish sauce and simmer for another 10 minutes. Return the chowder to a boil over high heat, then turn off the heat (or remove the pot from the burner if you have an electric stove). Add the razor clams, cover the pot, and let them poach for 2 minutes—do not overcook or they will become tough and rubbery. Season the chowder to taste with more fish sauce or some salt. Garnish with the celery leaves, reserved bacon, and crackers. Serve with Tabasco.

---

*If you avoid dairy, try making this chowder with cashew cream instead—it's just as good. To make cashew cream, simply soak 1 cup raw cashews in 1 cup water for 4 hours (or overnight in the refrigerator). Drain and discard the soaking water, combine the cashews with ¾ cup fresh water and a pinch of salt, and puree in a high-speed blender until very smooth, 2 to 3 minutes. Add more water depending on the desired consistency.

homemade fettuccine

with clams and marjoram

SERVES 4 AS A LUNCH
OR LIGHT DINNER

Kosher salt

2 pounds clams, scrubbed

½ cup dry white vermouth

2 sprigs fresh marjoram, plus
  1 tablespoon chopped
  marjoram leaves

2 sprigs fresh thyme

10 ounces Homemade
  Fettuccine (recipe follows) or
  store-bought fresh fettuccine

¼ cup extra-virgin olive oil

1 tablespoon unsalted butter

⅛ teaspoon red pepper flakes
  (more if you want it spicier)

1 cup roughly chopped fresh or
  canned tomatoes

¼ cup roughly chopped fresh
  Italian parsley

PAIRING: First choice is Orvieto;
second, pinot grigio.

When I was a little kid, I knew I had "arrived" in the culinary sense when my dad tapped me to make his signature clam dip. It consisted of sour cream, canned clams, Tabasco, Worcestershire sauce, and some more Tabasco. Fritos were involved. This dish is worlds away from that dip (best eaten while watching the New York Islanders play hockey), but chopping the clams brings me right back to my childhood kitchen, standing on my tiptoes and splashing hot sauce all over the counter.

Bring a large pot of water to a boil over high heat and add a heaping tablespoon of salt.

Meanwhile, in a medium saucepan, add the clams, vermouth, marjoram sprigs, and thyme. Bring to a boil over high heat, then reduce the heat to medium and cover the pot for 3 to 5 minutes, or until all the clams open. (Any clams that do not open can be cooked longer or discarded.) Using a colander, strain the clam liquor into a bowl, then pour it through a fine-mesh sieve or coffee filter to further remove any sediment. (This is especially important if you are using wild clams, which tend to be sandier than farmed.) Set aside.

Remove the marjoram and thyme sprigs and discard. Separate the clams from their shells (making sure to scrape out the adductor muscle where the clam attaches to the shell—it's tasty!). Chop the clams into small dice and set aside.

Boil the pasta until it is just barely al dente, about 3 minutes. Drain the pasta in a colander and set aside. In a large sauté pan over medium-high heat, add the oil, butter, and red pepper flakes. After 1 minute, add the tomatoes and cook for 2 to 3 minutes. Add the clams, marjoram leaves, parsley, pasta, and reserved clam liquor. Finish cooking the pasta in the sauce for 2 to 3 minutes, or until some of the sauce has been absorbed and the pasta is al dente. Check for seasoning and add more salt if necessary. Serve immediately.

CONTINUED

2 cups all-purpose flour
3 large eggs
1 tablespoon water, plus more
   as needed
½ tablespoon extra-virgin
   olive oil
¼ teaspoon fine sea salt

HOMEMADE FETTUCCINE

People are always shocked when they realize that making pasta dough takes ten minutes tops. The skill comes in rolling the dough, and here, practice makes perfect. Two tips that will help your experience: First, when mixing and rolling the dough, you can always add flour to make a slightly wet dough dryer, but I find it much harder to add moisture back to a dry dough. Second, never clean your pasta machine with water. The moisture will trap flour bits that will tear your dough or make it stick when you roll it out. Dust your machine with flour and clean it with a brush before storing. I recommend the Marcato Atlas pasta machine. One more note: You can roll out your dough by hand and eschew the machine. You will earn my respect. I did it once and understood immediately why Italian nonnas could crush my little pea-head in their massive biceps. This recipe doubles easily for larger groups.

To make the dough in a food processor: Add the flour, eggs, water, oil, and salt to the bowl of a food processor. Pulse until the mixture comes together into a ball. If it appears a bit dry, add small amounts of water until it comes together. Transfer the dough to a floured surface. Knead the dough for a few minutes and then wrap it in plastic wrap and let it rest for at least 10 minutes.

To make the dough by hand: In a large bowl, mix the flour with the salt. Make a well in the center of the flour; add the eggs, oil, and water to the well, and with a fork, gently beat the liquids. Slowly start incorporating flour from the inside edges until you have a thick paste, then gather the dough and knead it on a board until it comes together into a ball. Wrap it in plastic wrap and let it rest for at least 10 minutes.

To roll the dough: Using a hand-cranked pasta machine, divide the dough into two workable pieces (keep one wrapped while you roll out the other). Run each piece through the machine on setting #1 (the widest setting on your machine). Fold it into three pieces (like a letter), and run it through again, inserting the narrow end first. Set the machine to setting #2 and repeat the process, dusting with flour as necessary. At this point, you don't need to fold the dough. Keep running it through each setting down to #6 or #7, depending on how thin you want the dough. I think a thinner noodle works well for this recipe.

To cut and dry the pasta: Before cutting, I like to lay the pasta sheets on a lightly floured counter for 10 minutes or so, flipping them over after 5 minutes. This dries them slightly, which is a good thing at this stage, as it will keep the individual noodles from sticking to each other when you cut the dough. Run the pasta sheets through the fettuccine cutter attachment on your pasta machine. Dust the noodles with flour and keep them spread out on the counter until you are ready to boil them. If you want to freeze them, wait about 30 more minutes, until they have dried further, and pull the pasta together into several bundles. Freeze the noodles on a baking sheet, then transfer them to a ziplock freezer bag. Use within 2 weeks. You can cook the pasta directly from the freezer; just add a minute or so to the cooking time.

geoduck crudo
with shiso oil

SERVES 4 AS AN APPETIZER

½ pound geoduck siphon meat,
    well cleaned‡
½ cup extra-virgin olive oil
1 tablespoon seasoned rice
    wine vinegar
6 shiso leaves
Freshly ground pink
    peppercorns
Maldon or gray sea salt

---

‡ Go to GoodFishBook.com for
a demonstration of how to clean
a geoduck.

PAIRING: First and only choice is
Junmai-shu sake.

Random geoduck factoid: The oldest geoduck lived for 164 years. Let's take a moment to appreciate that. Somehow, this rather vulnerable clam, with the majority of its body outside of its protective shell, eluded predators and survived for a century and a half buried deep in the soft sand. Pretty incredible. Not-so-random geoduck factoid: No one—and I mean absolutely no one—can hold a geoduck and resist giggling.

Slice the geoduck paper thin with a very sharp knife and keep it cold in the refrigerator while you prepare the garnishes.

Combine the oil and rice wine vinegar with the shiso in a blender or food processor, and blend into a smooth light-green emulsion. Transfer the shiso oil to a squeeze bottle or a small jar with a narrow opening. (You will have some left over; refrigerate it and use on salads.)

Place the geoduck slices decoratively on a platter, each slice slightly overlapping the previous one. Generously drizzle the shiso oil over the top. Season to taste with the pepper and salt.

mussels

Shelton, Washington: January 2010. Gordon King, masterful mussel man and walking font of shellfish knowledge, whisks us out to the mussel rafts at Taylor Shellfish Farms. It's cold and windy and we're bundled up—hats, down coats, gloves, scarves. Gordon (in shorts) jumps out of the skiff and up onto the narrow, grated edging of the raft and shows us the lines where farmed mussels stretch far down into the water, filter feeding and thinking their mussel-y thoughts (which I imagine are quite limited).

Gordon is as passionate about farming mussels as I am about preparing them. The process is more straightforward than I had imagined it would be. Larvae are grown in a hatchery, placed onto mesh socks, dropped into Puget Sound, and then eighteen months later are harvested by hand and sent to the processing plant where they are separated and cleaned.

First we are shown the adult mussels—ready to be harvested later that day. Moments later Gordon pulls up a rope gripped tightly by black-brown adolescent mussels. Then he moves on to the other raft where the little babies, no bigger than a pinkie nail, are being lowered into their socks to take up residence for a time.

I draw my scarf tightly around my neck and turn away from the wind while scribbling notes in a little book. Later that night, a five-pound bag of mussels in the backseat, I stop by the market and pull out my notes. They say: Mussels. Bread. Guinness. Cream. Test this.

WHAT MAKES THIS A GOOD FISH	Whether they are wild or farmed, mussels act as filter feeders, improving ocean water quality. Like all shellfish, their needs are simple: they eat solely from the phytoplankton floating by (no wild fish meal required).

BY ANY OTHER NAME	For our purposes here on the Pacific Coast, let's focus on two species: Mediterranean mussels, or "meds" (*Mytilus galloprovincialis*), a nonnative species that is very easy to cultivate; and *Mytilus trossulus*, commonly known as the "Baltic" type. Washingtonians know the latter as Penn Cove mussels—which is sort of like saying Kleenex, as Penn Cove is a company in addition to being a place, but you get the idea. There is another species you might find if you go foraging, namely, the California mussel *Mytilus californianus*.

SEASON	Meds are at their best from June through October, which surprises many people who think all shellfish should be avoided in the summer—not true! Mussels, like other bivalves, are best in the months before they spawn and at their worst during and just after spawning. If you've ever purchased a mussel that only took up a tiny fraction of its shell, that puny, dried-out, sad, lil' thing probably just went through spawning. It's tired, and you don't want to eat it, trust me. The good news about *M. trossulus* is that this species is at its peak just when meds are petering out. The season for *M. trossulus*, aka Penn Cove mussels, is late fall through winter into early spring. If it helps you, you can think of meds being at their best in the heat of summer, just like the Mediterranean. Penn Coves are best in the cold months, just like a good hearty Northwesterner.

BUYING TIPS	Look for unbroken mussels that smell neutral or pleasant. If a mussel is open, tap it lightly or gently close it; if it springs back open and doesn't gently close itself, it is probably dead—do not cook these mussels as they could make you sick. Check the harvest date—there will be a tag with that information at the point of sale. Learn from my mistakes. I recently put my nose on some mussels that smelled just fine. I got them home, cooked them up, and it wasn't until their shells opened that it hit me: the unmistakable smell of baby diapers. I had forgotten to check the harvest tag on the mussels and was shopping at

a fish place I don't normally frequent. When I went back and took a peek at the tag, I realized those mussels had been harvested eight days prior. There is a theory that mussels, unlike clams and oysters, can go off even though they are still alive when you cook them. Eight-day-old shellfish would have had to be handled perfectly, in ideal circumstances, to still taste fresh. Check the tags and use your judgment, but I'm comfortable with anything up to five days from harvest—if you trust the handling has been sound. When cooking mussels, you may notice that a few don't open. You may have heard that eating these mussels will make you sick, but the truth is that they may be full of mud or just haven't been cooked long enough. Try cooking the closed ones a little longer, and if they still don't open, pitch them.

QUESTIONS TO ASK BEFORE YOU PULL OUT YOUR WALLET

Are these farmed or wild? (This will give you a sense of how dirty or gritty the mussels might be—farmed tend to be a lot cleaner.) Mussels, like clams, are an abundant coastal food, so ask if they are local. There is no need to fly in mussels from other places when we have them close to home. Ask what species they are so you can determine the quality (remember the different spawning times). Ask when they were harvested or look at the tag. I look for mussels harvested within five days of purchase.

CARING FOR YOUR GOOD FISH

Get your mussels home, put them in a bowl, and place a damp—not soaking wet—towel on them to keep them from drying out in the refrigerator. Use them quickly, within a day or two (keeping in mind their harvest date).

HOW THIS TYPE OF SEAFOOD IS RAISED OR HARVESTED

Mussels are either harvested in the wild by raking or dredging, or they are cultivated on ropes, mesh socks, or lines made from various materials, suspended most typically from rafts.

SUSTAINABLE SUBSTITUTES

Clams are an easy and widely available substitute for mussels.

mussels *with guinness cream*

2 pounds mussels
1 tablespoon extra-virgin
  olive oil
¼ cup minced shallots
⅛ teaspoon fine sea salt
¾ cup Guinness Extra Stout
¾ cup heavy cream
1 teaspoon freshly grated or
  prepared horseradish
2 teaspoons honey
⅛ teaspoon cayenne
2 tablespoons unsalted butter
2 tablespoons minced fresh
  Italian parsley
Good, crusty bread

‡ Go to GoodFishBook.com
for a demonstration of how to
debeard and clean mussels.

PAIRING: First and only choice is
Guinness beer, of course.

I try to eat fairly lightly, and that means I don't reach for cream every time I cook. Cream is a wonderful thing, but it can also be a crutch masking the flavors of the food it is paired with rather than elevating them. I tend to use cream judiciously, with the precision of a rifle, saving the cream cannon for ice cream. Then, one day, while developing mussel recipes, I hit on a major exception to this rule. It was on this auspicious day that Cream met Guinness, and a romance was born. Guinness elevated Cream into a decadent, malty, richer version of itself, and Cream elevated Guinness by rounding its caramel and chocolate edge with a warm white blanket. They lived happily ever after.

Scrub and debeard the mussels.‡ Set aside.

Heat a large pot over medium-high heat. Add the oil; when it is hot, add the shallots and salt. Sauté for 5 minutes, or until the shallots are lightly browned. Add the Guinness, cream, horseradish, honey, cayenne, and mussels. Toss the mussels, coating them with the sauce. Cover the pot, increase the heat to high, and cook for 3 minutes. Stir the mussels, and when most of them have opened and their meat has firmed up, transfer them with a slotted spoon to a large serving bowl. (Any mussels that do not open can be cooked longer or discarded.) Simmer the sauce gently until reduced by half. Turn off the heat, swirl in the butter and parsley, and taste for seasoning. If you find the sauce too bitter for your tastes, add more honey and salt. Pour the sauce over the mussels. Serve with bread to dip in the Guinness cream.

mussels *with apple cider and thyme glaze*

SERVES 4 AS A FIRST COURSE
OR LIGHT DINNER

2 pounds mussels
¼ cup hard apple cider
2 sprigs fresh thyme, plus
   1 teaspoon chopped
   fresh thyme
1 tablespoon unsalted butter
3 tablespoons minced shallots
¾ cup sweet apple or pear cider
¼ cup clam juice
1 teaspoon apple cider vinegar
1 tablespoon whole grain
   Dijon mustard
1 teaspoon chopped capers
Fine sea salt
Freshly ground black
   pepper (optional)

‡ Go to GoodFishBook.com
for a demonstration of how to
debeard and clean mussels.

PAIRING: First choice is
Savennières; second, Alsatian
pinot gris.

It seems that most mussel recipes fall into two camps. The first camp has mussels mingling with garlic, tomatoes, parsley, and white wine. It's a nice camp: familiar, warm, and predictable. The second camp is more exotic, where you'll find mussels dipped into a curry broth of coconut milk and chiles. I like both camps. I've been to them many times. But I'd like to take you to a different camp—a camp where mussels hang out with mustard and thyme and apple cider. I think you'll like it here.

Scrub and debeard the mussels.‡

In a large pot over high heat, add the hard apple cider and thyme sprigs. Add the mussels, cover, and cook for about 3 minutes, or until the mussels have opened and their meat firmed up. (Any mussels that do not open can be cooked longer or discarded.) Transfer the mussels to a large heatproof bowl, and cover to keep warm. Strain the mussel liquor through a fine-mesh sieve and set aside.

Melt the butter in a small saucepan over medium-low heat. Stir in the shallots and cook for about 1 minute, or until they are fragrant. Add the reserved mussel liquor, sweet apple cider, clam juice, and apple cider vinegar. Bring the sauce to a boil over medium-high heat, reduce to a simmer, and cook until the sauce is reduced by three-quarters, about 20 minutes. Remove the pan from the heat and stir in the mustard, chopped thyme, and capers. Season to taste with salt and pepper. Pour the sauce over the mussels and serve hot.

mussels *with pancetta and vermouth*

SERVES 6 TO 8 AS AN APPETIZER

2 pounds mussels

¼ cup dry white vermouth or
   dry white wine

2 ounces pancetta, prosciutto,
   or bacon

¼ cup finely minced shallots

Zest of 1 lemon (about
   2 teaspoons), plus lemon
   juice for finishing

¼ teaspoon cayenne

2 tablespoons mayonnaise

¼ cup panko or bread crumbs

2 tablespoons minced fresh
   Italian parsley

2 ounces (½ cup) grated
   Manchego cheese

Rock salt, for serving

---

‡ Go to GoodFishBook.com
for a demonstration of how to
debeard and clean mussels.

PAIRING: First choice is Chablis;
second, rosé.

My friend Ashlyn introduced me to a version of this recipe. She grew up in Louisiana and Mississippi and loved eating Oysters Bienville, a famous dish from New Orleans, which she then adapted by replacing the original seafood with mussels. In honor of Ashlyn, I'd like to tell you her favorite one-liner that she says every single time I mention I'm cooking mussels (or clams or oysters, for that matter): "Vanna," she says, "I'd like to bivalve."

Scrub and debeard the mussels.‡ Set aside.

Preheat the broiler. Place a rack in the lower middle position of the oven.

In a saucepan over high heat, place the mussels and vermouth and cover. Cook just until the mussels pop open and their meat has firmed up, 2 to 3 minutes. Remove them with tongs as they open. (Any mussels that do not open can be cooked longer or discarded.) When the mussels are done, strain the mussel liquor and set aside. Let the mussels cool.

In a wide sauté pan over medium heat, cook the pancetta until it releases some of its fat, about 5 minutes. Add the shallots and cook, stirring occasionally, until they are soft, about 5 more minutes. Add the reserved mussel liquor, lemon zest, and cayenne and deglaze the pan, letting the liquid evaporate completely. Transfer the contents of the pan to a medium bowl and fold in the mayonnaise. In a separate medium bowl, mix the panko and parsley.

When the mussels are cool, twist off the top shells and discard. Place the mussels in their bottom shells on a baking sheet. Top each mussel with a small amount of the pancetta mixture and then coat the top with some of the panko mixture. Finish each with a sprinkle of Manchego.

Broil the mussels until the topping is light brown, 1 to 2 minutes. Don't overcook them or they will get tough. Serve on a bed of rock salt with a squeeze of the lemon juice, if desired.

mussels *with bacon and israeli couscous*

SERVES 4 AS A LIGHT DINNER

2 pounds mussels

4 strips bacon, cut into
small dice

¼ cup small-diced onion

1 teaspoon sweet smoked
Spanish paprika or sweet
Hungarian paprika

⅛ teaspoon red pepper flakes

1 cup Israeli couscous*

⅛ teaspoon fine sea salt

1 cup water

½ cup dry white wine

½ cup heavy cream

⅓ cup roughly chopped fresh
Italian parsley

---

*Israeli couscous is a much larger
grain of pasta (about the size of
a salmon egg or BB gun pellet)
than regular couscous and can
be found at large supermarkets
or specialty stores.

---

‡ Go to GoodFishBook.com
for a demonstration of how to
debeard and clean mussels.

PAIRING: First choice is
California chardonnay; second,
white Burgundy.

Dear Grandma: I know when you see the ingredients in this dish, it might give you pause, as you raised me to be a good Jew, but I just want to remind you that, above all else, you taught me to see the humor in life. Isn't it funny how I combined bacon and Israeli couscous with shellfish? Love, Becky. P.S. I had originally called this recipe "Bad Jew Stew," but my editor thought that wasn't the best idea I've ever had, so it could've been worse.

. . . .

Scrub and debeard the mussels.‡ Set aside.

Heat a large pot over medium heat. Add the bacon and render the fat, about 10 minutes. Transfer the bacon with a slotted spoon to a paper-towel-lined plate and set aside. Add the onion, paprika, and red pepper flakes and cook for 3 to 4 minutes, or until the onions have softened. Add the couscous and salt. Sauté until the couscous is lightly browned, about 5 minutes. Add the water and wine and scrape the bottom of the pan. Reduce the heat to maintain a simmer, cover, and cook for 10 minutes, stirring occasionally. Add the mussels and cream, stir well, cover, and cook until the mussels open, another 3 to 4 minutes. (Any mussels that do not open can be cooked longer or discarded.) Add the parsley and reserved bacon, taste for seasoning, and serve.

mussels *with tomato-espelette butter*

SERVES 2 AS A LUNCH OR UP TO 4 AS A FIRST COURSE

1 pound unsalted butter, at room temperature

1½ tablespoons tomato paste

1 tablespoon piment d'Espelette pepper, or substitute ground Controne, Marash or Urfa flakes, or ½ teaspoon cayenne

1 teaspoon smoked sea salt

1 tablespoon extra-virgin olive oil

2 cloves garlic, crushed with the side of a knife

2 pounds mussels

¼ cup dry white vermouth

¼ cup chopped fresh Italian parsley

1 loaf crusty bread, sliced

---

‡ Go to GoodFishBook.com for a demonstration of how to debeard and clean mussels.

PAIRING: First choice is pinot noir–based rosé; second, Chablis.

This is just a slight twist on a very classic preparation. If you've made the compound butter the day before, this dish literally comes together in fifteen minutes. Make a winter citrus salad, grab a baguette, and place a big bowl for shells in the middle of the table. The mussels are great, of course, but the bread dipped into the buttery tomato-chile broth is insanely good. If you love the butter as much as I do, you can also garnish each bowl with another pat of it and let it slowly melt into the dish. The recipe for the butter will make more than you need. If you double the recipe, keep in mind that you won't need to double the butter.

In a stand mixer fitted with the paddle attachment, add the softened butter, tomato paste, piment d'Espelette, and salt and mix until well combined. (Alternatively, you can mix it by hand.) Transfer the butter onto a piece of plastic wrap and form it into a log. Wrap the butter well with the plastic wrap and refrigerate until firm. You can also freeze the butter in a ziplock freezer bag and cut off slices as you need them.

Scrub and debeard the mussels.‡ Set aside.

In a stockpot over medium-high heat, add the oil and smashed garlic. Let it sizzle for a minute or two. Add the mussels and vermouth, increase the heat to high, cover, and cook for about 3 minutes, or until the mussels open and their meat has firmed up. (Any mussels that do not open can be cooked longer or discarded.) Remove the mussels with a slotted spoon and allow the liquid to reduce on high heat for another minute. Reduce the heat to medium-low and add 3 tablespoons of the tomato-Espelette butter and the parsley, swirling the pot to incorporate the butter into the sauce. Taste the broth and adjust the seasoning. Let it all cook together for another minute. Serve with the bread.

oysters

I remember eating my first raw oyster just as surely as others remember their first lake dive, hands pointed together in prayer, toes death-gripped to the splintery edge of the dock. Truth be told, my experience was a culinary half step. I couldn't quite get myself to tackle the whole oyster, so I licked shyly at the liquor. Surprised at how delicious it was, I then drank it with gusto, letting my friend eat the oyster itself, while she puzzled at my strange workaround. When I finally went whole hog a few months later and tipped the entire oyster back, I realized all that fear and trepidation were for naught.

A little fear before trying something new is to be expected, but surely it is the wise who know that working through that fear as quickly as possible can lead to a lifetime of culinary enjoyment. For those still perched on the dock's edge: fried oysters are a damn fine baby step.

Whether they are wild or farmed, oysters act as filter feeders, improving ocean water quality. Like all shellfish, their needs are simple: they eat solely from the phytoplankton floating by (no wild fish meal required). Oysters are healthful: they are high in vitamin B$_{12}$, iron, and calcium; one oyster contains 370 milligrams of omega-3 fatty acids.

There are five species of oysters commonly found on the Pacific Coast:

Pacific oysters (*Crassostrea giga*) were brought to the Pacific Coast from Japan in the 1920s. Most Pacific oysters (as well as Eastern oysters) are named for the bay or inlet where they are grown rather than the species. For example, California's Tomales Bay or Drakes Bay oysters both happen to be Pacific oysters (ditto for Canada's Fanny Bay oysters), so it gets sort of confusing. Like all oysters, their flavor changes depending on where they grow. This is the ultimate pleasure of being an oyster aficionado—like wine, oysters have terroir. Pacific varieties can get really, really big (which, in my opinion, makes for better barbecue or chowder).

Olympia oysters (*Ostrea conchaphila* or *O. lurida*), aka Olys, are the tiniest and most celebrated oysters on the Pacific Coast, and also our only native species. Olys were so popular during the gold rush that they were nearly eradicated; back in the mid-1850s, single Olympia oysters went for a silver dollar, the equivalent of about thirty dollars per oyster today. Olympias are a great starter for a raw-oyster newbie—they're so small and they're cute, and it's hard to be intimidated by cute.

Kumamoto oysters (*Crassostrea sikamea*), aka Kumos, are appreciated by all for their sweetness; their beautiful deep, sculptured shell; and the fact that they are still at their best into the summer, when other oysters diminish in quality due to spawning. Kumos are sweet, briny, creamy, and nutty, with a distinct cucumber note. Kumos are also a great first oyster for half-shell virgins.

Eastern oysters (*Crassostrea virginica*), aka Virginicas, Gulf oysters, or American oysters, are truly American, ranging up and down the East Coast, along the Gulf of Mexico, and also here on the Pacific Coast. They tend to be firmer when grown in colder northern climes, which makes for a delicious oyster on the half shell. A Totten Inlet Virginica I had in Washington was one of my most favorite oysters ever, with a finish that lasted forever, like the very best kind of wine.

European flats (*Ostrea edulis*), aka Belons, were introduced to the Northwest in the 1950s and, not surprisingly, are native to Europe. Like the related Olympia oyster, the parent holds on to the developing larvae within the shell before releasing it into the water after a few weeks. European flats are round in shape with an extremely shallow cup. The shells are quite brittle, and the oysters are very briny.

SEASON

The rule "only eat oysters in months with an 'r' in them" (i.e. don't eat oysters in May, June, July, or August) is sort of right, sort of not. I don't eat oysters when they spawn, which is usually during the hotter months. An August oyster might be watery, gritty, and lacking in flavor. Generally speaking, oysters are better in the colder months, but modern refrigeration makes the rule less accurate. A nonspawning oyster harvested in the summer that is well handled can be delicious.

BUYING TIPS

You'll find live oysters either in saltwater tanks or stored on ice. As with all shellfish, you'll want to buy them live. You won't find oysters, unlike clams or mussels, slightly open. Or rather, if you find an oyster slightly open, it's probably dead. Oysters know how delicious they are—it's easier to get into Fort Knox than it is to get into a really fresh oyster.

QUESTIONS TO ASK
BEFORE YOU PULL OUT
YOUR WALLET

Ask to see the harvest tag so you know when the oysters were pulled out of the water. They can have a shelf life of up to two weeks, but when eating them raw, I prefer to get oysters that are as fresh as possible, harvested within five days of purchase. I feel they taste best when you're standing knee-deep in the water, shucking the oyster against your thigh and eating it right there. I think the quality and flavor lessens the longer and farther away you are from this idyllic picture.

CARING FOR YOUR
GOOD FISH

You'll commonly find fresh oysters in two forms: in their shell, live (also known as "shell stock"), or already shucked (usually packed in half-pint or pint-size containers; note that the jarred "smalls" are actually more like medium-size oysters in the shell). Store oysters in the shell in a bowl, and drape a damp—not soaking wet—towel over them to keep them from drying out in the refrigerator. If I'm going to eat oysters raw, I buy them the day I want to eat them. That's just me, but it probably should be you too. If you buy them shucked, be sure to check the packing date and keep them in the coldest part of your refrigerator. I typically cook preshucked oysters.

You'll find wild oysters clinging to rocks or clumped together in intertidal areas, a product of what's known as "natural set," in which larvae naturally attach themselves to old shells or rocky surfaces. Cultivated oysters develop from larvae that are, for the most part, grown in hatcheries and then encouraged to attach to shells (known as cultch). Cultivated oysters are grown in a variety of ways: in bags; suspended in the water column in trays or lantern nets; tumbled (to create a deep cup and smooth edges such as in Kushi and Shigoku oysters); or simply spread on the beach, what's known as bottom culture.

HOW THIS TYPE OF SEAFOOD IS RAISED OR HARVESTED

While I'd love to say there is a type of seafood you can easily substitute for oysters, I think that would be a disservice to how unique an oyster is. If you're craving oyster chowder, you can often find very high-quality oysters already shucked, in jars, that are great to use if you can't find them in the shell. Can't find shucked? Make a chowder with manila or razor clams instead.

SUSTAINABLE SUBSTITUTES

Oyster spawn on a half shell? Not exactly something you want to pay a premium for, so it's good to know what oysters look like during and after spawning so that you can avoid eating them. At this time, they are not at their best. Some oyster growers sell triploid oysters, which are essentially sterile. Triploids, or "trips," are plump and juicy when the others are reproducing. When an oyster spawns, the oyster will be milky and mushy, and after spawning, the oyster meat will be skinny, gray, and watery. Mmm, I'll take a dozen please! Typically this happens in the summer months, except for Kumamotos, which spawn during the winter, and of course the sterile trips. Oyster growers in France refer to triploids as *l'huître des quatre saisons*—the oyster for the four seasons.

oyster and artichoke soup

2 tablespoons unsalted butter

1 bunch green onions, light- and dark-green parts only, thinly sliced

2 ribs celery, thinly sliced

¼ teaspoon fine sea salt

¼ teaspoon freshly ground black pepper

2 tablespoons chopped fresh tarragon, divided (optional)

1 pint preshucked fresh oysters

2 (14-ounce) cans artichoke bottoms, drained

1 (8-ounce) bottle clam juice

4 ounces (1 cup) medium-diced oyster or cremini mushrooms

⅛ teaspoon cayenne

2 tablespoons cream sherry or dry sherry

2 tablespoons all-purpose flour

½ cup heavy cream

2 teaspoons lemon juice

PAIRING: First choice is white Burgundy; second, white Bordeaux.

Years ago, when a friend said she wanted to try a recipe for oyster and artichoke soup, I admit I wrinkled my nose. Some ingredient combinations can be truly terrible—others you nod your head up and down, a grin forming on your face because the oyster's sweet, soft brininess is a seafood sister to artichoke's creamy yet firm vegetal quality. If you use jarred high-quality preshucked oysters, the dish comes together really fast. It has become my new favorite soup.

In a stockpot over medium-high heat, melt the butter. Add the green onions, celery, salt, pepper, and 1 tablespoon of the tarragon. Sauté for 8 to 10 minutes, or until the vegetables are tender.

Meanwhile, drain the oysters, reserving the liquid. Rinse them under cold running water, dry them on a paper towel, then roughly chop them. Set aside.

Puree one can of the artichokes with the clam juice in a blender or food processor until smooth. Pour the puree into a 4-cup measuring cup, add the reserved oyster liquor, and then add water to make 4 cups of liquid. Set aside.

Roughly chop the other can of artichokes. Add them to the stockpot, along with the mushrooms and cayenne. Sauté over medium-high heat for about 3 minutes, or until the mushrooms release their juices. Add the sherry, stirring to loosen any bits clinging to the pot, and then add the flour. Sauté for another 2 to 3 minutes.

Add the pureed mixture to the pot and bring the soup to a boil over high heat. Reduce the heat and simmer for 10 minutes. Add the oysters, cream, and lemon juice. Season to taste with salt and pepper, turn off the heat, and let the soup sit for 5 minutes before stirring in the remaining 1 tablespoon tarragon. Serve immediately.

hangtown fry

Hangtown fry was invented during the 1850s gold rush in Placerville (Hangtown), California. Legend has it that a rich gold prospector coined the name when he demanded the most expensive dish at a local hotel. In those days, the costliest ingredients were bacon, eggs (likely cormorant eggs from San Francisco), and oysters (brought on ice or in saltwater barrels from the city).

SERVES 4

8 strips thick-cut bacon
½ pint preshucked fresh oysters, preferably "small," or 1 dozen medium-size oysters in the shell, shucked‡
1 cup buttermilk
8 eggs
1¼ cups roughly chopped arugula
¼ cup half-and-half
½ teaspoon Tabasco or other hot sauce
¼ teaspoon fine sea salt
1 tablespoon unsalted butter
½ cup panko or bread crumbs
1 tablespoon high-heat vegetable oil
4 slices good crusty bread, toasted
4 lemon wedges, for garnish

---

‡ Go to GoodFishBook.com for a demonstration of how to shuck oysters.

---

* Go to GoodFishBook.com to see how to bake bacon without a mess.

PAIRING: First choice is white Burgundy; second, Oregon chardonnay. A mimosa or Bloody Mary would be great too (hair of the dog and all that).

Lay the bacon on a parchment-lined baking sheet. Place in the cold oven, then turn the oven on to 400°F and set the timer for 20 minutes.*

Meanwhile, in a small bowl, soak the oysters in the buttermilk for 30 minutes in the refrigerator.

Whisk the eggs with the arugula, half-and-half, Tabasco, and salt. Allow the mixture to sit for 10 minutes for the creamiest eggs.

In a large sauté pan over medium heat, melt the butter. Pour the egg mixture into the pan and reduce the heat to medium-low. Grab a wooden spoon and start stirring. You will be tempted to increase the heat, but don't. If you keep stirring the eggs over medium-low heat, they will produce the creamiest, most delicious eggs you've ever had. It should take 6 to 8 minutes to set into small curds, but they will still have lots of moisture. Look for creamy, barely set eggs. When the eggs are done, place the pan at the back of the stovetop to keep warm.

When the bacon has finished cooking, remove it from the oven and transfer to a paper-towel-lined plate to drain. Drain the oysters and discard the buttermilk. Place the panko on a plate and dredge the oysters, coating them well on both sides.

In a clean sauté pan over high heat, add the oil. Pan-fry the oysters until they brown on one side, 1 to 2 minutes, then flip them and cook just 30 seconds more on the other side.

Serve each person a piece of toast and top with eggs, 2 slices of bacon, and a fried oyster or two. Garnish with a lemon wedge.

oysters on the half shell
with cucumber sorbet

SERVES 2 TO 6, DEPENDING ON YOUR FRIENDS' LOVE FOR OYSTERS

⅓ cup water

3 tablespoons sugar, plus additional for dusting

1 jalapeño, halved lengthwise, seeded, and sliced into thin half-moons

14 ounces (about 1 medium) cucumber, peeled and chopped

1½ tablespoons seasoned rice wine vinegar

¼ teaspoon fine sea salt

24 oysters in the shell, shucked‡

Rock salt or crushed ice, for serving

---

‡ Go to GoodFishBook.com for a demonstration of how to shuck oysters.

PAIRING: First choice is sauvignon blanc; second, muscadet.

I love oysters as naked as the day they were born. It takes a special accompaniment to a raw oyster to turn my head; most of the time, it seems to diminish the oyster's magnificence more than accent it. Until now. The combination of a slightly sweet, briny oyster with a refreshingly icy and vegetal cucumber sorbet would be special enough, but then you gild the lily by adding just a touch of candied jalapeño—another green note, but this time with a lingering fiery finish. After a few of these oysters, you can't help but feel completely alive, your taste buds dancing on your tongue.

In a small saucepan over high heat, add the water and sugar. Cook, stirring, until the sugar completely dissolves, about 2 minutes. Add the jalapeño. Simmer gently for 5 minutes. Strain the jalapeño, reserving the syrup. Lay the jalapeños out on parchment or wax paper to dry and dust lightly with more sugar.

Add the reserved syrup to a blender along with the cucumber, rice wine vinegar, and salt. Blend well and then strain through a fine-mesh sieve. Chill well and freeze in an ice cream or sorbet maker according to the manufacturer's instructions. Let the sorbet firm up in the freezer for at least 2 hours. Alternatively, if you don't have an ice cream maker, you can pour the mixture into a glass dish, place in the freezer, and stir every 20 minutes until it is frozen.

Spread the rock salt on a platter and arrange the oysters carefully on the salt. Scoop tiny balls (I use a melon baller) of cucumber sorbet and place them on the oysters. Quickly garnish each oyster with 1 piece of candied jalapeño and serve on the double, before the ice melts.

oysters

with lemon-thyme sabayon

SERVES 4 TO 6 AS AN APPETIZER

Rock salt, as needed

24 Pacific oysters in the
  shell, shucked‡

2 tablespoons oyster
  liquor, strained

2 large egg yolks

1 tablespoon lemon juice

1 scant teaspoon lemon zest

1 teaspoon minced fresh thyme

2 tablespoons unsalted butter*

Fine sea salt

---

*This is a great place to use extra tomato-Espelette butter from the recipe on page 51.

---

‡ Go to GoodFishBook.com for a demonstration of how to shuck oysters.

PAIRING: First choice is grüner veltliner; second, muscadet.

Sabayon is the sauce love child of a light and airy meringue and a rich, buttery hollandaise. I remember having to whisk this classic sauce when I worked in fine dining. The bowl was bigger than a bathtub, and we must have started with twenty yolks. When the chef would walk by, I'd whisk faster—a moment of daydreaming and you'd accidentally scramble the eggs. You were kindly rewarded for your hard work; before your eyes the yolks lightened and thickened into canary-yellow ribbons of emulsified velvet tracing trails in the shiny bowl, steam mixing with the perspiration on your brow. This is a great recipe to make for friends who are new to oysters and aren't quite on board (yet) with eating them raw. The oysters are blanketed with the bright sabayon, which puffs and caramelizes under the broiler, but the oysters themselves stay luscious, the best of both words, neither raw nor fully cooked.

Preheat the broiler.

Spread rock salt on a baking sheet to a ½ inch thickness. Arrange the oysters on the half shell over the salt. Place the pan in the refrigerator while you make the sabayon.

In the top of a double boiler, combine the oyster liquor, egg yolks, lemon juice and zest, and thyme. (If you don't have a double boiler, simply place a glass or metal bowl over a saucepan with 3 inches of boiling water; making sure the base of the bowl does not touch the water.) Whisk the mixture continuously, incorporating air into the sauce, until it becomes thick and reaches 160°F, about 5 full minutes, or until your arm falls off. Whisk in the butter. Turn off the heat and season the sabayon to taste with salt.

Remove the baking sheet from the refrigerator and spoon the sabayon over each oyster. Place the pan on the middle rack in the oven and broil the oysters for 2 to 3 minutes, or until the sauce browns. Watch very carefully because it burns easily. Serve immediately.

jet's oyster succotash

SERVES 4 AS A SIDE DISH

3 strips bacon, cut into small
dice (about ⅓ cup)

2 tablespoons unsalted butter

1 small carrot, cut into small
dice (about ½ cup)

¼ cup minced shallots

1 cup shelled edamame*

1 cup corn, thawed if
using frozen

1 teaspoon minced fresh lemon
thyme, or 1 teaspoon minced
fresh thyme plus ¼ teaspoon
lemon zest

½ pint preshucked fresh oysters,
or 6 large oysters in the shell,
shucked,‡ coarsely chopped,
and ¼ cup liquid reserved

2 teaspoons white wine vinegar

1 teaspoon lemon juice

Kosher salt and freshly ground
black pepper

Tabasco or other hot sauce

2 tablespoons minced fresh
Italian parsley

‡ Go to GoodFishBook.com
for a demonstration of how to
shuck oysters.

PAIRING: First choice is Chablis;
second, muscadet.

After a day spent scouring the beaches of southern Puget Sound for clams and oysters, my friends gathered together in my kitchen and a cooking frenzy ensued. My buddy Jet grabbed some corn and some herbs, and before long a version of this recipe was on the table: buttery, sweet, herbal, and smoky-salty. Oyster succotash goes from side dish to meal when you serve it with greens and some bruschetta. In the winter (since frozen edamame and corn are always available), it would be great alongside roasted chicken. In the summer, serve it with grilled flank steak or barbecued ribs.

In a large skillet over medium-high heat, cook the bacon until its fat is rendered and it is crisp, 6 to 7 minutes. Transfer the bacon with a slotted spoon to a paper-towel-lined plate and set aside. Add the butter, carrot, and shallots to the fat in the pan. Sauté for 5 minutes, or until the vegetables are soft. Add the edamame, corn, and lemon thyme, and sauté until the corn caramelizes, another 2 to 3 minutes.

Deglaze the pan with the oyster liquid and reduce until the mixture is dry. Add the oysters, vinegar, and lemon juice. Season to taste with salt, pepper, and Tabasco. Sprinkle with the parsley and reserved bacon.

*Edamame, or young soybeans in the pod, are sold in the frozen foods section of most supermarkets. You can also find shelled edamame, which are easy to thaw and add to recipes. If you have access to fresh fiddlehead ferns, you can use them in place of, or in combination with, the edamame. Salicornia, commonly known as beach asparagus or sea beans, would also be a lovely addition to this recipe, as would fava beans. All will need to be blanched in salted water for a few minutes then shocked in ice water before adding.

dungeness crab

I love me some Dungeness crab—all ways, but especially pure and simple, where the shortest distance between two points is a straight line from a cracked crab to my mouth. Butter is always a nice accompaniment, but good Dungeness crab seems to contain its own oceany butter: rich yet still crisp and clean. (An extra bonus is its onboard sea salt seasoning.)

When I worked at The Herbfarm Restaurant, I used to pick up our live crabs from the fish market. That long drive out to Woodinville was always punctuated by quick peeks into my rearview mirror to see if an army of rogue crustaceans was plotting to hijack the car. They never did, which was a very good thing, because what a loss if I had missed out on transforming these crabby warriors into the dishes of chef Jerry Traunfeld's imaginings: paper-thin pasta squares enfolding crabmeat with a delicate lemon beurre blanc, herbed crab cocktails with shiso, and delicate crab soufflés.

WHAT MAKES THIS A GOOD FISH

The Dungeness crab fishery is well managed and abundant up and down the coast, from California to Alaska. The population fluctuates year to year and, generally speaking, the allowable catch is restricted by size (only the bigger crabs—size minimums vary by area), sex (males only), and molt times (only nonmolting crabs may be harvested).

BY ANY OTHER NAME

Dungeness crabs (*Cancer magister*) are also known as "Dungies."

SEASON

Dungeness crabs molt many times in their first few years and once a year after that. Most commercial harvesting of Dungeness crab occurs in the fall and winter, though as you go north, the season extends into spring (in British Columbia) and summer (in Alaska). Crabs can be caught recreationally throughout the year in some areas. If you plan to go crabbing, check local sport-fishing regulations to make sure the season is open. Soft-shell crabs should be gently released to allow them to harden up (you get less yield by weight when the shell is soft).

BUYING TIPS

You will find Dungeness crab in many forms: live in saltwater or seawater tanks; cooked, cleaned, and on ice; as picked crabmeat; in sealed plastic tubs; or in cans (most canned crabmeat needs to be kept under refrigeration). I've found that the tubbed and canned Dungeness crab can be of surprisingly good quality. If you want a live Dungie, look for a spirited one and make sure it has both of its claws (sometimes they get knocked off or lost in a fight; amazingly, crabs can grow limbs back when they molt). Cooked crabs (known as whole cooks) are often less expensive than live ones because they don't need to be as perfect (they can be missing limbs) and, frankly, might have been the older crabs in the tank and not as lively as the others. Beware of bargain basement crab "sales."

If you get a chance to go crabbing, make sure you know how to "sex" a crab. Flip it onto its back; you'll see what's known as the apron. On males the apron looks tall and slender; on females it is wider and dome-shaped. Females hold their eggs under their apron (not a euphemism). Because they are needed to replenish the species, it's illegal to keep females, so make sure you are harvesting only males.

QUESTIONS TO ASK BEFORE YOU PULL OUT YOUR WALLET

If you're buying live Dungies, ask when the crab was caught and how long it's been in the tank. You'll want to buy live crabs soon after they've been pulled from the water, if possible. They can lose fat (and therefore flavor) the longer they sit in tanks. If your Dungie is already cooked, ask when it was cooked (you'll want to eat it within a day or two). If the picked crabmeat looks like it is sitting in a pool of water, walk on by—you'll pay for that water (and seafood sitting in a pool of water tells me all I need to know about the standards of that fish market).

CARING FOR YOUR GOOD FISH

If you buy a live crab, they will probably wrap it in newspaper and put it in a bag for you. I like to throw that bag immediately into the fridge—you'll want to cook the crab that day. Keep in mind that it is unadvisable to cook and eat dead crabs, even if they died while you had them, as bacteria multiply rapidly on dead shellfish. If you go crabbing and get lucky, keep those bad boys in a large bucket or cooler of seawater until you are ready to cook. About thirty minutes before I want to cook a crab, I start boiling a big pot of heavily salted water (or seawater, ideally); I get my steamer pot ready a little closer to cook time. (I've recently become a convert to the benefits of steaming over boiling. The crabmeat retains less water and, as a result, has a more pronounced flavor.) I then send the crab on a short tour of my freezer. This chill puts the crab into a trance of sorts, slowing its metabolism and making it easier to dispatch (the nice way of saying kill). For more information about humanely dispatching crab, go to GoodFishBook.com.

HOW THIS TYPE OF SEAFOOD IS RAISED OR HARVESTED

Crabs are wild caught, most typically in pots, though divers or waders can grab them by hand or with a net. I've even seen them being caught with a fishing pole/pot hybrid, the pot lowered on the reel. Asking any two crabbers what bait they use is sure to start a heated discussion: I've used everything from cat food (the stinkier the better) to fish heads to frozen turkey drumsticks. They've all worked. Crabs are voracious eaters.

SUSTAINABLE SUBSTITUTES

Because of their sweet flavor, shrimp or scallops are a good substitute for Dungeness crabmeat. There are also other Pacific Coast crabs not included in this book that would work well, such as Alaska snow crab and king crab legs. In particular, look for red rock crab that can be caught recreationally (they're delicious but mean little buggers).

CRAB THREE WAYS

When you need to purchase Dungeness crabmeat you can go one of three ways:

Pre-cooked, cleaned, and picked crabmeat. This is the most convenient option, but not necessarily the best option. It depends on the market and the depth of your pockets. Good markets will offer premium picked crabmeat that has no shells (though, just to be sure, give the meat an extra once-over). This convenience comes at a high cost, however.

Pre-cooked whole crab. You can ask the fishmonger to clean the crab for you, which means they will gut and rinse it. You will still have to crack and pick the meat yourself. This is an economical way to go, though it may be of a lesser quality than live or picked crab.

Live crab. This option is desirable for the ultimate in freshness and gives you total control over the cooking process. The price of live crab is typically the same or slightly more expensive than buying pre-cooked whole crab. Go to GoodFishBook.com for a video demonstration of how to kill, cook, and clean a crab. Boil or steam crabs that weigh around 2 pounds each, as most do, for about 14 minutes. Increase the cooking time by a few minutes if your crabs are larger or if you are cooking many at the same time.

A helpful conversion: Approximately one-quarter of the crab's weight is meat, so if you need 1 pound of crabmeat, you'll need 4 pounds of whole crab. Most Dungeness crabs are in the 1½ to 2 pound range.

dungeness crab panzanella

with charred-tomato vinaigrette

SERVES 4 AS A LIGHT LUNCH

2 cups halved cherry tomatoes

¼ cup plus 1 tablespoon extra-
  virgin olive oil, divided

2 teaspoons balsamic
  vinegar, divided

⅛ teaspoon fine sea salt

Freshly ground black pepper

½ cup roughly chopped fresh
  basil leaves, divided

2½ cups crust-on bread
  cubes cut from a good
  crusty artisan loaf

10 ounces Dungeness crabmeat

PAIRING: First choice is sparkling
rosé; second, Sancerre.

I think if I had been given the following as a word problem in junior high, I might have actually rocked math: If a fabulous bread salad was on a train traveling east at forty miles per hour, and a shipment of live Dungeness crabs was coming west traveling at ninety miles per hour, and just prior to impact someone threw some flaming tomatoes and fresh basil onto the tracks, how awesome would lunch be? You will have leftover dressing, which is a good thing, as you can spread it on toast, toss it with pasta or salad, serve it with Newspaper Crab with Three Sauces (page 71), or just eat it off a spoon.

Preheat the broiler. Place a rack in the top third of the oven.

Toss the tomatoes with 1 tablespoon of the oil, 1 teaspoon of the vinegar, the salt, and some grinds of pepper. Spread the tomatoes on a foil-lined baking sheet. Broil for 5 minutes, or until the tomatoes are charred in spots. Transfer to a bowl and set aside, leaving the broiler on.

Add half of the tomatoes to a blender, along with ¼ cup of the basil and the remaining ¼ cup oil and 1 teaspoon vinegar. Blend until the dressing is smooth. Season with salt and pepper to taste.

Toss the bread cubes with 2 tablespoons of the dressing. Spread them on the baking sheet and broil until lightly crispy in places, about 5 minutes. Stir the cubes and broil for another minute or two, until they are crispy all over. Set aside.

Double-check the crabmeat for any stray bits of shell. Gently squeeze out any excess moisture with your hands. Toss the crab with 2 tablespoons of the dressing. To serve, mix the crab with the reserved bread cubes, reserved tomatoes, and 2 more tablespoons of the dressing. Season with more salt and pepper if necessary, and garnish with the remaining ¼ cup basil leaves.

newspaper crab

with three sauces

SERVES 4 OUT-OF-TOWN GUESTS

4 cooked, cleaned Dungeness
   crabs
½ cup Soy Caramel Sauce
   (recipe follows)
½ cup Avocado Herb Sauce
   (recipe follows)
½ cup Lemon Panko Sauce
   (recipe follows)

PAIRING: First choice is
sauvignon blanc; second, beer,
such as Pike Place Brewery's
Naughty Nellie or Kilt Lifter.

One of my favorite things to do when friends come to Seattle for the first time is to take them to Pike Place Market, where we pick out cooked and cleaned crabs, grab some beers from Pike Place Brewery, then jump in the car and head to the Queen Anne neighborhood. I've got the Sunday paper, a blanket, and lots of paper towels in the car, and we lay out a picnic at this little park that overlooks the entire Seattle skyline. If it's raining—which, this being Seattle, it is wont to do—I take my guests back to my house, where I completely gild the lily by accompanying the crab with several sauces. I'm sure you'll prefer one sauce over the others, but I've yet to meet anyone who didn't shamelessly lick the bottom of the soy caramel bowl.

Lay several sheets of newspaper out on the table along with plenty of napkins and various tools for cracking (see my preferred crab tool on page 12). Serve the crabs with individual bowls of each sauce for dipping.

MAKES ABOUT ½ CUP

¼ cup sake
3 tablespoons mirin
2 tablespoons soy sauce
1 tablespoon lemon juice
1 teaspoon sugar
4 tablespoons (½ stick) cold
   unsalted butter

SOY CARAMEL SAUCE

In a small saucepan, add the sake, mirin, soy sauce, lemon juice, and sugar. Bring to a boil over high heat, then reduce to maintain a simmer. Cook the sauce until it is reduced by half, 5 to 7 minutes. Reduce the heat to its lowest setting and whisk in the butter 1 tablespoon at a time, adding each only after the previous one has melted. Taste and add more lemon juice if desired. You can make the reduction ahead and store in the refrigerator for up to 1 week; finish the sauce with the butter just prior to serving. You can also hold the sauce for about 2 hours in a thermos: preheat a thermos by filling it with boiling water for a few minutes, dump it out, and then pour in the sauce.

CONTINUED

AVOCADO HERB SAUCE

MAKES ABOUT ½ CUP

1 avocado, peeled and pitted
¼ cup packed fresh cilantro
   leaves and stems
¼ cup plain full-fat
   Greek-style yogurt
1 tablespoon mayonnaise
1 tablespoon freshly squeezed
   lime juice (about ½ lime)
½ teaspoon white wine vinegar
¼ teaspoon fine sea salt
¼ teaspoon Tabasco or other
   hot sauce

Combine all of the ingredients in a blender or food processor and blend to a smooth puree.

LEMON PANKO SAUCE

MAKES A GENEROUS ½ CUP

½ cup panko
¼ cup finely chopped fresh
   Italian parsley
½ tablespoon freshly
   grated lemon zest (about
   1 small lemon)
¼ teaspoon fine sea salt
Pinch of cayenne
¼ cup unsalted butter, melted

In a small bowl, mix the panko with the parsley, lemon zest, salt, and cayenne.

Serve the panko mixture and butter separately: instruct your guests to dip the crab into the melted butter and then into the lemon panko crumbs.

chilled cucumber-coconut soup

with dungeness crab

SERVES 4

1 tablespoon high-heat peanut
  or vegetable oil
1 cup small-diced yellow onion
¼ teaspoon fine sea salt
¼ teaspoon freshly ground
  black pepper
1 pound cucumbers,
  peeled, seeded, and sliced
  ½ inch thick
1½ cups chicken or
  vegetable stock
1 (14-ounce) can full-fat coconut
  milk, refrigerated for a few
  hours, ¼ cup of the thick
  cream reserved for garnish
1 cup packed fresh basil leaves,
  plus 2 tablespoons chopped
¼ cup packed fresh cilantro
  leaves and stems, plus
  1 tablespoon chopped
3 dashes of Tabasco or other
  hot sauce
Juice of 1 medium lime (about
  1½ tablespoons), divided
1 tablespoon fish sauce
¼ pound Dungeness crabmeat
1 tablespoon extra-virgin
  olive oil

PAIRING: First choice is
Washington riesling; second,
pinot blanc.

Jean-Georges Vongerichten is the chef/owner of the three-Michelin-starred Jean-Georges in New York City (among others all over the world). In one of his first cookbooks, I learned that fresh herbs and fish sauce are magical when combined with coconut milk and upping the amounts of herbs. Make the soup the day before; when you're ready to eat, simply mix the crab with the herbs, add it as a garnish, and serve.

Heat the vegetable oil in a stockpot over medium-high heat. Add the onion, salt, and pepper, and sauté for 3 to 4 minutes, or until the onion has softened. Add the cucumbers and sauté for 2 to 3 minutes more, then add the chicken stock, 1 cup of the coconut milk, 1 cup basil leaves, and ¼ cup cilantro. Bring to a simmer and cook for 2 minutes. Add the Tabasco, half of the lime juice, and the fish sauce.

Transfer the soup to a blender and blend to a smooth, bright-green puree—let the blender run for about 2 minutes. Strain the soup through a fine-mesh sieve, pressing on the solids to extract all of the liquid. Discard the solids. Taste and adjust the seasoning if necessary. The soup should have enough saltiness, acidity from the lime, and a bit of a kick from the pepper and Tabasco. Chill the soup in the refrigerator for at least 2 hours.

Shortly before serving, double-check the crabmeat for any stray bits of shell, and reserve any nice large crab pieces for garnish. Mix the 2 tablespoons chopped basil and 1 tablespoon chopped cilantro with the crabmeat and olive oil. Taste and adjust the seasoning, adding a pinch of salt if necessary.

Serve the chilled soup in shallow bowls with a small amount of crab salad in the middle. Lean a few of the larger crabmeat pieces against the salad. Drizzle some of the reserved coconut cream around the edges (thin the coconut cream with a little water if necessary).

dungeness crab mac and cheese

SERVES 4 TO 6

¼ cup (½ stick) unsalted butter, plus additional for greasing the pan

2 to 3 live Dungeness crabs, or about ¾ pound crabmeat

1 pound good-quality cheddar cheese (I like a mix of medium and sharp)

¼ cup minced shallots

¼ cup all-purpose flour

3 cups whole milk

1 tablespoon tomato paste

2 teaspoons Dijon mustard

2 bay leaves

¼ teaspoon regular or smoked paprika

⅛ teaspoon saffron, mixed with 1 tablespoon hot water

⅛ teaspoon cayenne

1 pound elbow or penne pasta

1 cup panko

¼ cup finely chopped fresh Italian parsley

¼ cup (½ stick) unsalted butter, melted

1 tablespoon freshly grated lemon zest (about 1 large lemon)

‡ Go to GoodFishBook.com for a demonstration of how to boil and clean Dungeness crab.

PAIRING: First choice is California chardonnay; second, white Burgundy.

For extra flavorful mac and cheese, cook the pasta in the same water you cooked the crab. As the pasta cooks, it absorbs the crab "stock," which then flavors the pasta from within. Tuck a napkin into your shirt and, as comedian Margaret Cho would say, "put on your eatin' dress."

Preheat the oven to 350°F. Grease a 13-by-9-inch baking dish with butter. Fill the sink with ice water.

Bring a large pot of salted water to a boil over high heat. Add the crabs. Once the water has returned to a boil, cook the crabs for 14 to 18 minutes. (Cook crabs that weigh around 2 pounds each, as most do, for about 14 minutes. Increase the cooking time by a few minutes if your crabs are larger or when cooking multiples.) While they cook, grate the cheddar and set aside. Using a pair of sturdy tongs, pull the crabs out of the cooking water and chill them in the ice water. Strain the crab cooking water through a sieve, return it to the pot, and return to a boil.

In a large saucepan over medium-low heat, melt the butter and add the shallots. Cook for 1 minute. Whisk in the flour gradually and then reduce the heat to low. Keep cooking and stirring the roux until it starts to smell nutty, about 5 minutes. Gradually add the milk while continuing to stir. Increase the heat to medium-high and add the tomato paste, mustard, bay leaves, paprika, saffron with water, and cayenne. Simmer gently until the sauce is slightly thickened, about 10 minutes. Add the grated cheese and cook until it has melted into the sauce. Taste for seasoning, then cover and set aside while you clean and crack the crabs.‡

Cook the pasta in the strained crab cooking water until it is al dente; drain and transfer to a large bowl. Stir the pasta and crabmeat into the sauce. Transfer this heart-stoppingly delicious concoction into the baking dish.

In a medium bowl, mix the panko with the parsley, melted butter, and lemon zest. Top the pasta with the panko mixture and bake for about 30 minutes, or until the mac and cheese is bubbly and browned on the top.

dungeness crab
with bacon-cider sauce

SERVES 4 AS A FIRST COURSE

1 pound Dungeness crabmeat

4 strips bacon, cut into
small dice

1 apple, such as Gala or Granny
Smith, sliced horizontally into
4 (⅓-inch) slices through the
core (remove the seeds with
the tip of a knife, leaving the
pretty star pattern)

⅓ cup small-diced shallot

¼ teaspoon fine sea salt

½ cup dry white wine

⅓ cup clam juice

¼ cup apple juice or cider

1 teaspoon minced fresh lemon
thyme or regular thyme

Heaping ¼ teaspoon freshly
ground black pepper

1 tablespoon unsalted butter

1 teaspoon minced
fresh tarragon

Cayenne (optional)

Maldon sea salt, for
garnish (optional)

PAIRING: First choice is
Savennières; second,
white Burgundy.

This is a sophisticated dish that I pull out in the fall as a first course to impress my family from back East, especially when they start in on the "blue crab is better than Dungeness" rhetoric. If you live in the Pacific Northwest, it is highly likely that you can make this dish with ingredients raised or grown very close to home: world-famous Washington apples and cider, Pacific Dungies, and locally cured bacon.

Double-check the crabmeat for any stray bits of shell. Place it in a medium bowl over another bowl partially filled with very hot tap water. Locate 4 nice large leg pieces to use as a garnish and set aside. Cover the top bowl. After 5 minutes, give the crabmeat a gentle stir. You want it to be room temperature or slightly warm when you serve the dish.

In a small skillet over medium-high heat, add the bacon. Reduce the heat to medium and cook the bacon until its fat is rendered and the bacon is crisp, about 10 minutes. Remove the bacon with a slotted spoon to a paper-towel-lined plate and set aside, reserving the fat. Pour the bacon fat through a fine-mesh sieve into a cup. Clean the skillet and place it back on the stove over medium-high heat. Add the bacon fat back to the skillet and, when it is hot, carefully slip the apples into the pan. Fry them until one side is nicely caramelized, 2 to 3 minutes, then flip and cook them for 30 seconds more. Transfer them to a plate and keep warm.

Without cleaning the skillet, add the shallot and salt, and cook over medium-high heat, scraping up any brown bits. Cook until the shallots are softened and just getting a little color, about 5 minutes. Deglaze the pan with the white wine, clam juice, and apple juice. Add the lemon thyme and pepper. Bring the sauce to a boil over high heat and reduce by half, about 5 minutes. Remove the skillet from the heat, then swirl in the butter, tarragon, and a pinch of cayenne. Taste and check for seasoning.

Serve each person a quarter of the crabmeat, placing it in the center of a warm plate. Place an apple slice (caramelized side up) to one side, leaning on the pile of crabmeat. Drizzle the sauce over the crab and apple, and garnish with some reserved bacon pieces and one piece of the reserved leg meat. Finish with a sprinkle of Maldon sea salt.

shrimp

When I was just a wee lass, I had a thing bad for shrimp cocktail. This habit started when I was six or so—an age that required me to kneel on my seat at my family's favorite local restaurant to reach the shrimp that perched on the sides of a soda fountain glass. I remember how cold and frosty that glass was; how the ice cupped a thimbleful of cocktail sauce in the middle; how five plump shrimp fanned out from the center like the orange-pink petals of a rare flower.

I feel wistful about those cheap and easy shrimp cocktails, those family meals that seemed to be devoid of the modern conversations about food that are fairly commonplace today. Being an ethical eater sometimes gives me an adult-size headache and a penchant for sounding like an old fogie who starts sentences with, "Remember when . . . ?" I no longer eat shrimp in the numbers I used to. I've learned to anticipate—with joy—the seasons for food.

Thirty-some-odd years later, with the feeling of the wooden chair on my knees and the smell of lemon still etched in my nasal passages, I find myself at the docks in Anacortes, Washington, where I happen upon some live spot prawns being sold off a local boat. The sun is shining and the striped and spotted orange prawns are lookers, stunning against the blue sky. I hang my legs over the side of the dock and twist off the shrimp heads, thanking each one for its life. My excitement builds as I plan a menu—I'm thinking some cocktail sauce, a lemon, a tall frosty glass, some crushed ice. Yes, that feels about right.

WHAT MAKES THIS A GOOD FISH	US-caught shrimp from the Pacific Ocean, generally speaking, are well managed, sustainable, and abundant. Shrimp grow very fast, produce many young in their short life spans, and have catch limits set by fishery managers. The pink shrimp fishery, in particular, has done a great job of reducing bycatch. The use of LED lights on the front of the net has reduced bycatch by 90 percent. Finfish see the lights and swim away. Pink shrimp, à la *Poltergeist*, go toward the light (and into the net).

....

BY ANY OTHER NAME	Pink shrimp (*Pandalus jordani*) are the tiny guys, no bigger than your thumbnail. They are also marketed as Oregon pink shrimp or cocktail shrimp, and are sometimes called bay shrimp, ocean shrimp, or salad shrimp. Spot prawns (*Pandalus platyceros*) are sometimes called spot shrimp, so-named for the distinctive white spots on the prawns' abdomens. There are two other species of shrimp that are very similar to spot prawns called sidestripe (*Pandalopsis dispar*) and coonstripe (*Pandalus hypsinotis*). Sidestripe and coonstripe prawns are often caught along with spot prawns and sometimes marketed erroneously under that name. All, regardless of name, are considered sustainable.

....

SEASON	Pink shrimp are in season from April through October in Oregon and Washington, but they most often come to market cooked, peeled, and frozen. Spot prawns are in season in the spring and summer in British Columbia, and can generally be found in Washington from May through August, though you can find frozen spot prawns year-round, especially through online sources. Alaska spot prawn season occurs in January and February and then again from May through October.

....

BUYING TIPS	If you are buying your shrimp or prawns frozen or previously frozen, make sure there is no sign of freezer burn (little white or dry-looking patches). Live spot prawns are a treat and a treasure: snap them up if you see them and make sure they are still alive—and lively! Pink shrimp and spot prawns are not sold in the "count per pound" size designations you often see when purchasing other shrimp and prawn varieties at fish counters (such as 21 to 25 for large, or 31 to 35 for medium). You will find pink shrimp and spot prawns listed instead by the price per pound alone.

QUESTIONS TO ASK BEFORE YOU PULL OUT YOUR WALLET	What species is this and where was it caught? Look for pink shrimp from Alaska, Washington, California, and Oregon. Spot prawns can come from British Columbia, Alaska, Washington, Oregon, or California.

....

CARING FOR YOUR GOOD FISH	Pink shrimp are often purchased frozen and can remain in your freezer for up to six months. They defrost very rapidly. I like to defrost them on paper towels since they tend to retain some water. Spot prawns can be purchased frozen or fresh (heads removed), or live. Thaw spot prawns under cool running water or over a drip pan in the refrigerator. If you purchase live spot prawns, you should remove their heads as soon as possible, as an enzymatic process will make the meat mushy if the heads remain on once the prawns have died. They are sometimes sold with their bright-orange eggs attached; I like to stir the eggs into a pasta sauce at the last moment for a little crunch and texture.

....

HOW THIS TYPE OF SEAFOOD IS RAISED OR HARVESTED	Pink shrimp are caught by trawling. Although trawling is often a destructive process, this fishery trawls midwater instead of on the seafloor and is therefore generally recognized as less damaging to the environment. Also, the trawl net has a bycatch reduction device that allows other non-target species to escape the net. Spot prawns are caught with traps, which have low bycatch issues and minimal negative impacts on habitat.

....

SUSTAINABLE SUBSTITUTES	Domestic farmed white shrimp, because they are grown in tank-based recirculating aquaculture systems, make a good, though not ideal, substitute for spot prawns. Spot prawns are sweeter than white shrimp, so lobster meat would be a more similar substitute. I find that scallops and prawns are interchangeable up to a point, and similarly, I think big chunks of crabmeat could stand in as a possible substitute. Whether fresh or frozen, it is best to purchase shrimp from the United States. US fisheries managers are making efforts to keep the catch sustainable and find solutions to bycatch issues. We don't have these assurances for imported shrimp and can't be guaranteed that the environmental standards or social justice issues for the workers who farm or fish for shrimp in other countries are adequate.

weeknight linguine

with spot prawns and basil

SERVES 4

1 tablespoon kosher salt
1 pound fresh or dried linguine
¼ cup extra-virgin olive oil
½ cup pitted kalamata olives
¼ cup capers, chopped
3 cloves garlic, minced
¼ teaspoon red pepper flakes
¼ cup dry white vermouth or
   dry white wine
2 fresh tomatoes, cut into
   medium dice, or 2 whole
   canned tomatoes, cut into
   medium dice, plus ½ cup of
   the juice
1 pound spot prawns, peeled
   and deveined‡
¼ cup roughly chopped fresh
   basil, plus some small leaves
   for garnish
Zest of 1 lemon (about
   2 teaspoons)
2 ounces goat cheese (optional)

‡ Go to GoodFishBook.com
for a demonstration of how to
devein shrimp.

PAIRING: First choice is pinot
grigio; second, grüner veltliner.

Legend has it that pasta puttanesca was a quick bite for busy "ladies of the evening" in Naples, Italy. This dish is based on a classic puttanesca but takes it in a slightly different direction by including our Pacific Coast spot prawns and the bright note of lemon zest. One of my favorite ways to dress this recipe up a bit is by adding goat cheese. Yes, cheese and seafood together are widely considered verboten. But there are also notable exceptions, such as crab mac and cheese (see page 75) and this linguine. In general, don't mix seafood and cheese except in those rare situations when it tastes really, really good.

Set a large pasta pot filled with water over high heat. When the water boils, add the salt. Add the pasta and cook until it is al dente. Drain in a colander, reserving ½ cup of the pasta cooking liquid. Set the pasta aside, shaking it from time to time to keep it from sticking.

While the pasta cooks, heat a large sauté pan over medium heat and add the oil. After a minute, add the olives, capers, garlic, and red pepper flakes, and cook, stirring, for 2 minutes to flavor the oil. Carefully add the vermouth, stirring to loosen any bits clinging to the pan. Add the tomatoes with juice and cook for 2 to 3 minutes more. If the sauce is dry, add a touch of the reserved pasta cooking water. Add the pasta, prawns, chopped basil, and lemon zest, and cook, tossing, for 2 more minutes. Season to taste with salt. Garnish with the basil leaves and goat cheese.

tom yum goong
(spicy shrimp and lemongrass soup)

SERVES 4

2 tablespoons high-heat
  vegetable oil, divided
2 ribs celery, cut into small dice
1 medium yellow onion, cut into
  small dice (about 1 cup)
½ small carrot, cut into small
  dice (about ⅓ cup)
1 pound spot prawns, peeled
  and deveined,‡ shells reserved
5 to 6 cups water
3 tomatoes, cut into medium
  dice, or 1 (14-ounce) can diced
  tomatoes with their juice
6 lime leaves, or zest of 1 lime
  (about 1 teaspoon)
6 thin slices fresh peeled
  galangal* or ginger
2 serrano chiles, halved (remove
  seeds and membranes for a
  milder soup)
½ cup sliced shallots
3 stalks lemongrass, woody
  top half discarded, cut into
  1-inch pieces
¼ teaspoon fine sea salt
3 ounces cremini or button
  mushrooms, sliced ½ inch
  thick (about 1 cup)
3 tablespoons fish sauce
3 tablespoons freshly squeezed
  lime juice (about 2 limes)
Whole cilantro leaves,
  for garnish

I was lucky enough to spend a month touring Thailand, eating my way through trains, outdoor markets, hole-in-the-wall wok stands, and little tucked-away places. What stands out for me is the way Thai cuisine is perfectly balanced between salty, sweet, sour, spicy, and bitter. The food in Thailand can be very hot. The weather in Thailand can be very hot. One thing that is not so hot in Thailand is a perspiring, red-faced woman like myself in need of rice to put out the fire in my mouth from the tom yum goong. This version has been rated WGS: white girl safe.

Set a stockpot over medium-high heat. Add 1 tablespoon of the oil, and when it is hot, add the celery, onion, and carrot. Sauté for 5 minutes, or until lightly browned. Increase the heat to high, add the prawn shells, and sauté until they are lightly browned, about 2 minutes. (Browning the shells at high heat gives the stock its distinctive flavor.) Add the water to the pot—if you are using canned tomatoes, pour off the juice, measure it, then add enough water to total 6 cups. Add the lime leaves, galangal, and serranos and bring to a boil over high heat. Scrape up any brown bits at the bottom of the pot. Simmer gently for 30 minutes.

Strain the stock through a fine-mesh sieve and set aside. Heat the remaining 1 tablespoon oil in the same stockpot over medium-high heat. Add the shallots, lemongrass, and salt and sauté until lightly browned, about 8 minutes. Add the tomatoes, mushrooms, and reserved stock. Bring the soup to a gentle boil, reduce to a simmer, and add the fish sauce. Simmer for 10 minutes. Add the prawns and turn off the heat. (The residual heat will fully cook them.)

*Galangal is in the ginger family and has aromas of citrus and pine that add pungency and perfume to dishes. The root looks like a larger, shinier version of gingerroot. It can be found in Asian markets or high-end supermarkets.

‡ Go to GoodFishBook.com for a demonstration of how to devein shrimp.

PAIRING: First choice is gewürztraminer; second, viognier.

Add the lime juice. Season to taste with salt, and add more fish sauce if desired. It's very important to taste the soup at this point and make sure it is balanced. If it is flat, add more salt. If it isn't bright, add more lime juice. A bit of sugar or honey can balance any excess tartness or spiciness.

Serve the soup garnished with cilantro leaves. Tell your guests that they can chew on the lemongrass but should not swallow it.

pink shrimp salad

with grapefruit and mint

SERVES 4

2 tablespoons freshly squeezed lime juice (1 medium lime)

2 tablespoons freshly squeezed grapefruit juice (½ small grapefruit)

1 teaspoon soy sauce

1 tablespoon fish sauce

1 teaspoon hot chile sauce, such as sriracha

1 teaspoon sugar

⅛ teaspoon fine sea salt, plus additional for the grapefruit

½ pound pink shrimp

1 small carrot, grated (about ¼ cup)

1 avocado, peeled, pitted, and cut into medium dice

¼ cup chopped cilantro stems and leaves

1 tablespoon high-heat vegetable oil

⅓ cup thinly sliced shallots

1 grapefruit (Texas Ruby Red, if available)

4 large butter lettuce leaves

¼ cup roughly chopped dry-roasted, salted peanuts, for garnish

¼ cup loosely packed fresh mint leaves, cut chiffonade, for garnish

---

PAIRING: First choice is New Zealand sauvignon blanc; second, Sancerre.

I used to teach a culinary program to new Vietnamese immigrants. Some of my students were painfully shy, so, to boost their confidence, I would have them teach the rest of the class a simple family recipe in English. I got a lovely education in Vietnamese regional cuisine just as surely as my students learned how to read and write recipes and work in a commercial kitchen. This dish reflects my love of the herbs and fresh vegetables in Vietnamese cooking, where the protein is used more as a garnish than as the entire focus of the meal.

....

In a large bowl, mix the lime juice, grapefruit juice, soy sauce, fish sauce, chile sauce, sugar, and salt. Add the shrimp, carrot, avocado, and cilantro. Mix well and let the shrimp marinate for 20 minutes in the refrigerator.

In a medium sauté pan over medium-high heat, add the oil. Add the shallots and cook until they are starting to brown, about 10 minutes. Let them cool and then add them to the shrimp mixture.

Cut the peel off the grapefruit, making sure to remove any of the white bitter pith from the flesh. Slice the grapefruit horizontally into ½-inch rounds and remove any seeds. Cut them into large cubes approximately 1-inch square. Salt the cubes lightly and set aside.

Place the lettuce leaves on a large platter. Spoon the grapefruit and then the shrimp mixture evenly over the leaves, drizzling excess marinade all around the platter. Garnish with the peanuts and mint.

grilled spot prawns
with "crack" salad

SERVES 4

For the crack salad:

1 underripe (still firm) mango, peeled, pitted, and cut into small dice

½ medium English cucumber, unpeeled, deseeded, and sliced into ¼-inch half-moons (about 2 cups)

1 Fresno chile, deseeded and minced, or ¼ red bell pepper, cut into small dice (optional)

⅓ cup dry-roasted, salted peanuts

⅓ cup chopped cilantro stems and leaves

¼ cup Thai sweet chile sauce,* such as Mae Ploy brand

1 tablespoon freshly squeezed lime juice (about ½ lime)

¼ cup unsweetened shredded coconut, toasted (optional)

For the spot prawns:

½ pound raw shell-on (head off) or live spot prawns

1 tablespoon high-heat vegetable oil

¼ teaspoon fine sea salt

Skewers (if using wooden skewers, presoak them in water for 1 hour)

PAIRING: First choice is riesling; second, pinot gris or Thai beer.

One reason I've never wanted to run a restaurant is that your customers get very attached to certain dishes and raise holy hell if you want to change the menu on them. I thought, therefore, as a private chef, I'd be free to change it up on my whim. That was until my clients had this dish, henceforth known as "crack" salad for its addictiveness. I'm not sure what it is exactly, but young and old, adventurous eaters and picky alike, everyone loves this dish.

....

To prepare the salad, in a large bowl, combine all of its ingredients and set aside.

To prepare the prawns, preheat an outdoor gas grill or an indoor grill pan to high heat. If you are working with live spot prawns, put them in the freezer for 30 minutes to numb them.

Season the prawns generously with the oil and salt. Skewer them using 2 skewers spaced 1 inch apart (this keeps the prawns from spinning around and holds them flat), or spear individual prawns lengthwise (as in the photo, see opposite page). Grill the prawns for about 2 minutes on each side, or until lightly charred. Spot prawns are very delicate, so be careful not to overcook them.

Serve the grilled prawns over the salad and provide lots of napkins.

---

*Thai sweet chile sauce is easy to find in the Asian foods aisle of any large supermarket.

scallops

If cooking seafood perfectly is the measure of a cook's skill, the scallop is a good measuring stick. Of all the things I've taught as a cooking instructor, it is the craft of perfectly searing a scallop that has most enthralled my students. No other seafood quite achieves its delectable duplicity: crispy, caramelized, sweet exterior meets creamy, silky, oceany interior.

In the male-dominated world of restaurant kitchens that I inhabited before venturing out on my own, I often found myself being measured up as I lowered scallops down into a smoking-hot pan. Did I wince or cry out as hot drops of fat met the delicate skin of my forearm? Did I place the scallops too close together so that wisps of steam rose from the pan and attracted the glare of my sous chef? Did my lips curl into a very subtle smirk when I flipped the scallops over with a flick of the wrist to reveal, thankfully, a tawny brown glistening crust? You bet.

WHAT MAKES THIS A GOOD FISH	Sea scallops are filter feeders just like clams, mussels, and oysters; this process contributes to better water quality. Like other farmed shellfish, scallops depend on clean waters to thrive, and as a result, shellfish farmers are often at the forefront of clean water advocacy initiatives. Look for both farmed and wild Pacific Coast scallops, especially weathervane scallops from Alaska. While harvested by mechanical dredge, which carries with it some habitat concerns that need to be more fully researched, dredging in areas with sandy, muddy bottoms results in less habitat destruction than in more sensitive ecologically diverse areas. An area of deep concern is ocean acidification, and this has been a major issue for shellfish growers. The excess carbon we humans create is graciously absorbed by the ocean. This causes the pH of the seawater to drop (become more acidic). Seawater with a lower pH negatively impacts shellfish growing conditions. Shellfish farmers have figured out how to adjust the pH of seawater in closed-containment systems when the larvae are growing, but shellfish are vulnerable to losses when moved to the ocean, where pH can't be controlled. For more information on ocean acidification, check the Sustainable Seafood Resources on page 313.

BY ANY OTHER NAME	Weathervane scallops (*Patinopecten caurinus*) are also known as giant Pacific scallops.

SEASON	Farmed scallops are available year-round (though they spawn from April to May). Weathervane scallop season in Alaska is from July through September, although very high-quality frozen weathervanes are available year-round.

BUYING TIPS	Some lesser scallops are soaked in sodium tripolyphosphate (STP), which can be used—or rather, abused—to minimize water loss when thawing frozen scallops. When applied to fresh scallops in excess, the scallops will take up extra moisture; more water equals diluted flavor and fewer scallops per pound. Buy "dry-packed" or "chemical-free," which is industry-speak for an unadulterated scallop. Dry-packed scallops will range from white to off-white to cream-colored: all are acceptable. Ask to smell the scallops: they should have a light, sweet ocean smell or hardly any at all. You'll find scallops sold in "count per pound" size designations. For example, large scallops are 10 to 20 per pound; medium scallops number 20 to 30 per pound. Of course,

you'll pay more per pound for the larger scallops. For most of the recipes in this book, the size of the scallop doesn't matter. I only specify "large" in one recipe because using a single scallop for each serving is visually appealing.

QUESTIONS TO ASK BEFORE YOU PULL OUT YOUR WALLET

After asking where and when the scallops were harvested, the most important question is whether they are fresh or were previously frozen. I ask this question only because if I end up not using all the scallops that day, I will freeze some raw ones to use at a later date, but only if they haven't already been frozen (too many freezing and thawing cycles will destroy their texture).

CARING FOR YOUR GOOD FISH

Unwrap fresh scallops when you get them home. Place them on a paper-towel-lined plate and cover well with plastic wrap. Use them that day or the next. If you are cooking the scallop, you'll want to remove the rectangular tag of tissue that connects the scallop to the shell. It is often, but not always, still attached to the scallop. It gets tough when cooked but can be left on for raw preparations. In the video about scallops at GoodFishBook.com, I show you what this piece looks like and how to remove it. If your scallops are frozen, thaw them according to the methods discussed in How to Safely Thaw Frozen Fish on page 18. If you're careful, and you're thawing a big block of scallops but only need some, you can "slack out" or thaw the corner of the package in cold water and then chip off just what you need, returning the rest to the freezer with no loss of quality.

HOW THIS TYPE OF SEAFOOD IS RAISED OR HARVESTED

Scallops can actually swim, pumping their adductor muscle (the part we eat), bellowing their shell open and closed, to escape prey or move to a different area. They prefer to hang out in sand, gravel, and rock bottoms. Commercially farmed scallops are raised in net cages that are hung in the water column offshore. The scallops go from hatchery to harvest in 18 to 24 months.

SUSTAINABLE SUBSTITUTES

Crab and shrimp are good substitutes for scallops. Halibut cheeks would also be a nice stand-in.

scallop crudo

SERVES 4 AS AN APPETIZER

½ pound sea scallops (see A
    Note on Eating Raw Seafood
    on page 311)
1 large orange
1 tablespoon lemon juice
Pinch of red pepper flakes
1 tablespoon chopped pumpkin
    seeds or pistachios,
    for garnish
4 teaspoons extra-virgin olive oil
1 teaspoon chopped fresh mint,
    for garnish
Maldon or gray sea salt

PAIRING: First choice is sauvignon
blanc; second, dry riesling.

Crudo is an Italian dish of raw fish dressed with olive oil, citrus, and sea salt. The beauty of a good crudo lies in its ability to preserve the subtlety of the fish flavor and bring out its richness with good olive oil while simultaneously balancing it with acid—in this case, orange juice. The best crudos have a textural component: here I use chopped bits of pumpkin seed and crunchy crystals of Maldon sea salt.

Place the scallops in a ziplock bag and freeze for 20 minutes to allow for easier slicing.

Zest the orange. (You will have about 2½ tablespoons of zest.) Cut a ¼-inch horizontal slice from the middle of the orange. Trim off the remaining pith, then cut the orange flesh into small dice. Set aside. Squeeze the remaining orange to yield ⅓ cup juice.

In a small saucepan over high heat, bring the orange juice, orange zest, lemon juice, and red pepper flakes to a boil over high heat. Cook the mixture until it reduces to a syrup (about 2 tablespoons remaining), about 3 minutes. Pour through a fine-mesh sieve, pressing on the zest to release its oil into the syrup. Discard the solids and allow the syrup to cool.

Toast the pumpkin seeds in a small skillet over high heat, stirring constantly, until they smell toasted and darken in color, about 2 minutes.

Using a very sharp, thin-bladed slicing knife, cut the scallops horizontally (against the grain) into ⅛-inch slices. Arrange the slices decoratively on 4 small plates. Spoon equal amounts of the syrup over the scallops. Drizzle approximately 1 teaspoon of the oil over each portion. Garnish with a sprinkling of pumpkin seeds, reserved diced orange, and mint. Carefully distribute a small pinch of Maldon salt over the scallop slices. Serve immediately.

TIPS FOR SEARING PERFECT CARAMELIZED SCALLOPS

First and foremost, start by purchasing high-quality, untreated scallops. See page 92 for more information about what to look for.

1. Dry your scallops very well on a paper towel before searing. A wet scallop will spurt and steam in the pan and take longer to caramelize. Remove the small side muscle if it is still attached to the scallop (it gets tough when cooked).

2. Use a pan that can get very hot, such as a cast-iron skillet. Don't use a nonstick pan because it is not made for high-heat use and doesn't caramelize protein very well.

3. Heat your pan over high heat. (Now, many of you will read that, defy me, and turn your heat down to medium-high. Trust me, and get your hand off that dial.) Add about 1 tablespoon high-heat vegetable oil. Roll your sleeves down to protect your arms; you may want to wear an apron as well. When the oil is very hot, carefully add the scallops, placing them away from you to minimize splattering oil on yourself. If you need to shriek when you do this, so be it.

4. Make sure to allow plenty of room between each scallop; cook them in batches if necessary. Crowded scallops will inhibit the evaporation of moisture and limit caramelization.

5. Very important: At this step, do *nothing*. Don't move the scallops. Don't touch them. Don't even look at them. Scallops will need at least 2 minutes of contact on this side with that hot pan to create good color (and therefore flavor).

6. After 2 minutes, carefully take the tip of a metal spatula and lift up a corner of a scallop so you can peek beneath it. If you've had problems with sticking in the past, either try a different pan or wait a bit longer (the protein will literally release itself from the pan most of the time if you've waited long enough and not panicked and gone in there with four spatulas and a crowbar). Do you see a pale, anemic scallop, or are you saying "Hello, beautiful"? If the former, wait a bit longer; if the latter, gently tease the scallop off the bottom of the pan and flip it over.

7. What you do next depends on your likes and dislikes. I cook my scallops, if they are somewhat large (at least ¾ inch tall), for only 1 minute on the opposite side (30 seconds if they are smaller). I like my scallops crusty and brown on the top and medium rare in the middle. If you've never tried a scallop this way, please do. It will literally taste like a different type of seafood compared to a well-done scallop—a better, more lovely type of seafood.

8. Transfer the scallops to a plate. Stand back and admire your handiwork.

If you're the visual type, go to GoodFishBook.com to see me demonstrate proper technique for handling and searing scallops.

scallops, grits, and greens

SERVES 4

For the greens:

1 tablespoon extra-virgin
  olive oil
1 bunch kale, stems
  removed, leaves chopped
  into bite-size pieces
1 bunch mustard greens, stems
  removed, leaves chopped into
  bite-size pieces
Pinch of red pepper flakes
¼ teaspoon fine sea salt
2 teaspoons honey
1 tablespoon apple
  cider vinegar
½ cup chicken or pork stock

For the grits:

2 cups whole milk
2 cups chicken or pork stock
¼ teaspoon fine sea salt
½ cup quick-cooking grits
  or polenta
1 cup (about 2 ounces) grated
  cheddar cheese
1 teaspoon orange zest

For the scallops:

1 pound sea scallops
1 tablespoon ancho chile
  powder* or other chile powder
¼ teaspoon fine sea salt
1 tablespoon high-heat
  vegetable oil

PAIRING: You *must* drink
Red Stripe Jamaican lager
with this dish.

You've probably heard of shrimp and grits, but what about scallops and grits? I wondered why I'd never thought of this dish or eaten it before. The sweet, caramelized scallop crust with a buttery soft interior mirrors the creaminess of the cheesy grits combined with earthy, spicy greens mellowed with honey. Turns out that this dish is a culinary oversight needing immediate rectification.

To prepare the greens, in a large pot over medium-high heat, add all of its ingredients. Stir well, cover, and cook for 10 to 15 minutes, or until the greens are tender. Taste for seasoning and adjust as needed. Keep warm.

To prepare the grits, in a large saucepan over high heat, add the milk, chicken stock, and salt. Bring to a boil over high heat and then reduce the heat to maintain a simmer. Gradually whisk in the grits. Reduce the heat to medium-low and stir the grits for 5 minutes, or until they are creamy and tender. Stir in the cheddar and orange zest. Keep warm.

To prepare the scallops, dry them with paper towels. Place them on a plate and season with the chile powder and salt. Heat a heavy skillet over high heat. Add the vegetable oil and, when it is really hot, carefully add the scallops to the pan, being careful not to splatter oil on yourself or crowd the pan with too many scallops. Cook the scallops for 2 minutes on one side without disturbing them, or until they are caramelized, then flip, cooking the other side for only a minute or so more. (See tips for searing scallops on opposite page.)

To serve, scoop the grits onto a platter or plates. Top with the greens and scallops.

---

*Look for ancho chile powder in the Mexican section of large supermarkets. You can also grind dried ancho chiles in a spice grinder to make your own powder.

scallops

with carrot cream and marjoram

SERVES 4 AS AN APPETIZER

For the carrot cream:
½ pound carrots, cut into large
   dice (about 2 cups)
1 teaspoon kosher salt
½ cup cream
Freshly ground black pepper

For the pickled carrots:
1 large carrot, sliced into short
   ribbons using a vegetable
   peeler (about 1 cup)
¼ cup seasoned rice
   wine vinegar

For the scallops:
1 pound sea scallops
¼ teaspoon fine sea salt
1 tablespoon high-heat
   vegetable oil

For serving:
2 tablespoons Herb Oil
   (recipe follows)
1 teaspoon marjoram leaves,
   for garnish

PAIRING: First choice is Sancerre;
second, Chablis.

About fifteen years ago, at Tulio Ristorante in downtown Seattle, I had a memorable pasta dish featuring fresh marjoram; it was just a small, fragrant amount tossed with butter and fresh pasta, but so many years later I can still smell its perfume. Oregano's sexier sister, as marjoram is sometimes called, is also a favorite of Jerry Traunfeld, former executive chef at The Herbfarm Restaurant, who taught me to combine it with carrots. There is something about the earthy sweetness of carrots paired with the delicate pine notes of marjoram that really works. The addition of sweet, briny scallops to that already solid combination throws this dish over the top.

To prepare the carrot cream, add the carrots and salt to a medium saucepan and cover with water. Bring to a boil over high heat and cook for 7 to 8 minutes, or until the carrots are tender. (Alternatively, you could steam them.) Drain the carrots and add them to a blender along with the cream and a pinch of pepper to taste. Blend until the mixture is a very smooth puree and set aside.

To prepare the pickled carrots, in a medium bowl, toss the carrots with the vinegar. Marinate the carrots for at least 20 minutes. Drain, reserving the vinegar for another use, and set aside.

To prepare the scallops, dry them with paper towels. Place them on a plate and season with the salt. Heat a heavy skillet over high heat. Add the oil and, when it is really hot, carefully add the scallops to the pan, being careful not to splatter oil on yourself or crowd the pan with too many scallops. Cook the scallops for 2 minutes on one side without disturbing them, or until they are caramelized, then flip, cooking the other side for only a minute or so more. (See tips for searing scallops on page 96.)

To assemble the dish, gently reheat the carrot cream, then spoon some on each of 4 plates. Top each plate with several scallops. Drizzle some Herb Oil around the scallops and garnish with a sprinkling of pickled carrots and marjoram leaves.

CONTINUED

¾ cup packed fresh Italian
  parsley leaves
1 tablespoon fresh marjoram
  leaves
¼ cup extra-virgin olive oil
¼ cup neutral vegetable oil,
  such as canola or safflower
⅛ teaspoon fine sea salt

HERB OIL

This recipe is infinitely flexible; many times I make it with basil and parsley. The reason I use both olive oil and a neutral oil is that sometimes the olive oil can dominate or make the oil a little bitter. The neutral oil allows the flavor of the herbs to shine.

In a blender, combine the parsley, marjoram, olive oil, vegetable oil, and salt. Blend until the oil turns a vibrant green color, about 3 minutes. You can strain the oil through a fine-mesh sieve if you'd like or leave it with some texture. Transfer the oil to a bowl, or if you'd like to be all fancy-pants, transfer it to a squeeze bottle.

summer scallops
with corn soup

SERVES 4

For the olive salad:
¼ cup pitted kalamata
  olives, minced
10 Castelvetrano or other fruity
  green olives, pitted and sliced
  into thin strips
1 tablespoon chopped fresh
  Italian parsley
1 teaspoon red wine vinegar
1 teaspoon Herb Oil
  (page 100)
Freshly ground black pepper

For the corn soup:
10 ounces frozen corn kernels,
  thawed, or 2 cups fresh corn
  kernels (cut from about 2 large
  ears of corn)
1 cup clam juice, warmed
1 teaspoon unsalted butter
Fine sea salt
Honey (optional)

For the tomato bread:
1 baguette
Extra-virgin olive oil
1 tomato, cut into
  4 (¼-inch) slices, the rest
  cut into small dice
Fine sea salt

Do not be deceived into thinking this dish is difficult to make because of its many components. Each part is extremely simple, and the result is a symphony of summer flavors: sweet corn; juicy, meaty tomatoes; the world's best fruit—the olive; and buttery scallops. All of it served with crusty, tomato-juice-soaked, toasted bread and two bright, piquant oils. This is the dish I would take with me to a desert island.

To prepare the olive salad, in a small bowl, combine the olives, parsley, vinegar, and Herb Oil. Add pepper to taste and set aside.

To prepare the corn soup, if you are using fresh corn kernels, fill a small saucepan with salted water and bring to a boil over high heat. Meanwhile, fill a medium bowl with ice water. When the water is boiling, add the corn. Cook until it is barely cooked through but still tender, about 2 minutes. Transfer the corn to a colander, drain, and then plunge it into the ice bath. When cool, drain in a colander.

In a blender, combine the corn, clam juice, and butter until smooth. (You can then pass the soup through a fine-mesh sieve if you want a more luxurious texture.) Season to taste with salt. Add some honey if you feel the soup needs a bit more sweetness. Set aside and keep warm until you're ready to assemble the dish.

Preheat the broiler. Place a rack in the top third of the oven.

To prepare the tomato bread, slice the baguette into eight 1-inch-thick slices. (Freeze the remaining baguette for another day.) Brush each slice with some olive oil. Arrange the slices on a baking sheet and broil the bread until it is lightly brown on one side, 1 to 2 minutes. (Keep a close eye on it!) Remove from the oven and, using a fork, press the diced tomato onto the browned sides of the bread slices. Sprinkle each with a little salt. Reserve the tomato slices for when you assemble the dish.

For the scallops:
12 sea scallops
¼ teaspoon fine sea salt
2 tablespoons high-heat
  vegetable oil

For serving:
2 tablespoons Herb Oil
  (page 100)
2 tablespoons chile oil

PAIRING: First choice is rosé;
second, white Burgundy.

To prepare the scallops, dry them with paper towels. Place them on a plate and season with the salt. Heat a heavy skillet over high heat. Add the vegetable oil and, when it is really hot, carefully add the scallops to the pan, being careful not to splatter oil on yourself or crowd the pan with too many scallops. Cook the scallops for 2 minutes on one side without disturbing them, or until they are caramelized, then flip, cooking the other side for only a minute or so more. (See tips for searing scallops on page 96.) Set aside and keep warm until ready to assemble dish.

To assemble the dish, ladle some corn soup into each of 4 wide, shallow bowls. Lay a tomato slice sprinkled with a little salt in the middle of each bowl. Place 3 scallops around the tomato. Spoon some olive salad on top of each scallop. Drizzle ⅓ tablespoon Herb Oil and ½ tablespoon chile oil around the edges of the soup. Serve with the tomato bread.

scallops with tarragon beurre blanc

SERVES 4 AS A SMALL PLATE OR
2 AS A LIGHT ENTRÉE

**For the pea and
asparagus puree:**

4 ounces asparagus
(5 to 7 spears), chopped,
tips reserved

1 teaspoon kosher salt

¼ cup fresh or frozen peas

¼ cup fresh Italian
parsley leaves

3 tablespoons plain full-fat
Greek-style yogurt

1 tablespoon extra-virgin
olive oil

1 teaspoon lemon juice

⅛ teaspoon fine sea salt

For the tarragon beurre blanc:

¼ cup dry white wine

1 tablespoon champagne
vinegar

1 tablespoon minced shallot

1 teaspoon chopped fresh
tarragon

⅛ teaspoon fine sea salt

5 tablespoons cold
unsalted butter

For the vegetable sauté:

1 ounce prosciutto, cut into
small dice

1 tablespoon minced shallot

Reserved asparagus tips

Reserved 1 tablespoon peas

Freshly ground black
pepper (optional)

I suppose this is the place where I could wax poetic about spring: the chartreuse profusions of new leaves and sweet, sweet peas and the majesty of asparagus. But I won't. You've heard all that before. What I'll say instead are two things: rich, creamy herbal butter and crispy prosciutto. Spring is great and all, but it's also a confusing time, when the weather is as bipolar as Sylvia Plath and you're not sure how to dress. This dish has one foot firmly in fatten-up wintertime and the other foot in healthy, vegetal summertime, just like spring itself.

Do-ahead tip: The tarragon beurre blanc can be prepared the day before, without adding the butter. Before serving, just reheat on the lowest setting and whisk in the butter. The pea and asparagus puree can be made the day before and warmed to serve.

To prepare the puree, chop the asparagus stems into 1-inch pieces. Fill a small saucepan with water. Add the kosher salt and bring to a boil over high heat. Meanwhile, fill a medium bowl with ice water. When the water is boiling, add the asparagus pieces. Cook until the pieces are barely cooked through but still tender, about 4 minutes. Remove them immediately with a slotted spoon and plunge them into the ice bath. When the pieces have cooled, remove them from the ice bath.

If using fresh peas, blanch them for 1 minute in the boiling salted water, then shock them in ice water, as described above. If using frozen, thaw them under cool running water and drain. Reserve 1 tablespoon peas for later use in the vegetable sauté.

In a blender, puree the blanched asparagus stems and peas, along with the parsley, yogurt, olive oil, lemon juice, and sea salt, until smooth. Push the puree through a fine-mesh sieve using a rubber spatula; taste and adjust seasoning, if desired. Warm in a small saucepan before assembling the dish.

For the scallops:

4 large (10 to 20 count) sea
  scallops, about 1½ ounces
  per scallop

⅛ teaspoon fine sea salt

1 tablespoon high-heat
  vegetable oil

For serving:

1 teaspoon fresh tarragon
  leaves, as garnish

PAIRING: First choice is
grüner veltliner; second,
white Bordeaux.

To prepare the beurre blanc, in a small saucepan over high heat, add the wine, vinegar, shallot, tarragon, and sea salt. Bring to a boil over high heat, then reduce the heat to a simmer and cook until the liquid is reduced to just 1 tablespoon, 6 to 7 minutes. Reduce the heat to its lowest setting and whisk in the cold butter, 1 tablespoon at a time, adding each only after the previous one has been incorporated. Taste for seasoning and then set the beurre blanc aside in a warm place. It will hold for about half an hour; if it should "break," mix it in a blender for 1 minute to re-emulsify.

To prepare the vegetable sauté, in a sauté pan over medium heat, add the prosciutto. Cook the prosciutto until its fat is rendered and it starts to crisp, 6 to 8 minutes. Add the shallots and asparagus tips and cook for another 2 to 3 minutes, or until the shallots are tender. Add the reserved peas. Taste and add a few grinds of pepper, if desired. Set aside and keep warm.

To prepare the scallops, dry them with paper towels. Place them on a plate and season with the salt. Heat a heavy skillet over high heat. Add the vegetable oil and, when it is really hot, carefully add the scallops to the pan, being careful not to splatter oil on yourself or crowd the pan with too many scallops. Cook the scallops for 3 minutes on one side without disturbing them, or until they are caramelized, then flip, cooking the other side for 2 minutes more. (See tips for searing scallops on page 96.) Set aside and keep them warm until you're ready to assemble the dish.

To assemble the dish, place a little pea and asparagus puree on each of 4 plates. Top with some of the vegetable sauté and a seared scallop. Pour some tarragon beurre blanc over the scallop. Garnish with tarragon leaves.

squid

Squid is one of those galvanizing types of seafood. It has its share of lovers and haters, and for the most part, the hater camp is stocked with the poor folks who've had to chew through overcooked squid better served as projectile weapons. The lovers—myself included—have tasted the divinity found in a piece of grilled or wok-seared squid that has been removed from the flame with the urgency and focus one would employ if their own hand was on fire. Like many, I stumbled through several years wondering why these rubbery rings were worthy of menu real estate until a trip to Italy where, at the famous restaurant Guido da Costigliole, a Michelin one star restaurant in Piedmont, I was served a bowl of squid that changed my perspective forever. I can only guess at its preparation, but it seemed to be poached in butter that had been flavored with fresh bay leaves. It was insanely good. The squid was so surprisingly tender. I heard my teeth meet with too much force, so prepared was my mouth to do battle. I went back to the same restaurant the next night. I ordered the exact same dish.

WHAT MAKES THIS A GOOD FISH	Squid grow quickly and are, generally speaking, caught toward the end of their short life cycle (about six months to a year). Good management of this fishery is crucial because squid are a very important link in the food chain. Like sardines and anchovies, they are food for sea lions, salmon, dolphins, whales, and seabirds. Currently, most of the Pacific Coast squid is coming from California. The California Department of Fish and Game manages this fishery consistent with a federal fishery management plan. The state regulates catch limitations, time and seasonal closures, monitoring programs, and a permit system.
BY ANY OTHER NAME	You may why wonder why squid are in the shellfish section. Shell or no shell, they are scientifically classified as members of the phylum Mollusca, alongside with shellfish. As for the species, California squid (*Loligo opalescens*) are also called market squid, California market squid, Monterey squid, or opalescent inshore squid. Squid are called *ika* in sushi bars, but it is often not squid at all, but rather Vietnamese cuttlefish harvested from unregulated fisheries. This practice can negatively impact other organisms that depend on the cuttlefish as an important food source. Squid are also called calamari in Italian, a name that has become synonymous with "squid" in the English language.
SEASON	There are two squid fisheries in California: the summer Monterey Bay fishery and the fall and winter fishery in Southern California. You can pretty much say squid are available year-round. You can also find frozen squid from California year-round, though an estimated 90 percent gets exported (and, ironically, processed and sold back to us as frozen calamari from China).
BUYING TIPS	Squid are sold fresh both whole and cleaned (separated into tubes and tentacles), as well as frozen (whole and cleaned).
QUESTIONS TO ASK BEFORE YOU PULL OUT YOUR WALLET	Where was it caught? Try to buy domestic Pacific Coast squid.

**CARING FOR YOUR
GOOD FISH**

If you're not going to use your squid right away, put it in the coldest part of your fridge or throw the package in a colander over a bowl and put some ice on top of it to keep it at its best. Thaw frozen squid according to How to Safely Thaw Frozen Fish on page 18.

**HOW THIS TYPE OF
SEAFOOD IS RAISED OR
HARVESTED**

Market squid are caught at night by purse seining. Boats shine bright lights to attract massive numbers of squid from their spawning grounds. Small boats then harvest the squid by drawing the net around them and pulling it closed.

**SUSTAINABLE
SUBSTITUTES**

I substitute spot prawns or scallops for squid when necessary.

quick squid

with red chile sauce and herbs

**SERVES 4 FOR LUNCH OR
AS AN APPETIZER**

1 pound cleaned squid, tubes
  cut into rings and tentacles cut
  in half lengthwise‡
1 tablespoon fish sauce
1 tablespoon freshly squeezed
  lime juice (about ½ lime)
2 green onions, minced
Heaping ¼ teaspoon freshly
  ground black pepper
⅛ teaspoon fine sea salt
1 head butter lettuce, washed
  and dried, whole leaves picked
  off the stem
2 cups fresh cilantro leaves
1 cup fresh Thai or regular
  basil leaves
1 carrot, grated or cut into fine
  julienne, or 1 cup bean sprouts
1 cup Thai sweet chile sauce
1 tablespoon high-heat
  vegetable oil

‡ If using whole squid, go
to GoodFishBook.com for a
demonstration of how to clean
and cut up a squid.

PAIRING: First choice is riesling;
second, gewürztraminer.

This is the recipe to make for people who are convinced that healthy food can't be made quickly and inexpensively. In no time, the table will be overflowing with fresh herbs, lettuce, and quickly seared salty-sour squid. You can tell your guests to place all the ingredients in a piece of lettuce before dipping into the sweet chile sauce or, alternatively, make themselves a salad and use the sauce as dressing.

In a large bowl, combine the squid with the fish sauce, lime juice, green onions, pepper, and salt. Set aside while you heat a wok or large sauté pan over high heat. Decoratively assemble the lettuce, cilantro, Thai basil, carrots, and a bowl of chile sauce on a large platter.

Add the vegetable oil to the wok and, when it is hot, add the squid. Cook, stirring constantly, for 2 to 3 minutes only, just until the squid ring edges curl up a bit and turn white. Transfer the squid to a bowl with a slotted spoon, leaving the liquid in the wok. Reduce the liquid down to a thick glaze (making sure to add any juices that accumulate at the bottom of the bowl the squid is resting in), about 5 minutes. Pour the glaze back over the squid and serve it on the platter with the accompaniments.

squid

with chickpeas, potatoes, and piquillo peppers

SERVES 4 FOR LUNCH OR AS AN APPETIZER

1 (15-ounce can) chickpeas, drained and rinsed

A really nice, fruity Spanish olive oil

½ teaspoon smoked bittersweet or sweet paprika

Heaping ¼ teaspoon freshly ground black pepper

¼ teaspoon fine sea salt, divided

1 small leek

⅓ pound small-diced Yukon Gold potatoes, skin on

⅛ teaspoon cayenne

⅓ cup piquillo or roasted red peppers, sliced into ¼-inch rings

¼ cup manzanilla or other flavorful, cured olives, pitted and roughly chopped

½ teaspoon minced fresh thyme

1½ tablespoons good-quality sherry vinegar (Arvum Gran Reserva is my favorite)

1 pound cleaned squid, tubes cut into ¼-inch rings and tentacles cut in half lengthwise, or whole squid, cleaned and cut‡

1 tablespoon roughly chopped fresh Italian parsley, for garnish

---

PAIRING: First choice, vinho verde; second, albariño.

Squid and potatoes have a fabulous affinity for one another; the potatoes, when browned act as flavor sponges, soaking up any juices and providing a fluffy contrast to the tender toothsomeness of the perfectly cooked squid. When good extra-virgin olive oil and piquillo peppers are added, you are transported right to Spain—standing shoulder to shoulder at a tapas bar drinking wine out of little cups, the sun hitting your shoulders and music playing.

....

Preheat the oven to 450°F.

On a baking sheet, toss the chickpeas with 1½ tablespoons olive oil, paprika, pepper, and ⅛ teaspoon of the salt. Taste and add more salt if the chickpeas need it. Roast for about 10 minutes, or until the chickpeas are browned. Set aside. Leave the oven on.

Prepare the leek by cutting off the dark-green tougher part (which you can save to make stock). Cut off the root end. Cut the leek in half lengthwise and wash well. Slice into ½-inch half-moons.

In a medium sauté pan over medium-high heat, add ¼ cup olive oil and, when it is hot, add the potatoes, the remaining ⅛ teaspoon salt, and cayenne. Cook the potatoes until they are crisp on the outside and tender on the inside, 6 to 7 minutes. Add the leeks and sauté for 3 to 4 minutes, or until they are soft. Add the peppers, olives, thyme, and vinegar, and sauté for another few minutes. Pull the pan off the heat and immediately add the squid and chickpeas. Mix well and scoop the mixture into 4 small oven-safe dishes, such as Spanish *cazuelas* or medium ramekins. Place the dishes on a baking sheet and bake for 5 minutes, or until the squid is tender and cooked through.

Remove from the oven and garnish with the parsley and a drizzle of olive oil, about 1 teaspoon per person. Serve immediately.

---

‡ If using whole squid, go to GoodFishBook.com for a demonstration of how to clean and cut up a squid.

wok-seared squid

with lemongrass, chile, and basil

SERVES 4 FOR LUNCH OR AS A
LIGHT DINNER

1 stalk lemongrass

2 tablespoons high-heat
vegetable oil, divided

1 pound cleaned squid, tubes
cut into rings and tentacles cut
in half lengthwise, or whole
squid, cleaned and cut‡

⅛ teaspoon fine sea salt

½ small red onion, sliced into
thin half-moons

1 tablespoon grated fresh
peeled ginger

½ cup medium-diced red
bell pepper

1 tablespoon Thai roasted
red chile paste (I like Thai
Kitchen brand)

¼ cup clam juice

½ cup roughly torn fresh
basil leaves

1 teaspoon fish sauce

2 medium limes, one juiced, the
other cut into wedges
for garnish

Cooked rice noodles or rice,
for serving

‡ If using whole squid, go
GoodFishBook.com for a
demonstration of how to clean
and cut up a squid.

PAIRING: First choice is
riesling; second, Thai beer,
such as Singha.

Stir-frying is high-heat cooking from start to finish. It is extra important to have all your ingredients ready before you turn on the heat (what the French call *mise en place*). Be prepared for some active stirring, as the squid is in and out of the hot wok very quickly. By the time the heady scent of the lemongrass has reached your nostrils, the squid is probably done. Feel free to serve the lemongrass pieces in each person's bowl: just be sure to tell your diners not to eat them outright, unless they are really into a high-fiber diet. Add a little kick by including thinly sliced serranos when stir-frying the vegetables.

Prepare the lemongrass by cutting off the top half of the stalk (where it is thinner and darker); discard this. Trim the very bottom and discard, then cut the stalk into 1-inch lengths. Smack each piece of lemongrass with the side of a knife to help it release its flavor into the dish.

Heat a wok or large sauté pan over high heat. Add 1 tablespoon of the oil to the wok, along with the lemongrass. Cook for 1 minute, or until the lemongrass just starts to brown. Add the squid and salt and cook for 1 to 2 minutes, or just until the squid ring edges curl up a bit and turn white. Transfer the squid and lemongrass, along with any juices, to a large bowl and reserve. Wipe the wok clean with a paper towel.

Add the remaining 1 tablespoon oil to the wok (still at high heat), along with the onions, ginger, bell pepper, and chile paste. Pick the lemongrass from the bowl and add it back to the wok. Sauté, actively stirring, for 3 to 4 minutes, or until the onions start to soften. Add any juice that has collected from the squid (but not the squid itself) and the clam juice. Cook over high heat until there is hardly any liquid left, about 2 minutes. Add the squid, basil, and fish sauce, and cook for 1 more minute. Season to taste with more fish sauce if desired and add the lime juice.

Serve immediately, over rice noodles or rice, with lime wedges on the side.

chorizo-and-apple-stuffed squid

with sherry pepper sauce

SERVES 6 AS AN APPETIZER

For the chorizo-and-apple stuffing:

2 tablespoons extra-virgin olive oil

3 ounces Spanish chorizo, cut into small dice

¼ cup small-diced leeks, white and light-green parts only

½ cup small-diced Granny Smith or other tart green apple

⅛ teaspoon fine sea salt

⅛ teaspoon cayenne

1 teaspoon tangerine zest (from 1 large tangerine or sub with orange zest)

2 tablespoons red wine

For the sherry pepper sauce:

1 tablespoon diced shallot

½ teaspoon fresh thyme leaves

⅛ teaspoon fine sea salt

½ cup piquillo peppers

¼ cup extra-virgin olive oil

¼ teaspoon honey

1 teaspoon sherry vinegar

For the squid:

½ pound cleaned whole squid tubes‡

Toothpicks, for securing squid

2 tablespoons extra-virgin olive oil

For serving:

Good crusty bread

PAIRING: First choice is Vouvray sec; second, Alsatian pinot gris.

Recipes are the currency of chefs. My conviction is that when chefs share recipes and ideas with each other, they spread goodwill and foster creativity and collaboration. Thanks to chef Ashlyn Forshner for this fabulous, original, and unforgettable stuffed squid dish, spicy and savory with Spanish chorizo, sweet with apples and leeks, and tart with a sherry-vinegar-laced pepper sauce.

To prepare the stuffing, heat the olive oil over medium-high heat in a large skillet. Add the chorizo and cook for 5 minutes, or until crispy and brown around the edges. Add the leeks, apples, salt, cayenne, and tangerine zest and sauté for 3 to 4 more minutes, or until the apples soften. Turn the heat up to high and deglaze the pan with the wine until all the liquid evaporates, about 2 minutes. Let the mixture cool for 5 minutes.

To prepare the sauce, add all of the ingredients to the bowl of a food processor and blend thoroughly, stopping occasionally to scrape down the sides. Check seasoning and set aside.

To prepare the squid, using a small spoon or your fingers, stuff a squid tube with a portion of chorizo-apple filling, packing it in tightly. Secure the squid closed with a toothpick. Repeat with the remaining squid.

In a large skillet over medium heat, add the olive oil. When the oil is hot, caramelize the stuffed squid, cooking for 1 to 2 minutes, then flipping and cooking for another minute or two on the other side, being careful not to overcook. Set aside.

Serve each guest a small plate with one stuffed squid and a spoonful of pepper sauce on the side. Pass around some bread to dip in the sauce.

‡ Go to GoodFishBook.com for a demonstration of how to clean a squid.

grilled squid
with tamarind and orange

SERVES 4

1 teaspoon minced shallot

1 tablespoon grated fresh
peeled ginger

1 tablespoon minced serrano
chile (seeds left in)

1 small orange, first zested, then
juiced (about 1 teaspoon zest
and 3 tablespoons juice)

2 teaspoons tamarind paste (or
substitute with lemon juice)

½ teaspoon fine sea salt

1 teaspoon plus 1 tablespoon
extra-virgin olive oil, divided

1 pound whole squid, cleaned,
tentacles cut from the tubes‡

High-heat vegetable oil, for
oiling the grill

1 teaspoon minced fresh mint,
for garnish

Maldon or gray sea salt, for
garnish (optional)

‡ Go to GoodFishBook.com for
a demonstration of how to clean
and cut up a squid.

PAIRING: First choice is albariño;
second, grüner veltliner.

Primum non nocere. First, do no harm. All medical students are taught this, and I am of the opinion that it should also be taught in culinary schools. In medicine, sometimes the cure can do more damage than the sickness, and similarly, overzealous culinary students and chefs can sometimes do more damage to food than if they had simply let the poor ingredient be. I'm a big fan of sauce, don't get me wrong, but some foods shine the brightest when prepared the most simply. Great ingredients don't require heroic culinary interventions.

In a small bowl, combine the shallot, ginger, chile, orange zest, 2 tablespoons of the orange juice, tamarind paste, salt, and 1 teaspoon of the olive oil. Pour over the squid and let it marinate for 15 minutes.

Preheat an indoor or outdoor grill to high heat. When the grill is very hot, oil the grates well with the vegetable oil and place the squid tubes and tentacles on the grates. (You may need to do this in two batches.) Grill for a few minutes, or until you see grill marks. Flip the squid and grill for another 30 seconds to 1 minute. Transfer the grilled squid to a platter and repeat with the remaining squid pieces.

To serve, lay the grilled squid out on a small platter and drizzle with the remaining 1 tablespoon olive oil and orange juice. Garnish with the mint and some Maldon salt.

FINFISH

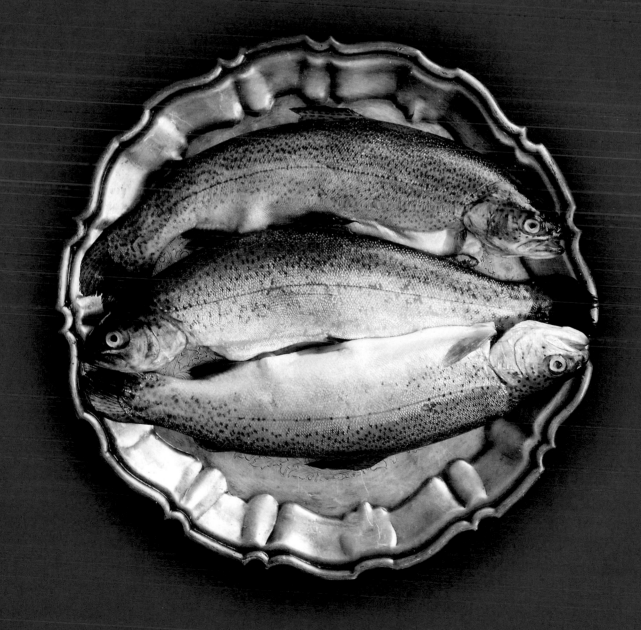

wild salmon

In 2006 I ran the galley of a seventy-five-foot yacht headed up to Ketchikan, Alaska, by way of the Inside Passage. My sole motivation for taking this job—aside, of course, from the stunningly beautiful landscapes—was what I had hoped would be access to some of the freshest and most delicious seafood I'd ever laid my hands on. I was not disappointed.

The boat was a day outside Queen Charlotte Sound and its nauseatingly rolling sea. When we arrived at the Shearwater Marina, near Bella Bella, British Columbia, my sea legs were barely beneath me, so the dock planks felt especially comforting. Matt, the marina manager, greeted me on the dock and quickly offered me a freshly caught twenty-pound king salmon that some sport fishermen had left them that day. By way of an answer, I jogged up the dock, trailing after him, a smile on my face like a delightfully simple-minded Labrador retriever. I remember holding that salmon tenderly to my chest, thanking him profusely, and coddling it the whole way back to the boat, grinning like an idiot.

I busily got to work cleaning, scaling, and cutting the salmon into portions that would fit in the boat's refrigerator and freezer. I threw the backbone and tail over the side of the boat and watched as little fish instantaneously darted at it, taking their share as it slowly descended. I watched the bones sink until I could no longer see them and then caught up with the rest of the group. I smelled like a salmon. I couldn't have been happier.

WHAT MAKES THIS A GOOD FISH

In the United States we love our salmon! So much so that we almost loved it to the brink of extinction. Luckily, we were able to show our affection for the silver-sided beauties by changing our voracious fishing ways and improving fisheries management. We can now have our salmon and eat it too.

The health of Alaskan salmon stocks is a testament to good management practices. In 1857 the United States bought Alaska from Russia, and along with it came the seemingly endless supply of wild salmon. In 1959, Alaska became a state and inherited from federal authorities the problem of an overfished salmon population. With great foresight, the new State of Alaska included guidelines for the sustainable management of all its natural resources in its constitution. Likewise, West Coast salmon fisheries have reformed their management to reflect sustainable fishing practices. You can feel good eating salmon from US salmon fisheries. British Columbia has also reformed its fisheries management. With the exception of its South Coast gill net and purse seine fisheries, British Columbia's salmon fisheries are considered sustainable.

With fishing reforms now in place, the biggest issue for wild salmon on the West Coast is habitat. This is because there are so many more of us living in the Lower 48 and in the same regions that wild salmon pass though on their way to spawn. Meeting human needs for energy, food, and shelter has caused salmon habitat loss and degradation due to dams, logging, manure and chemical runoff from agriculture, and development. Our cars are another big contributor: they leak oil, spread copper-containing dust from their brakes, and spit out exhaust with invisible chemicals; all of these pollutants find their way into the waterways where salmon return.

But don't despair! As eaters of wild salmon, there are things we can do to assure our land-based lives are not in conflict with those of salmon and their need for a pristine habitat in which to reproduce the next generation of fish. Little things can make a big difference. For example, turn off the water when you're brushing your teeth for less water down the drain and thus more in streams. Use a carwash instead of washing your vehicle in the driveway. Carwash facilities filter wastewater, whereas your soapy, dirty water goes into the ocean by way of the storm drain on the street. Keep your car tuned up to minimize leaks of all kinds. You get the idea. Look for more tips on the Oregon and Washington Salmon Safe websites, which are listed in the Sustainable Seafood Resources on page 313.

BY ANY OTHER NAME

I made up a mnemonic to remember the five salmon: Can (chinook) Pink (pink) Socks (sockeye) Keep (keta) you Covered (coho)?

Chinook (*Oncorhynchus tshawytscha*), aka kings, springers, and tyee, are the largest of the salmon species (often more than 25 pounds, the record chinook weighed in at 146 pounds!) and the one with the most fat. Chinook salmon are beloved throughout the world. Like oysters that are often known by the waters in which they grow, salmon differ in fat content and flavor depending on the rivers they were spawned in and what they ate on their way home to spawn. Copper River salmon is a well-known example of a fish marketed by its river's name. A rare genetic variation that affects only 1 percent of chinook causes its flesh to be white; the meat is sold as "white king" or "ivory king." Even more rare is the marbled chinook caught off the Washington coast. Try white or marbled chinook if you happen to see it.

I encourage you (as does your wallet), however, to explore the other four species of wild salmon. Think of chinook as you would a New York steak or filet mignon: best for occasional eating, whereas more reasonably priced cuts are great on a more regular basis. There is much to enjoy in a well-handled fresh or carefully frozen pink, sockeye, coho, or chum salmon.

Pink salmon (*Oncorhynchus gorbuscha*), aka humpback or humpies, are the smallest of the salmon species (weighing from 3 to 12 pounds) and the most plentiful. They are typically sold in cans or smoked, though if you find them fresh, I encourage you to cook with the fillets. Keep in mind that pink salmon is softer in texture and quite lean and therefore less forgiving in the overcooking department.

Sockeye (*Oncorhynchus nerka*), aka reds or blueback, average 6 to 9 pounds and have deep-red flesh and thinner fillets than the much bigger chinook. Sockeyes are valued for their delicious fat (second to chinook), firm texture, and pronounced flavor.

Coho (*Oncorhynchus kisutch*), aka silvers, are a popular sport fish in the Pacific Northwest, valued for their reckless, spirited chase of a lure. They average 6 to 12 pounds. Of the five salmon species, coho has the third highest amount of fat and should be considered a great value: it has good flavor and is much more affordable per pound than sockeye or chinook.

Keta (*Oncorhynchus keta*), aka chum or dogs, ranging from 6 to 17 pounds, are the last salmon species to spawn, and are considered the least valuable commercially. Chum often get a bad rap in the culinary world. I find this to be a crisis of imagination and a waste of a good protein source. Because of how lean they are, I prefer to steam or smoke them, or cook them in chowders to preserve their moisture. *Ikura* (see page 298) are the eggs from keta salmon.

Salmon fishing seasons vary from state to state, but in general, here are some guidelines. Chinook: May to September, with a southeast Alaska winter season from mid-October to mid-April; Southern Oregon is the only region in the Lower 48 to have a chinook season in October. Pink: June to November. Sockeye: May to September. Coho: June to October. Keta: June to November.

....

BUYING TIPS

A salmon's pin bones run along the dorsal side of both fillets. Want a crystal ball into the salmon's recent past? Look carefully at the pin bones. Think of it this way: pin bones are just like any bone, and the older the flesh gets, the more it pulls away from the bone. If you see a divot (flesh pulled back from the bone) around the pin bones, it's a sign that the fillet is old. A fresh salmon will have pin bones that are right at the surface of the flesh or slightly beneath. Furthermore, if you see gaping or tearing of the flesh, it's usually a sign that the fish was mishandled. If you are buying salmon whole (typically sans head and gutted), look for bright, shiny, intact scales. When the fish is pressed gently, the flesh should bounce back. Check the belly cavity—it should smell like nothing or a light ocean breeze. If the fish was bled quickly and carefully you won't see blood left in any of the capillaries of the belly walls. Make sure there is no bruising, which is a sign of poor handling.

....

QUESTIONS TO ASK BEFORE YOU PULL OUT YOUR WALLET

Most importantly, is this salmon wild or farmed? Stick with wild. Stick with wild. Stick with wild. I feel so strongly about this I said it three times. There are some farmed salmon operations that use tank-based recirculating aquaculture systems (RAS); that is my only current exception to this rule. If you are going to buy farm-raised salmon, make sure it was raised in a RAS and not a net pen.

Here's a quick recap from Farmed Versus Wild on page 19: Salmon farms are a challenge to wild salmon. Farmed salmon raised in net pens have been shown to spread diseases and parasites to the wild fish. Escaped farmed salmon compete with wild salmon for food and spawning grounds, both of which can affect survival rates for wild salmon. Problems associated with farmed salmon in British Columbia and the Lower 48 don't affect Alaska's wild salmon as significantly, as Alaska does not allow salmon to be farmed in its waters.

CARING FOR YOUR GOOD FISH

If you're not going to use your salmon right away, put it in the coldest part of your fridge or place the package in a colander over a bowl and put some ice on top of it to keep it at its best. Thaw frozen salmon according to How to Safely Thaw Frozen Fish on page 18.

HOW THIS TYPE OF SEAFOOD IS RAISED OR HARVESTED

There are three main ways to catch a wild salmon.

Purse seining: Think of a purse seine as a big net that is pulled from the back (stern) of the boat into the sea by a smaller skiff (boat). Once in the water, the skiff pulls the net in a circle around a school of salmon as they swim by. Then the purse line at the bottom of the net is pulled closed, forming a purse shape, to keep the fish from swimming out of the bottom of the net. The whole net is then hauled onboard the boat and the fish are stored in the fish hold.

Trolling (hook and line): As mentioned previously, trolling is the commercial equivalent of rod and reel fishing: several lines, each with one hook, are pulled behind the boat. Individual fish are caught and handled one at a time. This fishing technique produces the highest-quality salmon.

Gill-netting: Gillnets trap the salmon in the mesh of a net as they swim by. As the fish try to back out of the net, their gills get caught in its holes. At sea, drift gillnets are a bad scene and some call them a "wall of death." These gillnets can be miles long, are randomly deployed, and generally not closely monitored while in the water. On the other hand, salmon fishermen use much shorter gillnets and never leave their net once it is in the water. They set their gill-nets in nearshore areas where salmon are known to annually pass through on their migratory swim and at a time when the fish are likely to have schooled together. This is known as time and area management and it increases the likelihood of catching the targeted salmon with little bycatch of other species. Additionally, regulating the size of the mesh allows smaller juvenile salmon to swim through and larger fish to be caught.

SUSTAINABLE SUBSTITUTES

Salmon has a lot of flavor and, depending on which species you get, varying levels of fat. You'll want to substitute a fatty fish such as black cod for a piece of chinook or sockeye salmon. Leaner salmon species, such as keta, pink, and coho, could be substituted with arctic char or trout.

THE ANATOMY OF A FLAKE

There's a lot in a word. It seems that most of fish cookery has boiled down to five letters: F-L-A-K-E. If you are comfortable with the concept of "flake," "flaking," or often, "just flaking," then proceed to the recipes. If, though, this concept is one of the world's great mysteries to you, as it was to many of my cooking students over the years, then you might need some helpful clarification.

First, a story. I once knew someone who had a temp job copyediting recipes. She was most definitely not a cook and could burn water, bless her heart. In her one day at this job, she took out the word "just" every single time it appeared before "flakes" in all the fish recipes, so that, for example, "Cook the salmon until it just flakes" became "Cook the salmon until it flakes." She thought whomever was writing the recipes had terrible grammar. I gently teased her that there is a world of culinary difference between "just flaking" and "flaking," which is why I began this lesson by saying there's a lot in a word.

So, to brass tacks. I feel pictures are in order here.

Here I am pressing on a piece of salmon (a) and halibut (b) that is not flaking, not "just flaking," not even thinking about flaking. It's totally not there yet, unless it's a piece of albacore or a scallop and then, well, I'd eat it anywhere from raw to just seared on the outside.

This is exactly the doneness you are looking for. A press of the finger reveals a sliding away, ever so gently, of the fish into the beginning of individual flakes. The center of the halibut is still glistening with juices and ever so slightly translucent; the salmon is a nice medium rare. I call this the "thinking about flaking" stage, a phrase I prefer to "just flaking," which is confusing to some. I removed the fish from the pan about one minute before these photos were taken. Then I lightly covered the fish, which kept it warm and allowed it to finish cooking to the perfect stage of doneness.

Oh boy, we've gone too far here. This is where my copy editor friend was trying to send all those unwitting recipe readers. Behold: Fish. Flaking. This fish still has some moisture, but I guarantee, by the time it hits your plate, it will have that squeaky, almost mealy, dry, tooth-grabbing texture that is the calling card of the fish *flake*. When the moisture finally returns to your mouth, get a fresh piece of fish and practice, practice, practice.

The most accurate way for beginner and intermediate cooks alike to determine perfect doneness for fish is by taking its temperature—I recommend a Thermapen or ThermaPop (see page 12). When you stick the probe in, make sure the tip is situated in the center of the fish and isn't hitting the pan or passing through and taking the air temperature. These are the temperatures I recommend for the best flavor and preservation of moisture in the fish featured in this book. Keep in mind that the FDA recommends cooking fish to much higher temperatures than what's recommended here. If you cook fish to the FDA's recommended temperature, it is true that nothing can possibly survive the cooking process, including flavor. If cardboard is your thing, I highly recommend it. If not, follow my guidelines:

110–115°F: seared albacore (rare to medium-rare in the center)

115–120°F: salmon (rare)

120–125°F: salmon (medium-rare)

125°F: wahoo

125–130°F: halibut, scallops, mahi, char, trout, cod, lingcod, sardines, and herring (cover lightly with foil after removing from the pan; they will continue to cook while resting)

135°F: black cod

Salmon Variety:
Pink and Keta

SERVES 4

1 tablespoon extra-virgin
olive oil

1 medium yellow onion, cut into
small dice

2 cloves garlic, minced

2 ribs celery, cut into small dice

¼ teaspoon fine sea salt

1 medium Yukon Gold or small
russet potato, peeled, cut into
small dice

1 teaspoon minced fresh thyme

1 bay leaf

¼ teaspoon cayenne

¼ cup dry white wine

1 (14-ounce) can diced tomatoes

1 cup water

1 cup clam juice

⅓ cup heavy cream

½ pound pink or keta salmon
fillet, skinned, pin bones
removed,‡ and cut into
1-inch cubes

¼ cup minced fresh
Italian parsley

---

‡ Go to GoodFishBook.com
for a demonstration of how to
remove the skin and pin bones
from a fillet.

PAIRING: First choice is
Cru Beaujolais; second,
white Burgundy.

wild salmon chowder
with fire-roasted tomatoes

I adore this chowder. The trick here, just like with Halibut Coconut Curry with Charred Chiles and Lime (page 171), is to add the fish to the stockpot and then turn the heat off. This cooks the salmon gently, with the residual heat from the liquid in the pot finishing the job. This is especially important when using salmon species that are lower in fat, such as pink and keta. This is the kind of recipe I teach my students when they say they don't have time to cook. I am tempted to point out that they are sitting through a two-and-a-half-hour cooking class and could have made this recipe five times over, but I don't. I'm hoping they buy this book so I can get the last word in, because being right and eating this soup—now that's delicious!

Grab yourself a large stockpot, add the oil, and heat over medium-high heat. Sauté the onion, garlic, celery, and salt for 5 minutes, then add the potato. Sauté for another 5 minutes. Add the thyme, bay leaf, cayenne, and white wine, stirring to loosen any bits clinging to the pot. Add the tomatoes, water, and clam juice, and bring to a boil over high heat. Lower the heat to medium and simmer for 15 minutes, or until the potatoes are soft. Bring the chowder back to a boil, then add the cream, salmon, and parsley; stir gently, tucking the salmon under the liquid. Immediately turn off the heat and cover the pot. (Remove the pot from the burner if you have an electric stove.) Let the soup sit for 5 minutes to poach the fish gently. Taste and adjust the seasoning before serving.

The chowder is great the next day and keeps well in the freezer for 2 months. You can also make the chowder base up to the point of adding the cream, salmon, and parsley and freeze it. Defrost the base, bring to a boil over high heat, and use fresh fish, cream, and parsley that day.

hajime's steamed banana leaf salmon

SERVES 4

½ cup sake

½ cup mirin

¼ cup soy sauce

½ teaspoon grated fresh
    peeled ginger

1 teaspoon lime juice

⅛ teaspoon fine sea salt

1 pound keta or pink salmon
    fillet (ask for a cut that includes
    the belly), pin bones removed,‡
    cut into 4 equal portions

Banana leaves,* cut into
    4 (8½-by-11-inch) pieces

1 ounce dried shiitake
    mushrooms, rehydrated, stems
    removed, caps sliced thin

¼ cup thinly sliced onion

2 tablespoons chopped fresh
    shiso leaves (or substitute with
    fresh mint)

4 teaspoons unsalted butter

---

*Banana leaves can be found
frozen in most Asian supermarkets. If you can't find them,
steam the fish in parchment
paper (but you'll lose the wonderful perfume of the banana
leaves, so use them if you can).

---

‡ Go to GoodFishBook.com
for a demonstration of how to
remove pin bones from a fillet.

PAIRING: First choice is pinot
gris; second, Beaujolais.

As if Hajime Sato wasn't badass enough, riding his motorcycle around Seattle and ruling over his sushi bar with his webcams and sushi rules, he decided, after fifteen years of running his restaurant Mashiko, to stop contributing to the problems of the oceans. In 2009 he went 100 percent sustainable: no more bluefin tuna, unagi, or farmed imported shrimp. It turns out Hajime does have a soft spot; he saves it for the fish and for those customers with an open mind. (When the first edition of this book went to press, Mashiko was one of only four sustainable sushi bars in the United States; as of 2017, there are upwards of twenty-five sustainable sushi bars in the country.)

In a medium bowl, combine the sake, mirin, soy sauce, ginger, lime juice, and salt. Add the salmon pieces and let them marinate for 20 minutes.

Lay the banana leaves out on a counter. On each leaf, place a quarter of the mushrooms, onions, and shiso leaves. Top with a piece of the salmon, reserving the marinade. Top each salmon piece with 1 teaspoon of butter. Fold the left and right sides of the leaves over the fish and then tuck under the top and bottom edges to form a square packet. Place the packets into a steamer basket. In a medium saucepan over high heat, add 2 cups water; when it boils, reduce the heat to low, place the steamer basket into the pan, and cover. Cook for 7 minutes, then check the internal temperature by pushing a thermometer probe through the banana leaf and into the center of the fish. Remove the packets from the steamer when the fish reaches 120°F. (They will continue to cook after removal.)

Meanwhile, add the marinade to a small saucepan over high heat, and reduce the marinade until it has a syrupy consistency, about 15 minutes. Remove the salmon packets from the steamer basket and let them sit, undisturbed, for about 3 minutes. Serve each person a banana packet and pass a bowl of the sauce.

SERVES 4 AS AN APPETIZER

2 cups cold water

4 dried shiitake mushrooms

5 grams (0.2 ounce)
kombu (kelp)

10 grams (0.4 ounce)
katsuobushi (bonito flakes)

¼ pound asparagus, cut into
2-inch pieces

2 tablespoons mirin

1½ tablespoons soy sauce

½ pound keta or pink
salmon fillet, skinned, pin
bones removed,‡ cut into
1-inch cubes

½ teaspoon *shichimi togarashi*,
plus additional for serving

½ teaspoon lemon zest

¼ cup potato starch

¾ cup high-heat vegetable oil

1 tablespoon salmon roe (*ikura*),
for garnish

4 lemon wedges, for serving

---

‡ Go to GoodFishBook.com
for a demonstration of how to
remove pin bones from a fillet.

PAIRING: First choice: Junmai-
shu sake; second, champagne.

agedashi salmon
with asparagus, shiitakes, and salmon roe

A twist on a classic Japanese dish, this healthy fish recipe swaps in wild salmon for the traditional tofu. I add an extra kick with the inclusion of *shichimi togarashi*, a Japanese chile pepper blend, available in well-stocked markets or online. Even though there is some frying involved, this dish is extremely light and makes a great first course. Follow it up with sushi, Roasted Black Cod with Bok Choy and Soy Caramel Sauce (page 180), or Char Katsu with Ponzu Sauce and Cucumber-Hijiki Salad (page 226).

To make the dashi (stock), in a medium saucepan, combine the water, shiitakes, and kombu. Let sit for 30 minutes. Bring the mixture just to a boil over high heat. When you start to see bubbles form around the kombu, remove it and the shiitakes to a cutting board. Slice the kombu into very thin ribbons and set aside. Thinly slice the shiitakes.

Add the *katsuobushi* to the water, return to a boil, and let simmer for 2 minutes. Turn off the heat and let the dashi sit for 5 minutes before straining it through a fine-mesh sieve. Rinse out the pot and return the dashi to it, along with the sliced shiitakes. Add the asparagus, mirin, and soy sauce to the pot. Bring to a boil over high heat, then reduce to a simmer and cook gently until the asparagus is tender but still bright green. Keep it warm while you prepare the salmon.

In a medium bowl, gently mix the salmon cubes with the *shichimi togarashi* and lemon zest. Add the potato starch and toss gently to coat.

Heat the oil in a small, high-sided saucepan over medium-high heat until it reaches 350°F. Carefully add the salmon (you may need to cook in batches) and cook just until it crisps up a bit, 1 to 2 minutes per side for perfect medium-rare. It will continue to cook a bit off the heat. Transfer the salmon to a paper-towel-lined plate.

To serve, divide the vegetables and sauce between 4 small bowls. Place the salmon pieces on top. Garnish with the sliced kombu and *ikura*. Offer each person a wedge of lemon to squeeze over the fish.

Salmon Variety:
Pink and Keta

SERVES 4

2 tablespoons extra-virgin olive oil, divided
2 cups fresh corn kernels (cut from about 2 large ears of corn), or hell, just use frozen
1 pint cherry tomatoes, halved (or leave whole)
½ bunch green onions, trimmed, halved crosswise
1 lemon, zested and then cut into thin slices
½ teaspoon fine sea salt, divided
1 pound keta or pink salmon tail fillets, skin on (this will save time since the tails have no bones)
1 teaspoon soy sauce
Pinch of cayenne (optional)
1 small bunch Thai or regular basil, leaves picked and roughly chopped (or leave whole)
1 tablespoon unsalted butter
Garlic bread, for serving

PAIRING: First choice is whatever you have at home; second, whatever your neighbor has at home.

the easiest recipe in this book

We need more honesty in cookbooks. What if authors titled their recipes more accurately? "This Recipe Will Take You Days," "Fifty-Six Dollars Worth of Ingredients," "Not as Good Homemade as in My Restaurant," "You've Never Heard of Four of the Ingredients and You'll Go to Three Stores Looking for Them," and hat tip to my friend Jill for "Go Ahead and Substitute Half the Ingredients with Other Things." But truly, this is the easiest recipe in this book, and you can replace the corn and tomatoes for whatever vegetables are in season: asparagus and peas in the spring, thinly sliced carrots, garlic, and kale in the winter.

Preheat the oven to 400°F.

Line a baking sheet with aluminum foil, letting it extend over the edges of the pan. Drizzle 1 tablespoon of the oil in the middle of the foil. Put the corn, tomatoes, and green onions on top of it. Toss the vegetables with the oil to coat lightly and spread them evenly in the pan. Sprinkle with the lemon zest and ¼ teaspoon of the sea salt. Arrange the salmon on top of the vegetables. Drizzle the soy sauce and remaining 1 tablespoon oil over the fish. Sprinkle with the cayenne and scatter first the lemon slices and then the basil leaves on top. Top it all with the butter.

Lay another big piece of foil over the pan and crimp all the edges together nice and tight. Place in the oven and set a timer for 8 minutes. Unwrap and serve straight from the pan with garlic bread and a salad. Clean the kitchen in 5 minutes. Feel like a rock star.

Salmon Variety:
Pink and Keta

SERVES 4

1 stalk lemongrass

2 tablespoons high-heat
  vegetable oil

¼ cup minced shallot

2 tablespoons sugar

¼ teaspoon fine sea salt

¼ teaspoon red pepper flakes

1½ cups medium-diced green
  cabbage

2 bulbs baby bok choy, white
  bases cut crosswise into
  ¼-inch slices, tender green
  leaves reserved

1 serrano chile, minced

¼ cup dry white wine or dry
  white vermouth

1 quart water

2 Roma tomatoes, cut into
  small dice

½ cup medium-diced fresh
  pineapple

3 tablespoons fish sauce

2 tablespoons tamarind paste

1 pound pink or keta salmon
  fillet, skinned, pin bones
  removed,‡ cut into 1-inch cubes

¼ cup fresh cilantro leaves and
  stems, for garnish

Cooked rice or naan, for serving

PAIRING: First choice is New
Zealand sauvignon blanc;
second, Torrontés.

salmon in spiced tamarind soup

This is my take on a *rasam*, a South Indian soup that is light and refreshing and feels restorative. It is commonly based around tamarind, a rich sour-sweet fruit, and I bump up the sour-sweet combo by adding pineapple. A big bowl of rice on the side brings the energy back down to earth. Healthy and warming, this is the perfect soup to make in the early fall, on that first day when you smell the change in season and the temperature of the wind is just slightly chilly.

Prepare the lemongrass by cutting off the top half of the stalk (where it is thinner and darker); discard this. Trim the very bottom and discard, then cut the stalk into 2-inch lengths. Smack the lemongrass with the side of a knife to help it release its flavor into the dish.

Heat a soup pot over medium-high heat. Add the oil, shallot, sugar, salt, red pepper flakes, and lemongrass and sauté for 3 minutes, or until the shallots soften. Increase the heat to high and add the cabbage, bok choy white parts, and serrano and saute for another 2 minutes. Deglaze with the wine and cook until it fully evaporates. Add the water, tomatoes, pineapple, fish sauce, and tamarind. Bring to a boil over high heat, then reduce to a simmer and cook for 10 minutes. Return to a boil, and then add the salmon, tucking the fish under the liquid, and bok choy green leaves. Cover the pot and turn off the heat. (Remove the pot from the burner if you have an electric stove.) Let the salmon gently poach in the hot soup for 5 minutes. Taste the soup for seasoning, and adjust with salt, fish sauce, and sugar to your liking. Remove the lemongrass (or tell your guests they can chew on it but shouldn't swallow it), garnish with cilantro, and serve with rice or naan.

‡ Go to GoodFishBook.com for a demonstration of how to remove the skin and pin bones from a fillet.

SERVES 4

1 teaspoon red pepper flakes

1 tablespoon coriander seeds

¼ teaspoon fenugreek seeds

2 tablespoons coconut oil

30 fresh or frozen curry leaves

1 teaspoon mustard seeds

2 medium shallots, sliced ⅛ inch thick (about 1 cup)

3 serrano chiles (seeds and membranes removed from 2), cut into ¼-inch slices

5 cloves fermented black garlic (optional)

2-inch piece fresh peeled ginger,* cut julienne

1-inch piece fresh peeled turmeric,* very finely grated

1 teaspoon fine sea salt

1 (14-ounce) can full-fat coconut milk

1 cup water

1 tablespoon tamarind paste

1 pound keta or pink salmon fillet, skinned, pin bones removed,‡ cut into 1-inch cubes

---

‡ Go to GoodFishBook.com for a demonstration of how to remove the skin and pin bones from a fillet.

PAIRING: First choice is Torrontés; second, Oregon pinot gris

kerala curry
with coconut milk and curry leaves

Kerala, a southern state in India on the tropical Malabar Coast, is known for its fish curries speckled with the glossy green of curry leaves. Curry leaves contribute that magical "Wow, what's that awesome flavor?" whenever I make dishes using them for my non-Indian friends. Monica Bhide, author of *Modern Spice* (and many other great books), admonishes readers at the beginning of her *New York Times* article on curry leaves: "Curry leaves have nothing to do with curry powder." Curry, or karri, leaves look similar to lime leaves or bay leaves in that they are green and aromatic—and that's the extent of the similarities. They add a lemony essence to food, but don't even think that you can just substitute with lemon zest. There is a quality to them that defies description. Is it tea-like? Slightly floral? A bit earthy? Yes. They are an exceptional ingredient and *make* this dish. Oh, and bonus points because they are edible. If you can't find them at a local Indian or Asian market, they can be ordered online.

....

In a medium skillet over medium-high heat, toast the red pepper flakes, coriander, and fenugreek until fragrant and darkened, 2 to 3 minutes. Grind the mixture in a spice grinder and set aside.

Grab a splatter guard if you have one. In the same skillet, heat the coconut oil over medium-high heat, add the curry leaves and mustard seeds, and set the splatter guard on top. When the seeds pop and the leaves crisp up, add the shallots, serranos, black garlic, ginger, turmeric, reserved spice mixture, and salt. Sauté for 2 to 3 minutes, then add the coconut milk, water, and tamarind paste. Bring to a boil over high heat, then reduce to a simmer and cook until oil comes to the top of the curry. Add the salmon, tucking the fish under the simmering liquid. Immediately turn off the heat (or remove the pot from the burner if you have an electric stove) and cover the pot. Let the salmon gently poach in the hot curry for 5 minutes.

---

*If the ginger and turmeric are organic, there is no need to peel them. Just grate away!

KING / CHINO

KING / CHINO

SOCKEYE

COHO / SILV

Salmon Variety:
Coho, Sockeye, and King

SERVES 4

¼ teaspoon black peppercorns

1 (1-inch) piece cinnamon stick, broken up into smaller pieces

¾ teaspoon fine sea salt, divided

¼ teaspoon cumin seeds

¼ teaspoon allspice berries

¼ teaspoon red pepper flakes (or ½ teaspoon for a spicier rub)

1 pound coho or sockeye salmon fillet, skin on, pin bones removed,‡ cut into 4 equal portions

2 large orange sweet potatoes (marketed as "yams"), peeled (or not) and cut into 4-by-½-inch pieces (about 4 cups)

1 tablespoon plus 2 teaspoons extra-virgin olive oil, divided

1 bunch kale leaves, stems removed, chopped into bite-size pieces (about 4 cups)

Heaping ¼ teaspoon freshly ground black pepper

1 (14-ounce) can black beans, drained and rinsed

1 (14-ounce) can full-fat coconut milk

1 tablespoon apple cider vinegar

1 tablespoon high-heat vegetable oil

1 lime, cut into wedges, for garnish

jerk-spiced salmon

with coconut pot liquor and sweet potato fries

The food indulgences I love tend not to be very good for me: quality tequila, candy, deep-fried anything . . . especially doughnuts. Imagine my excitement when I developed a recipe that I could eat over and over again and which included some of the world's most healthful foods: wild salmon, dark leafy greens, beans, and sweet potatoes. Who needs doughnuts when you can eat kale that tastes this good? OK, well I still do—but now, not as often.

. . . .

Preheat the oven to 400°F.

Grind the peppercorns, cinnamon stick, ¼ teaspoon of the salt, the cumin seeds, allspice berries, and red pepper flakes in a spice grinder until fine. Reserve 1 teaspoon of the spice rub for the sweet potatoes. Coat the salmon pieces on all sides with the remainder of the rub and set them aside on a plate in the refrigerator for 30 minutes.

In a large bowl, toss the sweet potato pieces with 2 teaspoons of the olive oil, the reserved teaspoon spice rub, and ¼ teaspoon of the salt. Spread them out on a baking sheet and bake for 25 to 30 minutes, or until browned in spots. Remove the sweet potatoes from the oven and cover to keep warm. Leave the oven on.

In a large pot over medium-high heat, add the remaining 1 tablespoon olive oil. Add the kale, the remaining ¼ teaspoon salt, and the pepper, and sauté for 2 to 3 minutes, or until the greens start to wilt. Add the black beans, coconut milk, and apple cider vinegar. Stir and then simmer for 10 minutes, or until the greens are tender. Season to taste and keep warm until you are ready to serve.

CONTINUED

‡ Go to GoodFishBook.com for a demonstration of how to remove pin bones from a fillet.

PAIRING: First choice is viognier; second, Red Stripe Jamaican lager.

JERK-SPICED SALMON, CONTINUED

In an ovenproof skillet over high heat, add the vegetable oil. When it is hot, carefully add the salmon fillets, skin side up. Cook for 2 to 3 minutes, or until the fillets are browned, then flip them carefully and place the skillet in the oven for 5 to 6 minutes, or until the salmon reaches 120°F.

To serve, divide the greens and beans among 4 bowls and top each with a piece of salmon. Ladle some of the coconut "pot liquor" all around the outer edge of the bowl. Tuck some sweet potatoes alongside the salmon and garnish with a lime wedge.

Salmon Variety:
Coho, Sockeye, and King

SERVES 4

1 tablespoon coriander seeds
2 teaspoons cumin seeds
1 teaspoon red pepper flakes
6 cardamom pods
2-inch piece cinnamon stick,
  broken into smaller pieces
1 teaspoon ground turmeric
1 pound coho salmon fillet,
  skinned, pin bones removed,‡
  cut into 4 equal portions
1½ teaspoons fine sea salt,
  divided
3 tablespoons ghee, divided
½ cup small-diced shallot
4 ounces shiitake or cremini
  mushrooms, cut into quarters
  (stem the shiitakes, if using)
1 tablespoon minced garlic
1 tablespoon minced fresh
  peeled ginger
⅓ cup dry white vermouth or
  dry white wine
3 medium canned whole
  tomatoes
1 cup water
½ cup plain full-fat
  Greek-style yogurt
½ cup heavy cream
2 teaspoons honey
1 medium Yukon Gold potato,
  cut into medium dice (about
  1½ cups)
1 cup fresh peas (frozen are fine)
Cilantro, for garnish
1 lime, cut into wedges,
  for serving
Naan, for serving

seared salmon
tikka masala

This recipe appears to be much harder than it really is. I rated it "2 fish" in difficulty simply because it has many ingredients, you need to toast some spices, and use a spice grinder and a blender, but truly no step in this recipe requires special skill or much time. It's well worth the effort. I believe in you, and I know you can do it. That being said, I suspect that for many of you, you're just reading this recipe for the food porn—you know you don't intend to actually make it. I know this because I flip through cookbooks doing exactly the same thing. Do you feel like I'm talking directly to you? I am. I'm writing this from inside your house. I really like that shirt you're wearing.

....

Preheat the oven to 400°F.

In a dry medium skillet over medium-high heat, toast the coriander seeds, cumin seeds, red pepper flakes, cardamom, and cinnamon stick until they darken lightly and start to smell good, 1 to 2 minutes. Transfer the toasted spices along with the turmeric to a spice grinder and grind into a very fine powder.

Season the salmon pieces with ½ teaspoon of the salt and ½ teaspoon of the spice mixture. Set aside.

In a large sauté pan over medium-high heat, add 2 tablespoons of the ghee. Once hot, add the shallot and remaining 1 teaspoon salt and sauté for 2 to 3 minutes, or until translucent. Add the mushrooms and increase the heat to high. Cook, stirring occasionally, until the mushrooms begin to brown around the edges, 4 to 5 minutes. Add the garlic and ginger and sauté for 1 minute, or until aromatic. Deglaze the pan with the vermouth.

Meanwhile, in a blender, puree the tomatoes, water, yogurt, cream, honey, and the remainder of the spice mixture. Add the puree and the potato to the pan with the mushrooms. Bring to a boil over high heat, then reduce to a simmer and cook for 15 minutes, or until the potato is tender. Add the peas and cook for 1 more minute. Season to taste with salt and lime juice if it needs acidity.

‡ Go to GoodFishBook.com for a demonstration of how to remove the skin and pin bones from a fillet.

PAIRING: First choice: Kabinett riesling; second, gewürztraminer.

Heat a separate medium oven-proof skillet over high heat and add the remaining 1 tablespoon ghee. Once hot, swirl the ghee to coat the pan, then add the salmon. Cook for 2 to 3 minutes, or until the fillets are browned, then flip them over carefully and place the skillet in the oven for 5 to 6 minutes, or until the salmon reaches 120°F.

Serve a portion of the tikka masala in each of 4 bowls. Top with the salmon, garnish with cilantro, and serve with a lime wedge and naan.

What's that white stuff you sometimes see on salmon when it cooks? A lot of people think it's fat, but it is actually a protein called albumin (also found in egg whites). In perfectly cooked salmon, the albumin will show—just barely—on the top at the thickest point of the fish and look like someone spilled a little skim milk on it. If it thickens up, appears all across the top, and looks like curdled cream, the fish is way overcooked. See the final salmon photograph on page 127: albumin has formed and is clearly visible between the flakes on the top of the fish. This is exactly what you want to avoid. A little thick albumin forming around the bottom or sides is fine (and unavoidable because of the convection of heat off the pan), but when the albumin comes out of the top in great quantity, the fish is definitely overcooked.

Salmon Variety:
Coho, Sockeye, and King

SERVES 4

½ cup buttermilk

3 tablespoons mayonnaise

1 tablespoon apple
cider vinegar

1 teaspoon Dijon mustard

1 teaspoon chopped fresh dill

1 small clove garlic, minced

2 to 3 shakes of your favorite
hot sauce

1 pound coho or Chinook
salmon fillet, skin on, pin
bones removed,[‡] cut into
4 equal portions

Fine sea salt

Freshly ground black pepper

2 bunches watercress

2 cups rye croutons*

¼ cup purple sauerkraut (or use
any favorite sauerkraut)

Pickled mustard seeds,**
for garnish (optional)

———————————————

[‡] Go to GoodFishBook.com
for a demonstration of how to
remove pin bones from a fillet.

———————————————

PAIRING: First choice is
Washington chardonnay;
second, grüner veltliner.

grilled salmon
*with watercress salad, rye croutons,
and buttermilk dressing*

This dish leans heavily on some classic German ingredients. Rye croutons, mustard, and sauerkraut, it turns out, pair beautifully with rich salmon. Most large supermarkets sell sauerkraut in the refrigerated section; if you can't find purple sauerkraut, feel free to use green (or make your own!). A rich dill-infused buttermilk dressing brings it all together.

....

Preheat a grill over high heat. (Make sure the grates are clean and oiled.)

In a small bowl, whisk together the buttermilk, mayonnaise, apple cider vinegar, mustard, dill, garlic, and hot sauce. Set aside.

Season the salmon with salt and pepper and grill (with the lid down), skin side down, for 7 to 10 minutes, or until the internal temperature reaches 120°F for medium-rare. Transfer the salmon to a plate and keep warm.

Toss the watercress with half of the dressing. Mound the salad onto plates or a platter and top with the salmon. Garnish with the rye croutons, sauerkraut, and pickled mustard seeds. Serve with extra dressing on the side.

———————————————————————————

*Make rye croutons by tossing ½-inch cubes of rye bread with 1 teaspoon extra-virgin olive oil and a pinch of sea salt; bake in a 350°F oven for 10 to 15 minutes, or until crisp.

———————————————————————————

**Make pickled mustard seeds by combining ½ cup yellow mustard seeds, ½ cup rice vinegar, ⅓ cup water, ⅓ cup mirin, 1 teaspoon sugar, and ½ teaspoon sea salt in a small saucepan; simmer gently for 45 minutes, or until the seeds plump up, adding more water as needed. They will keep in the refrigerator for a month or two.

Salmon Variety:
Coho, Sockeye, and King

coriander-and-lemon-crusted salmon

with poached egg, roasted asparagus,
and hazelnuts

SERVES 4

8 cups water

1 tablespoon distilled
white vinegar

4 very fresh large eggs

1 tablespoon extra-virgin
olive oil, divided, plus
additional for drizzling

1 tablespoon coriander seeds

½ teaspoon red pepper flakes

¾ teaspoon fine sea
salt, divided

Zest and juice from 1 lemon

1 pound coho or sockeye
salmon fillet, skin on, pin
bones removed,‡ cut into
4 equal portions

1 pound asparagus, tough
ends trimmed

1 tablespoon chopped
fresh tarragon

1 tablespoon chopped
fresh mint

⅛ teaspoon freshly ground
black pepper

¼ cup hazelnuts, toasted and
roughly chopped

Part of me is really resistant to put a recipe in this book with an egg on top because, man, we got a little crazy there with putting an egg on everything. Americans! Not everything is better with an egg on it. But—ahem—this is, so it's not the time or place to make such an argument. If you want this dish to come together more quickly at serving time, you can crust the salmon and peel the asparagus up to two hours before broiling; you can also poach the eggs and chill them in ice water in the refrigerator up to a day in advance.

....

Fill a medium bowl with ice water. In a large saucepan, bring the water and vinegar to a boil over high heat. Carefully tip an egg into a small ramekin. (Pro tip: For neater, less shaggy poached eggs, hold each egg in a fine-mesh sieve for 10 seconds, letting any loose egg white drain through; discard.) Reduce the boiling water to a bare simmer. Gently stir in a circle so that the water is swirling around the pot. Tip each egg, one at a time, into the middle of the swirling water, and keep swirling the water in between. Cook each egg until the whites are set but the yolks are still runny, 3 to 4 minutes. Remove the eggs with a slotted spoon to the ice water, but leave the hot water in the pot. You can hold the chilled poached eggs in the water in the refrigerator and reheat later (within 24 hours).

Position a rack in the upper third of the oven. Preheat the broiler to high. Drizzle a rimmed baking sheet with 1 teaspoon of the oil.

Combine the coriander seeds, red pepper flakes, and ¼ teaspoon of the salt in a spice grinder and blend until finely ground. Transfer to a small bowl and stir in the lemon zest. Coat the salmon pieces with this mixture and place on the baking sheet.

‡ Go to GoodFishBook.com for a demonstration of how to remove the skin and pin bones from a fillet.

PAIRING: First choice is sauvignon blanc; second, pinot blanc.

Cut 2 inches off the tips of the asparagus and set them beside the salmon, tossing them through the oil on the pan. Sprinkle ⅛ teaspoon of the salt over the asparagus tips.

Using a peeler, shave the asparagus spears lengthwise into long curls. (You'll be left with some of the spear center intact; discard or save these for making soup). Toss the asparagus curls in a medium bowl with the tarragon, mint, lemon juice, remaining 2 teaspoons oil, ⅛ teaspoon of the salt, and pepper. Set aside to soften for at least 10 minutes.

Broil the salmon and asparagus tips about 6 inches from the element until the salmon reaches 120°F for medium-rare. Let the salmon rest while you reheat the eggs. Bring the water back to a gentle boil. Carefully lower the eggs into the hot water for 30 seconds to reheat. Pat dry on paper towels.

Create a "nest" with the shaved asparagus salad. Serve the poached egg inside the nest, seasoning the eggs with the remaining ¼ teaspoon salt and the pepper, if desired. Serve the salmon to the side, scatter the toasted hazelnuts around the plate, and drizzle with a little oil.

SERVES 4

For the fennel salt:
1 tablespoon fennel seeds
1 teaspoon fine sea salt
½ teaspoon black peppercorns

For the vegetables:
1 large fennel bulb, stems
    removed, cut into ½-inch-thick
    wedges, small frond pieces
    reserved for garnish
1 red onion, cut into thick slices
1 tablespoon extra-virgin
    olive oil

For the salad:
¼ cup plain full-fat
    Greek-style yogurt
1 teaspoon Dijon mustard
Pinch of cayenne
½ teaspoon honey
4 cups salad greens (mixture of
    arugula, frisée, mizuna, etc.)

For the salmon:
1 pound sockeye salmon fillet,
    skin on, pin bones removed,‡
    cut into 4 equal portions
High-heat vegetable oil, for
    oiling the grill

‡ Go to GoodFishBook.com
for a demonstration of how to
remove pin bones from a fillet.

PAIRING: First choice is
California pinot noir; second,
grüner veltliner.

grilled sockeye salmon
with fennel two ways

When I was a child, I despised black jellybeans. I went so far as to think of them as assault weapons designed by adults to keep the candy bowl away from the children (see also: Good & Plentys). But tastes change, children mature into adults, and suddenly I'm the one foisting licorice-tasting fennel onto children's plates. Fennel has become one of my favorite vegetables; it marries perfectly with the strong character and richness of wild salmon. In this recipe, it is featured two ways: as a fennel salt rub and in wedges, smoky and sweet from the grill.

To prepare the fennel salt, grind the fennel seeds, salt, and peppercorns together in a spice grinder. Reserve.

To prepare the vegetables, in a medium bowl, toss the fennel and onion with the olive oil and 1 teaspoon of the fennel salt.

To prepare the salad, in a small bowl, combine the yogurt, mustard, cayenne, and honey. Season to taste with salt. Right before serving, lightly coat the greens with 2 tablespoons of the dressing. Reserve the rest to use as a sauce for the salmon.

To prepare the salmon, coat the pieces on all sides with the remaining fennel salt and set them aside on a plate in the refrigerator.

Preheat an outdoor gas grill or indoor grill pan to high heat. Oil the grill rack with vegetable oil.

Grill the fennel wedges and onion slices for 6 to 8 minutes, or until crisp-tender. Grill the salmon, skin side up, until the grill marks are clearly visible. Sockeye is fairly thin, so it will cook quickly. Remove it from the grill when it reaches 120°F at the center for medium-rare.

This is a great dish to serve family-style on a large platter. Place the salad in the middle of the platter and top with the salmon. Scatter the vegetables all around the platter. Garnish with small fennel fronds. Serve with the reserved sauce on the side.

roasted salmon

with wild mushrooms and pinot noir sauce

SERVES 4

For the pinot noir sauce:
¼ cup minced shallots
1 teaspoon fennel seeds,
  lightly crushed with the side
  of a knife
1 star anise pod
2 teaspoons honey
1 bottle pinot noir
4 cups low-sodium vegetable
  or chicken stock
1 cup (2 sticks) cold unsalted
  butter, cut into large dice

For the vegetables:
1 large turnip or rutabaga, cut
  into medium dice
1 tablespoon extra-virgin olive
  oil, plus additional for drizzling
½ teaspoon fine sea salt
¼ teaspoon freshly ground
  black pepper
1 small leek, white and light-
  green parts only, cut into
  medium dice
3 ounces fresh wild mushrooms
  (morels, black trumpet,
  porcini), cleaned well and cut
  into bite-size pieces

I once thought butter sauces were a cop-out. Of course it tastes great; it's a butter sauce! On principle, I wouldn't make one. Then I got older and realized that the French didn't build their civilization upon the semifirm back of butter and barrels of wine on a whim. Sure, first there was that cook who drunkenly tipped his Burgundy into the butter pot, but then they codified that drunken miracle into the very fabric of their cuisine. We are all the beneficiaries of this legacy, and it was naïve bluster that kept me from embracing dishes such as this one, where copious amounts of pinot noir meet butter, coating and enhancing the fatty goodness of a perfectly cooked piece of salmon.

To prepare the pinot noir sauce, in a wide saucepan over high heat, combine all its ingredients except for the butter. Bring the liquid to a boil over high heat, then reduce the heat to a gentle simmer. Reduce the sauce until you have 1½ cups, about 40 minutes. (If you want to speed this up, the sauce can be reduced over slightly higher heat.) While the sauce reduces, prepare the vegetables.

Preheat the oven to 400°F.

To prepare the vegetables, spread the turnips on a baking sheet lined with parchment paper. Drizzle with 1 tablespoon oil and season with the salt and pepper. Cover the turnips with foil and roast in the oven for 20 minutes. Uncover the turnips, add the leeks and mushrooms, and stir well. Drizzle with a little more oil, if desired. Roast the vegetables, uncovered, for 20 more minutes. Remove the baking sheet from the oven, taste, and add more salt if desired. Cover with foil and set aside. Reduce the oven temperature to 250°F.

For the roasted salmon:

1 pound chinook salmon fillet, skinned, pin bones removed,‡ and cut into 4 equal portions

1 tablespoon extra-virgin olive oil

¼ teaspoon fine sea salt

---

‡ Go to GoodFishBook.com for a demonstration of how to remove the skin and pin bones from a fillet.

PAIRING: First choice is red Burgundy; second, Oregon pinot noir.

To finish the sauce, first strain it through a fine-mesh sieve. Return the sauce to the saucepan over low heat. Whisk the cold butter into the sauce a little at a time until it's all incorporated. Keep the sauce warm at the back of the stove, off the heat, while you prepare the salmon.

To prepare the salmon, lay the salmon pieces on a baking sheet lined with parchment paper. Drizzle the fillets with the oil and season with the salt. When the oven has cooled to 250°F, roast the salmon for 8 to 10 minutes, or until the salmon reaches 120°F for medium-rare.

To serve, spoon a small amount of sauce onto each plate and top with the vegetables and salmon.

coffee-and-spice-rubbed salmon tacos

with charred cabbage, mango salsa, and avocado cream

SERVES 4

1 avocado, peeled and pitted

⅓ cup plain whole-fat yogurt

2 tablespoons lime juice, divided

2¾ teaspoons fine sea salt, divided

Dash of Tabasco

3 tablespoons whole coffee beans

1 tablespoon coriander seeds

1 tablespoon ancho chile powder

1 tablespoon brown sugar

½ teaspoon cumin seeds

1 pound coho or sockeye salmon fillet, skin on, pin bones removed,‡ cut into 4 equal portions

2 serrano chiles

1 mango, cut into small dice

1 cup minced cilantro (about ½ bunch)

1 clove garlic, minced

1 tablespoon virgin coconut oil, melted

2 tablespoons high-heat vegetable oil, divided

½ small head red cabbage, cut into medium dice

8 small corn tortillas

I know, I know. It's so stereotypical. A chef in Seattle combines iconic Pacific Northwest salmon with our city's biggest beverage cliché. But don't let the predictability stop you from trying this recipe because: a) I didn't make you use Starbucks beans, and b) these tacos are really, really good. You'll have leftover coffee rub, so you can save it for a rainy day. See what I did there?

To make the avocado cream, combine the avocado, yogurt, 1 tablespoon of the lime juice, ½ teaspoon of the salt, and Tabasco in a blender. Blend until the mixture is a smooth puree. Season to taste with more lime juice and salt, if desired.

To make the spice mixture, grind the coffee beans, coriander seeds, chile powder, brown sugar, cumin seeds, and 1½ teaspoons of the salt to a fine powder in a spice grinder. Coat the salmon on the flesh side only with half of the spice mixture and set aside while you prepare the salsa. (Save the other half of the spice mixture for another day.)

Char the serranos until blackened over a gas flame (thread a metal skewer through each end to help hold them flat) or under the broiler, then mince them. Place in a medium bowl with the mango, cilantro, garlic, coconut oil, and ½ teaspoon of the salt. Mix well and adjust seasoning to taste.

Heat an outdoor grill or grill pan over medium-high heat. Add 1 tablespoon of the vegetable oil to the pan, or brush some oil on the grill and the salmon if you are grilling. Cook the salmon, skin side up, for 30 seconds only, to keep the spices from burning. Flip the salmon over and cook, skin side down, until the skin is crisp and a thermometer measures 120°F. Transfer the salmon to a plate, gently pull off the skin, and set it aside on a cooling rack.

CONTINUED

‡ Go to GoodFishBook.com for a demonstration of how to remove pin bones from a fillet.

PAIRING: First choice is Beaujolais; second, a porter or stout brewed with coffee, or a pilsner.

Add the cabbage and remaining ¼ teaspoon salt to the pan and sear over high heat until the cabbage is charred, about 5 minutes total. (Alternatively, you could grill oiled cabbage leaves and then chop after charring.) Transfer to a medium bowl. Heat the tortillas in the pan until they soften, about 1 minute per side. Chop the salmon skin into bite-size pieces and break the salmon into chunks. Serve the tacos immediately, layering the tortillas with avocado cream, salmon, cabbage, mango salsa, and salmon skin chips.

Salmon Variety:
Coho, Sockeye, and King

SERVES 4

½ box (8 ounces) dried
vermicelli, broken into
½-inch pieces

2 tablespoons extra-virgin
olive oil (preferably Spanish
arbequina), divided, plus
additional for drizzling

1 yellow onion, cut into
small dice

2 bay leaves

½ teaspoon red pepper flakes

½ teaspoon smoked paprika

½ teaspoon fine sea
salt, divided

½ cup small-diced
Spanish chorizo

1 pound king salmon fillet,
skinned, pin bones removed,‡
cut into 4 equal portions

½ cup dry white wine or dry
white vermouth

2 cups water

4 whole canned tomatoes
(Muir Glen fire-roasted are
great here)

1 pound manila clams

1 teaspoon sherry vinegar (preferably Arvum Gran Reserva)

1 roasted red pepper (preferably
piquillo), cut into strips

Herb Oil (page 100)

PAIRING: First choice is albariño;
second, rosé.

fideos *with salmon, clams, and smoked paprika*

Fideos means "noodles" in Spanish. You start with vermicelli and then break them up into small pieces, sauté them in oil until they brown, and then cook in just enough liquid to soften them. The dish is essentially a pilaf or paella using noodles instead of rice. Think of them as long, skinny pieces of couscous, or a creative way to use up the broken bits at the bottom of a bag of pasta. Some of the best dishes of the world probably came about this way. This dish marries the Pacific Northwest (salmon and clams) with classic Spanish flavors (chorizo, sherry vinegar, and smoked paprika). The quality of the ingredients is everything to this dish, so choose care-fully! I offer my suggestions in the ingredient list.

Toast the vermicelli in a dry skillet over medium-high heat, stirring constantly, until browned. Set aside.

Heat a Dutch oven or braising pot over medium-high heat and add 1 tablespoon of the oil. Add the onion, bay leaves, red pepper flakes, paprika, and ¼ teaspoon of the salt. Sauté for 5 minutes, or until the onion softens. Add the chorizo and continue to cook, stirring occasionally, for 10 minutes. Push the onions and chorizo to the side of the pot and add the remaining 1 tablespoon oil to the center of the pot. Sprinkle the remaining ¼ teaspoon salt over the salmon fillets and place them in the pan, skin side up. Reduce the heat to medium and cook the salmon until it develops a nice brown crust on the bottom, 3 to 4 minutes, then immediately remove from the pan. (Do not cook the second side.) Set aside.

Add the wine to the pot to deglaze it. Add the water and tomatoes, breaking the tomatoes up with a spoon. Bring to a boil over high heat and add the vermicelli, clams, and sherry vinegar. Reduce the heat to a simmer and cook until the clams open and the vermicelli is tender, about 10 minutes. Divide among 4 bowls and garnish each one with red pepper strips and a drizzle of Herb Oil.

‡ Go to GoodFishBook.com for a demonstration of how to remove the skin and pin bones from a fillet.

seared salmon, morels, and peas

with green goddess sauce

No one can deny how beautiful the Pacific Northwest is; it's why I moved here twenty years ago from the East Coast. The local ingredients are magical, and the constant rains are a big part of the reason we have so much abundance. It's why mushrooms grow in every corner of this region (and our homes). Come spring, the rains have been so constant, the gray so bleak, that you can find us standing outside pushing our faces into the sun like hopeful but extremely weak daffodils. When spring Chinook salmon return to their home rivers, and you see the first mighty little leaves of your parsley growing back in the garden, and spring morels hit the mountains and the farmers' markets, it causes more than just the regular joy normal people get at the change of the season. Indeed, it's like the world's biggest Prozac raining down onto our moldy souls. Enjoy the recipe! Lord knows we will.

SERVES 4

For the green goddess sauce:
½ cup whole fat plain yogurt
3 tablespoons extra-virgin olive oil
½ cup fresh Italian parsley
¼ cup packed fresh basil leaves
2 tablespoons chopped fresh chives
2 tablespoons chopped fresh dill
2 tablespoons chopped fresh mint
2 tablespoons chopped fresh tarragon
1 tablespoon lemon juice
1 anchovy fillet
¼ teaspoon fine sea salt
⅛ teaspoon freshly ground black pepper

For the salmon and vegetables:
8 ounces fresh morels, trimmed, or 1 ounce dried morels, soaked*
1 pound chinook salmon fillet, skin on, pin bones removed,‡ cut into 4 equal portions
½ teaspoon fine sea salt, divided
2 tablespoons extra-virgin olive oil, divided
3 cups fresh or frozen (thawed) peas
1 clove garlic, minced
¼ teaspoon freshly ground black pepper

To make the green goddess sauce, combine all the sauce ingredients in a blender and puree until very creamy and bright green. Set aside.

To prepare the salmon and vegetables, first briefly swish fresh morels in a large bowl of tepid water. Drain and repeat to remove all the dirt. Gently but thoroughly pat them dry with an absorbant towel and cut in half if large.

Pat the salmon skin very dry with a paper towel and sprinkle the flesh with ¼ teaspoon of the salt. Heat 1 tablespoon of the oil in a large cast-iron skillet over medium-high heat until shimmering. Swirl to coat the pan, then add the salmon pieces, skin side down. Using a spatula, gently press on the salmon to keep the pieces relatively flat; cook until the skin begins to crisp, 4 to 5 minutes. Lift up the salmon and carefully touch the skin: it will be firm if it's crispy. Turn the salmon over and cook for 1 to 3 minutes more, until the internal temperature reaches 120°F for medium-rare. Carefully transfer to a plate.

½ cup low-sodium mushroom
  broth or soaking liquid
¼ cup chopped mixed fresh
  herbs, such as parsley, dill,
  and/or tarragon

---

† Go to GoodFishBook.com
for a demonstration of how to
remove pin bones from a fillet.

PAIRING: First choice is white
Burgundy; second, Sancerre.

Reduce the heat to medium. Add the remaining 1 tablespoon oil, the morels, peas, garlic, pepper, and the remaining ¼ teaspoon salt. Cook, stirring, for 2 minutes. Add the mushroom broth and cook until most of the liquid has evaporated, 2 to 3 minutes. Stir in the mixed herbs and remove the pan from the heat. Serve the salmon over the green goddess sauce. Drape the salmon with the morel and pea mixture.

---

*When rehydrating dried morels, I recommend a 5-minute soak in warm water followed by some agitation with your hands to release any grit or dirt. Pull the morels up and out of the warm water and then soak them in enough boiling water to cover for 10 minutes to rehydrate. Both soaking liquids can be poured through a fine-mesh sieve to get rid of grit and then used as you would a mushroom stock.

pacific halibut

My first dealings with a whole halibut came soon after a career change, having bailed early on a track toward medical school. I chose sautéing over surgery, though I was pleased when I realized that white jackets, knife work, and a certain amount of blood were still in my future. I was a third-quarter culinary student when my chef-instructor heaved a large halibut up onto a stainless-steel worktable. I learned that day that a "fletch" is not Chevy Chase, but rather a halibut fillet (there are four, unlike round fish, such as a salmon, which have two). I sharpened my knives and joined my fellow students in filleting the big beast, two fletches on the top, flip, two fletches on the bottom.

That halibut went through an early career change of sorts as well. A halibut starts its life as a round fish with an eye on either side of its head, as you might expect. However, by the time a halibut is six months old, it has settled down to the bottom of the ocean and made a transition to life as a flatfish. From then on both eyes—having shifted to the top side of its body—stare up at the world swimming by. This life change seems to suit the halibut, and I can say the same for myself. I chose the right career, shifting my gaze toward a life in food, and I, too, have never looked back.

WHAT MAKES THIS A GOOD CHOICE	Pacific halibut in Alaska, Washington, Oregon, California, and British Columbia is managed by the International Halibut Commission (IPHC). Every year the IPHC researches the health of the halibut population and sets annual catch limits, known as Total Allowable Catch (TAC), which are then divided among the established fishing areas. Management in each fishing area determines how the catch will be divvied up. This fishery is recognized as one of the best managed in the world and has a very long history, dating back to the nineteenth century.
BY ANY OTHER NAME	A small Pacific halibut (*Hippoglossus stenolepis*) is called a "chicken," and a large one is called a "barn door."
SEASON	The first sign of spring on the Pacific Coast is when fresh halibut appears in the markets. The season is March through November.
BUYING TIPS	Pay attention to the halibut's color: It should be white or off-white. If it has a yellow tinge, it's old. Dull white spots are a sign of freezer burn. Look for halibut cheeks; they are a nice treat—the finfish equivalent of crabmeat.
QUESTIONS TO ASK BEFORE YOU PULL OUT YOUR WALLET	Where is the halibut from? Atlantic halibut is terribly overfished at this point, so make sure you are getting Pacific halibut, which is caught primarily in Alaska, but also in Oregon, Washington, and British Columbia.
CARING FOR YOUR GOOD FISH	If you're not going to use your halibut right away, put it in the coldest part of your fridge or place the package in a colander over a bowl and put some ice on top of it to keep it at its best. Thaw frozen halibut according to How to Safely Thaw Frozen Fish on page 18.
HOW THIS TYPE OF SEAFOOD IS RAISED OR HARVESTED	Halibut are flatfish that live deep in the ocean. They are caught by bottom long-line gear that is set along the ocean floor. Bait is put on hooks every few yards. When the gear is pulled in, the halibut are brought onto the boat one by one, killed, and iced down.
SUSTAINABLE SUBSTITUTES	Halibut is a firm yet delicate fish, meaty and mild tasting; some say it is a steak in fish form. Substitute with Pacific cod, lingcod, or mahi-mahi.

roasted halibut

with radicchio-pancetta sauce, peas, and artichokes

SERVES 4

1 pound halibut fillet, skinned[‡]
   cut into 4 equal portions

⅛ teaspoon fine sea salt

1 tablespoon high-heat
   vegetable oil

1 tablespoon extra-virgin
   olive oil

2 ounces pancetta, lightly
   smoked bacon, or prosciutto,
   cut into medium dice

½ cup sliced shallots

¼ pound radicchio,
   chopped into bite-size
   pieces (about 3 cups)

1 teaspoon honey

1 tablespoon white wine vinegar

1 tablespoon white wine or
   dry vermouth

1 cup fish stock, clam juice, or
   vegetable broth

½ cup frozen, canned, or jarred
   artichoke hearts, quartered
   (thawed and patted dry, if
   using frozen)

½ cup fresh or frozen peas
   (thawed if using frozen)

½ lemon

[‡] Go to GoodFishBook.com
for a demonstration of how to
remove the skin from a fillet.

PAIRING: First choice is
muscadet; second, rosé.

Since halibut comes into season in the spring, it makes sense to pair it with peas and artichokes, two vegetal harbingers of the kinder, gentler season. I love the fact that this is a one-dish dinner—from the stove top to the oven to serving right from the skillet—a weeknight meal that seems fancier than it is. As with all the halibut recipes, really lean on the side of undercooking the fish. You can always cook it for another minute longer if it is not to your liking, but, unless you know something I don't about the progression of Father Time, a piece of overcooked fish has nowhere to go but more overcooked.

Preheat the oven to 350°F.

Lightly season the halibut fillets with the salt. In a large ovenproof skillet over high heat, add the vegetable oil and sear the fillets for 3 minutes, or until they are browned on one side. Transfer them to a plate, and reduce the heat to medium-high. Add the olive oil, pancetta, and shallots, and cook until the pancetta starts to crisp, 5 to 6 minutes. Add the radicchio and honey, and cook for another 3 to 4 minutes, or until the radicchio wilts and caramelizes. Add the white wine vinegar, white wine, and fish stock, stirring to loosen any bits clinging to the skillet. Add the artichokes and peas, stir, then nestle the halibut pieces back in the pan, browned side up. Place the pan in the oven and cook for 3 to 4 minutes, or until the internal temperature of the halibut reaches 125 to 130°F. Finish with a squeeze of lemon juice over the top. Serve each person a piece of fish and a portion of vegetables, ladling the broth over the top of the fish.

steamed halibut

with sizzling chile-ginger oil

SERVES 4

1 bunch green onions, white and light-green parts cut julienne, dark-green parts reserved

1 pound halibut fillet, skin on, cut into 4 equal portions

2 teaspoons Shaoxing rice wine or pale dry sherry

¼ teaspoon fine sea salt

2 tablespoons finely julienned fresh peeled ginger

1 teaspoon red pepper flakes (use less if you want it less hot)

2 teaspoons soy sauce

2 tablespoons refined coconut oil or peanut oil

1 tablespoon toasted sesame oil

Leaves (and small, tender stems) from 1 small bunch cilantro, for garnish

---

PAIRING: First choice is Kabinett riesling; second, Vouvray sec.

I've adapted a classic Chinese preparation typically done to a whole bone-in fish to fillets instead. Maybe I don't get out much, but it's really exciting when you pour the hot oil over the fish and everything crackles and sizzles. This is quick weeknight cooking at its best. Serve with rice and the blackened broccolini from page 271 or the cucumber salad from page 183. Feel free to substitute Pacific cod for the halibut, especially if you're cooking on a budget.

Bring 4 inches of water to a boil over high heat in a pasta pot with insert or a saucepan with a collapsible steamer insert. Reduce to a simmer. Lay the dark-green onions in the bottom of the steamer insert. Lay the halibut pieces on the scallions, skin side down. Drizzle the rice wine over the fillets and sprinkle with the salt. Cover the pot and steam the fish until the halibut reaches 120°F in the center, 8 to 10 minutes. (It will continue to cook off the heat.) Transfer the fish to a platter. Lay the ginger, light-green onions, and red pepper flakes on top. Drizzle the soy sauce over the fillets.

Heat a small saucepan over high heat. Add the coconut oil and sesame oil and heat until they shimmer and just start to smoke. Pour this very hot oil over the fish. You'll hear the ginger and green onions sizzle. Garnish with a generous amount of cilantro.

smoked halibut

with stinging nettle sauce and nettle gnocchi

SERVES 4

3 ounces fresh morels (about
  1 cup), or 1 ounce dried morels
Nettle Gnocchi (recipe follows)
1 cup blanched, drained, and
  chopped nettles,* reserved
  from the Nettle Gnocchi
1 bunch fresh Italian parsley
  (stems OK)
1 cup plain whole-fat Greek-
  style yogurt
2 teaspoons freshly squeezed
  lemon juice
1 teaspoon fine sea salt, divided
¼ teaspoon freshly ground
  black pepper
¼ cup extra-virgin olive oil
½ cup mushroom stock (from
  rehydrating the dried morels
  or store-bought)
1 pound halibut fillet, skinned,
  cut into 4 equal portions
½ cup apple wood or alder
  wood chips (optional)
2 tablespoons high-heat
  vegetable oil, divided
¼ cup salmonberry
  blossoms** (optional)

---

*Nettles are a noxious weed to
many, a spring tonic and elixir
to others. You will not find them
sold in stores. Some vendors
may sell them at farmers'
markets or head to the woods
and harvest them yourself (wear
gloves!) in early spring.

We must have a deliriously starving person who got lost in the woods to thank for discovering that nettles are delicious and healthful. This person must have fallen into a stinging nettle patch mouth agape, and while screaming in pain, decided to eat the plant to exact revenge upon the aggressor. This dish is a celebration of spring vitality and the foraging spirit. So many delicious edibles come together here: halibut from the ocean, wood from the trees to use for smoking, nettles so easily dismissed as weeds, salmonberry blossoms for color, and morels found in secret spots deep in the woods, hidden in the dirt and brush. To the victor go the spoils.

If you are using fresh morels, briefly swish them in a large bowl of tepid water. Drain and repeat to remove all the dirt. Dry them on an absorbent towel. Pan-fry a test mushroom to see if it is sandy or gritty. If so, repeat the cleaning process. Halve any large morels lengthwise and keep any small ones whole. If you are using dried morels, I recommend a 5-minute soak in warm water followed by some agitation with your hands to release any grit or dirt. Pull the morels up and out of the warm water and then soak them in enough boiling water to cover for 10 minutes to rehydrate. Both soaking liquids can be poured through a fine-mesh sieve to get rid of grit and then used as mushroom stock.

Make the Nettle Gnocchi.

Add the reserved blanched nettles, parsley, yogurt, lemon juice, ½ teaspoon of the salt, pepper, olive oil, and mushroom stock to a blender or food processor and blend well (for up to 3 minutes), until smooth. Push the sauce through a fine-mesh sieve if you desire a smoother texture. Taste and adjust seasoning. Set aside.

Boil the gnocchi (see page 165) and set aside.

Season the halibut with ¼ teaspoon of the salt. Smoke the halibut according to the instructions on the opposite page.‡ Alternatively, you can pan-sear it: In a large sauté pan over high heat, add

** When foraging for spring nettles in the wild, keep a watchful eye out for deep pink–red salmonberry blossoms in bloom at the same time.

‡ Go to GoodFishBook.com for a demonstration of how to wok-smoke fish.

PAIRING: First choice is Sancerre; second, California sauvignon blanc.

1 tablespoon of the vegetable oil. When the oil is hot, add the halibut to the pan and cook it until browned on one side, 3 to 4 minutes. Flip the fillets carefully and continue cooking until the internal temperature of the fish reaches 125 to 130°F. Transfer the fish to a platter. Add the remaining 1 tablespoon vegetable oil to the pan and then the morels, gnocchi, and the remaining ¼ teaspoon salt. Sauté until the edges of the mushrooms crisp up a little, 4 to 5 minutes. Set aside and keep warm.

To serve, ladle a small amount of nettle sauce in the center of each of 4 plates. Carefully spoon a portion of the morels and gnocchi to one side of the sauce. Top with a piece of halibut and garnish with salmonberry blossoms.

CONTINUED

HOW TO SMOKE FISH AT HOME

If you have an actual, legitimate smoker, I'm jealous! For the rest of us: you can turn a wok into a makeshift smoker. If you don't have a good kitchen fan, I recommend an outdoor grill. (But if you do, turn on the fan, disable your smoke alarm, open a few windows, and get started.) Go to GoodFishBook.com for a demonstration of this wok-smoking technique.

Set the wok over high heat. Line the bottom with a piece of aluminum foil. Place about ½ cup wood chips (I prefer apple wood or alder) in the bottom of the wok. I use a propane torch to quickly ignite the chips, then I leave them to burn for about 1 minute, blow out the flames, cover the wok, and allow it to fill with smoke (about 2 minutes). Lacking a torch, you can instead simply cover the wok and wait for the high heat to get the wood smoking (this will take a little longer, 3 to 4 minutes). Once the wok is filled with smoke, carefully lay a circular rack (sprayed or brushed with oil) inside the wok. Season your fish with salt. Lay the fish carefully on the rack. Cover and smoke the fish until the internal temperature reaches the desired degree (see the temperature chart on page 127). You'll see the flesh turn a nice golden color when the smoke has penetrated. This method is called "hot-smoking," which cooks the fish all the way through.

1 tablespoon kosher salt

1¼ cups packed nettle leaves*
  (or substitute spinach)

2 pounds (about 2 large) russet
  potatoes

1 egg, beaten

¾ cup all-purpose flour, plus
  additional as needed

½ teaspoon fine sea salt

---

*See the note about nettles on
page 162.

NETTLE GNOCCHI

Preheat the oven to 350°F.

To prepare the nettles, bring a large pot of water to a boil over high heat. While the water heats, fill a medium bowl with ice water. When the water is boiling, add the kosher salt and, using gloves or tongs, carefully add the nettles, making sure they are submerged. Cook for exactly 5 minutes. Remove them immediately with a slotted spoon or tongs and plunge them into the ice bath. When the nettles have cooled, remove them from the ice bath and with your hands squeeze out all the water. Finely chop the nettles. Divide into two portions: set aside ¼ cup for making the gnocchi and reserve 1 cup for making the sauce (see page 162).

Pierce the potatoes all over with the tines of a fork. Bake them in the oven directly on a rack for about 1½ hours, flipping them after 45 minutes, until they are tender, dry, and have crackly skins. While they are still hot (and using towels to protect yourself), cut the potatoes in half and use a spoon to scoop out the centers. Discard the potato skins or eat with sour cream. Run the potato through a ricer or food mill, or mash the potatoes really well by hand and then mix the nettles into the potatoes. Cool on a baking sheet.

When the potatoes are cool, transfer them to a large bowl and stir in the egg, flour, and sea salt. Mix well with a wooden spoon and then knead the dough gently in the bowl until it forms a ball, adding more flour if necessary (but keep in mind the more flour you add, the tougher the gnocchi will be). Transfer the dough to a wooden board and divide it into 8 pieces. Roll each piece into a long rope about ¾ inch in diameter. When all the pieces are rolled out, cut each rope into gnocchi approximately ¾ inch long. If desired, use a fork to press down each gnocchi, lightly dragging it back to shape them. For a different look, you can pick up the gnocchi and roll them off the tines of the fork.

To freeze the gnocchi for later use, place them on a parchment-paper-lined baking sheet (make sure they are not touching each other), and put them in the freezer for about 1 hour. When the gnocchi are frozen, transfer them to a ziplock bag and use within 3 months.

If cooking the gnocchi immediately, bring a large pot of water to a boil over high heat. Season the water generously with kosher salt and add the gnocchi in batches. Cook until they float to the surface and then, after about 1 minute, taste one: it should be light and fluffy, not dense. Cook a little longer if necessary; then, using a slotted spoon, transfer the gnocchi to a bowl.

If you are not serving them right away, drizzle the gnocchi with some olive oil or butter to keep them from sticking together. Or transfer the cooked gnocchi immediately into a sauté pan to brown them.

halibut escabèche

with anchovy-almond salsa verde

SERVES 4

For the spice rub:
½ teaspoon black peppercorns
¼ teaspoon cumin seeds
½ teaspoon coriander seeds
2 bay leaves
¼ teaspoon brown sugar
¼ teaspoon fine sea salt

For the salsa verde:
½ cup extra-virgin olive oil
⅓ cup roughly chopped fresh
   Italian parsley (stems are fine)
2 canned or jarred anchovies
2 tablespoons sherry vinegar
1 teaspoon capers
½ tablespoon raisins
6 whole almonds
¼ teaspoon red pepper flakes
¼ teaspoon fine sea salt

For the halibut:
1 tablespoon high-heat
   vegetable oil
1 pound halibut fillet, skinned,‡
   bones removed, cut into
   4 equal portions

This is my version of escabèche, a dish of Spanish origin with variations in many cuisines, in which you sear or poach fish or meat and then marinate it in a vinegary sauce. A refreshing dish, it is usually served cold or at room temperature in hot climates. Halibut is mild and somewhat delicate, and most people treat it so—serving it simply pan-fried with light butter sauces or in broths. I think there is also a firmness and blank-slate quality to halibut that make me want to spice it up for a night, send it to Spain, and see what trouble it gets into. Escabèche with anchovy salsa verde does just that.

To prepare the rub, finely grind the peppercorns, cumin seeds, coriander seeds, bay leaves, brown sugar, and salt in a spice grinder. Coat the halibut fillets with the rub and set aside in the refrigerator while you make the salsa verde.

To prepare the salsa verde, add all of its ingredients to a blender and blend to a smooth puree. Set aside.

To prepare the halibut, in a large sauté pan over high heat, add the vegetable oil. When the oil is hot, add the fillets skin side up and cook until the fish is browned on one side, 3 to 4 minutes. Flip the halibut carefully and continue cooking until the internal temperature reaches 125 to 130°F. Remove the halibut from the pan, lightly cover, and set aside.

For the garnish:

1 teaspoon extra-virgin olive oil

¼ cup diced red onions

⅛ teaspoon fine sea salt

1 tablespoon roughly chopped
   Marcona or regular almonds

1 small carrot, sliced into
   short ribbons using a
   vegetable peeler

1 tablespoon raisins

1 teaspoon smoked paprika

¼ cup water

2 tablespoons sherry vinegar

---

‡ Go to GoodFishBook.com
for a demonstration of how to
remove the skin from a fillet.

PAIRING: First choice is vinho
verde; second, verdelho.

To prepare the garnish, add the olive oil to the pan you cooked the fish in and turn the heat to medium high. Add the red onion and salt, and sauté for 4 to 5 minutes, or until the onions have softened. Add the almonds, carrot, raisins, and paprika. Sauté for 2 minutes, or until the nuts are toasted, and then deglaze the pan with the water. Reduce until there is no liquid left and then add the sherry vinegar. Stir well and pour the mixture over the halibut. Cover the fish to keep it warm and allow it to marinate with the garnish for 10 minutes. Uncover and serve with the salsa verde on the side.

halibut tacos
with tequila-lime marinade and red cabbage slaw

SERVES 4

For the red cabbage slaw:
¾ pound red cabbage,
   shredded (about 4 cups)
1 tablespoon kosher salt
1 Granny Smith apple, cored
   and grated
½ teaspoon brown
   mustard seeds
½ bunch cilantro leaves and
   stems, roughly chopped
   (about ¾ cup)
2 tablespoons apple
   cider vinegar
2 tablespoons extra-virgin
   olive oil

For the tequila-lime marinade:
Zest and juice of 1 lime
   (about 1 teaspoon zest and
   2 tablespoons juice)
2 tablespoons tequila*
½ teaspoon fine sea salt
2 large serrano chiles, halved,
   seeds and membranes
   removed, sliced crosswise into
   half rings
1 small red onion, sliced into
   thin half-moons (about ⅔ cup)
2 tablespoons extra-virgin
   olive oil

For the halibut:
1 pound halibut fillet, skinned,‡
   bones removed
1 tablespoon high-heat
   vegetable oil

I present to you the godfather of fish tacos that I wait all winter for, pining longingly for the spring season when the first wild Alaska halibut comes to market. It's typically early March when halibut hits Pacific Northwest markets, vying for attention along with rhubarb and asparagus. If you have a bit more time, make some home-made, not Pacific Northwest, guacamole. It is painfully simple: smash 2 ripe avocados with a fork, and add 1½ tablespoons lime juice, ¾ teaspoon salt, and 1 teaspoon hot sauce of your choice—mine is Tabasco.

To prepare the slaw, toss the cabbage with the salt. Place in a colander. Locate a bowl that will fit nicely into the colander, fill it with water, and set it on top of the cabbage. Set this in the sink. The weight of the bowl of water will help force water from the cabbage, concentrating its flavor.

Lightly press the grated apple to drain any liquid. In a large bowl, mix the apple with the mustard seeds, cilantro, apple cider vinegar, and olive oil. Give the cabbage a squeeze with those fancy kitchen tools of yours called "hands." Rinse the salt off the cabbage and squeeze again, getting all the liquid out. Combine the cabbage with the rest of the slaw ingredients and season to taste with salt. Set aside.

To prepare the marinade, in a small bowl, combine all of the marinade ingredients.

To prepare the halibut, place it in a large pan. Pour the marinade over the fillet and set aside for 20 minutes.

In a grill pan or sauté pan over high heat, add the vegetable oil. Add the halibut, reserving the marinade, and cook until the fish is browned on one side, 3 to 4 minutes. Flip the halibut carefully and continue cooking until the fish is thinking about flaking, but not quite yet flaking (see page 126), and the internal temperature

CONTINUED

For the taco bar:
Corn or flour tortillas, warmed
Sour cream
Guacamole (optional)
Lime wedges
Tequila
Beers, of course

---

*Get good-quality tequila
so you can sip it while you
cook—my favorite is Cazadores
Reposado, a great clean flavor
for the price.

---

‡ Go to GoodFishBook.com
for a demonstration of how to
remove the skin from a fillet.

PAIRING: First choice is
Red Stripe Jamaican lager;
second, tequila.

HALIBUT TACOS, CONTINUED

reaches 125 to 130°F. The fish will continue to cook a bit more after you remove it from the heat. Transfer the fish to a platter. Add the marinade to the pan (or get out a fresh pan if you grilled the fish) and cook over high heat for 5 to 7 minutes, until the liquid evaporates and the serranos and onions are lightly charred. Spread the marinade on top of the halibut, which, by this point, should be perfectly done.

Set up the best taco bar you've ever seen, with warmed tortillas; bowls of sour cream, guacamole, and red cabbage slaw; the platter of halibut (which you can flake up with a fork so people can easily portion into their tortillas) with charred serranos and onions; limes; shot glasses filled with good tequila; and beer, lots of beer.

halibut coconut curry

with charred chiles and lime

SERVES 4

2 jalapeños, seeds and
   membranes removed from one
   or both (if you want less heat)
2 stalks lemongrass,
   woody top half discarded,
   roughly chopped
½ cup roughly chopped shallots
¼ cup cilantro stems
1 clove garlic
2 tablespoons chopped fresh
   galangal or peeled ginger
1 teaspoon coriander seeds,
   ground in a spice grinder
1 teaspoon cumin seeds, ground
   in a spice grinder
¼ teaspoon fine sea salt
¼ teaspoon dried turmeric, or
   1 teaspoon grated peeled
   fresh turmeric
5 lime leaves, or zest of 2 limes
   (about 2 teaspoons)
Chicken or vegetable stock
   or water
1 tablespoon high-heat
   vegetable oil
1 (14-ounce) can full-fat
   coconut milk
1 tablespoon fish sauce
½ pound halibut fillet, skinned‡
   and cut into 1-inch cubes

I don't know what it is about this dish that brings me so much joy—perhaps it starts with the color: bright-green curry set off against the vivid red onion and charred chile garnish, with little bits of lime. Or perhaps it's the texture: silky coconut milk meeting tender, yielding halibut contrasted with tiny, crunchy sesame seeds and the slight bite of jalapeño. It could be the flavor: sweetness balanced with spice and the savor of garlic and shallot, the cilantro hitting the herbal high note, clean and fresh until the cumin brings you back down to earth. Perhaps it's all of it, washing over your senses the way food hits you on the streets of Bangkok—impossible to tease out the flavors from the high-pitched moped whine, the assault of fish sauce on your nasal passages, the sun beating down on your shoulders, a well-used bottle of red chile oil within arm's reach.

....

Add the jalapeños, lemongrass, shallots, cilantro, garlic, galangal, coriander, cumin, salt, turmeric, and 1 of the lime leaves to the bowl of a food processor or a high-speed blender and blend, using up to ¼ cup chicken stock to help the mixture process into a smooth puree. You'll have to scrape down the curry once or twice. Blend well for at least 3 minutes.

In a medium saucepan over medium-high heat, add the oil. Add the curry and fry it for 2 to 3 minutes. Add the coconut milk, fish sauce, and the remaining lime leaves. Bring to a boil over high heat, then reduce the heat to medium-low and simmer for 10 minutes. Return to a boil and add the halibut, tucking it under the liquid. Immediately turn off the heat and cover the pot (remove the pot from the burner if you have an electric stove). Let the curry sit for 5 minutes so that the fish poaches gently. Taste and adjust the seasoning.

CONTINUED

For the topping:

1 teaspoon high-heat
vegetable oil

4 Fresno chiles, seeded and
minced (or substitute 1 small
red pepper, minced)

2 tablespoons minced red onion

⅓ cup chopped cilantro leaves

2 limes, peeled and flesh cut
into small dice

Fine sea salt

Black sesame seeds, for
garnish (optional)

---

‡ Go to GoodFishBook.com
for a demonstration of how to
remove the skin from a fillet.

PAIRING: First choice is riesling;
second, gewürztraminer.

To prepare the topping, heat the oil in a small sauté pan over medium-high heat. Fry the chiles and onion until they are browned, about 10 minutes. Remove the pan from the heat and stir in the cilantro and lime. Season to taste with salt. Serve a spoonful on top of each person's curry. Garnish with sesame seeds.

halibut

with vanilla, kumquat, and ginger

SERVES 4

2 tablespoons ghee or
    unsalted butter
1 (2-inch) stick cinnamon
½ vanilla bean, split,
    seeds scraped
6 whole green cardamom pods
1 pound halibut fillet, skinned,‡
    cut into 4 equal portions
¼ teaspoon fine sea salt
1 small fennel bulb, halved
    lengthwise and then cut
    crosswise into ¼ inch thick
    slices, fronds broken into little
    pieces and reserved
    for garnish
6 kumquats, sliced very thin
    crosswise, seeded
¼ cup chardonnay
½ cup unsalted fish stock
    or water
1 tablespoon grated fresh
    peeled ginger
½ teaspoon freshly ground
    black pepper (keep the grind
    pretty rough)
2 tablespoons unsalted butter

‡ Go to GoodFishBook.com
for a demonstration of how to
remove the skin from a fillet.

PAIRING: First choice is a
moderately oaked chardonnay;
second, albariño.

Does the combination of these ingredients sound a little strange in your ear? Yeah, they did to me too, but I persisted and I think you should too. The idea started with wanting to create a halibut dish with vanilla. I thought about the flavors in chai—cinnamon, vanilla, cardamom—and I took it in that direction. I had friends over for a tasting night where they got to put on their most critical food reviewer hats and tell me how they thought the dish could be improved. Janet said "kumquats," and everyone paused, some looked at her funny, and I jumped up and ran to my fridge where (when has this ever happened?) I had three kumquats in my crisper drawer. I sliced them thinly, and we all tasted the dish again. BINGO. Serve this dish with the roasted asparagus from page 144 or, what the hell, whatever happens to be in your crisper drawer at the moment.

....

Add the ghee to a large sauté pan over medium heat. Add the cinnamon, vanilla bean and seeds, and cardamom pods to the ghee. Let the aromatics sizzle in the ghee until it becomes very fragrant, about 1 minute. Dry the halibut pieces with a paper towel and then season with the salt. Increase the heat to high and slide the halibut into the pan. Sear on just one side until browned, about 3 minutes. Using a fish spatula, release the halibut and set aside. (You'll cook the other side later.)

Add the fennel and half of the kumquat slices to the pan, reduce the heat to medium-high, and cook until the fennel is tender and just starting to brown, 8 to 10 minutes. Add a little water if it threatens to stick or burn. Remove the cinnamon stick, vanilla bean pod, and cardamom pods; discard. Deglaze the pan with the chardonnay and let it reduce until the wine is mostly evaporated. Reduce the heat to medium and add the fish stock, the remainder of the kumquats, ginger, pepper, and butter. Swirl the pan until the butter melts into the sauce. Return the halibut to the pan, uncooked side down, and tilt the pan slightly to spoon some sauce over the fish until the internal temperature reaches 130°F. Taste the sauce and add more salt if desired. Serve garnished with the reserved fennel fronds.

black cod

Names are secondary to experiences when you're a child. Somewhere deep down in my childhood mind I might have known the fish I kept returning to was called sablefish, but that seemed beside the point. The point was reaching across the table with fork extended before my stupid brothers could take it all.

Sablefish was brought to our family table in what we called "the spread." The spread happened when Uncle Vic and Aunt Selly would come in from "the city" (New York) and bring with them "the fixin's" from Russ and Daughters. There would be bialys and bagels, sablefish and whitefish, herring, lox, and pickles. My grandmother would contribute onions, cream cheese, wedges of lemon, black olives, and big slices of her garden tomatoes. Bagel sandwiches would get piled so high we couldn't stuff them in our mouths and instead had to deconstruct them with knife and fork. The spread, the accompaniments, the extended family around my grandparent's big dining room table—this is what I think of when I taste black cod.

It wasn't until years later that I realized sablefish and black cod are the same thing. In fact, I do believe I've said at a cocktail party or two that my two favorite fish were sablefish and black cod. At least I'm consistent.

WHAT MAKES THIS A GOOD FISH

Black cod can be found from California up to Alaska, with most of the catch coming from Alaska. Black cod are caught with bottom long-lines and pots, which are selective fishing gear types that limit bycatch. Black cod can also be caught using trawl gear. In this fishery, the use of fish-excluder devices has greatly reduced the amount of bycatch. Habitat destruction isn't as much of an issue because they prefer swimming in areas with sandy, muddy bottoms. While I've warned you to stay away from fish caught with trawl gear, black cod is an exception that some experts say is OK.

BY ANY OTHER NAME

Black cod (*Anoplopoma fimbria*) is also known as sablefish, butterfish, skil, skilfish, and coalfish.

SEASON

Alaska: March through November. British Columbia: year-round (but peak is January through April). California, Oregon, Washington: year-round.

BUYING TIPS

I like to buy fish fillets that are center-cut versus buying tail pieces, so that I get a thicker piece that is more resistant to overcooking. With black cod, on the other hand, I sometimes prefer tail pieces because they are boneless (black cod bones are not difficult to remove once the fish is cooked, but sometimes it's nice to eat with abandon). Besides, overcooking is very difficult with black cod. This fish is full of fat and flavor, high in healthy omega-3 fatty acids. You'd literally have to walk completely away from the kitchen for 30 minutes to dry this fish out (not that I'm encouraging you to do that). If you can find black cod collars (the fatty meat inside the gill frame), you are in for an extra-special, decadent treat if you marinate and broil them.

QUESTIONS TO ASK BEFORE YOU PULL OUT YOUR WALLET

Where is the black cod from? Look for US wild caught.

CARING FOR YOUR GOOD FISH

If you're not going to use your black cod right away, put it in the coldest part of your fridge or place the package in a colander over a bowl and put some ice on top of it to keep it at its best. Thaw frozen black cod according to How to Safely Thaw Frozen Fish on page 18.

HOW THIS TYPE OF SEAFOOD IS RAISED OR HARVESTED

Black cod is caught in the wild using many different methods: longlining (see page 19 for an explanation), by handline, in pots, or by trawling (see page 19 for an explanation). There are black cod farms in British Columbia that raise the fish in open ocean in net pens. Reports state that there are fewer incidents of disease and lower use of chemicals in black cod farming than in salmon farming, but there are still issues. My feeling is why buy farmed black cod when there is a sustainable fishery for wild?

SUSTAINABLE SUBSTITUTES

Hmm, a stick of butter comes to mind. Or perhaps a piece of halibut coated with butter, wrapped in bacon, and finished with more butter. A really fatty piece of chinook would be the closest substitute for the richness of black cod.

roasted black cod

with bok choy and soy caramel sauce

SERVES 4

5 ounces red cabbage, thinly
   sliced (about 2 cups)
2 bulbs baby bok choy, halved
2 small tomatoes, halved, or
   1 pint whole cherry tomatoes
4 green onions, white and
   light-green parts only, cut into
   3-inch lengths
⅛ teaspoon fine sea salt
4 teaspoons toasted sesame oil
4 teaspoons seasoned rice
   wine vinegar
4 (¼-inch slices) lime
1 serrano chile, sliced (optional)
1 pound black cod fillet or
   steaks, skin on, cut into
   4 equal portions
½ cup Soy Caramel Sauce
   (page 71)
Cooked rice, for serving

PAIRING: First choice is Oregon
pinot gris; second, Savennières.

Typically when I develop a recipe, I do my utmost to roll out a red carpet for the star ingredient. I may add other ingredients to boost the star, but it's clear they play second fiddle. A great piece of fish deserves top billing. Herbs, spices, and sauces are relegated to the role of supporting cast—until now. Let me be frank: this dish is all about the soy caramel. It was always all about the soy caramel. The black cod is merely a delicious platform on which the sauce sits. The bok choy and cabbage are vegetal intermissions. When the house lights dim, the soy caramel upstages them all.

....

Preheat the oven to 400°F. Line a baking sheet with parchment paper.

You're going to make 4 separate piles on the pan. Each pile will get ½ cup cabbage, a bok choy half, a tomato half (or a few cherry tomatoes), and a quarter of the green onions. Sprinkle the salt evenly over the piles. Drizzle each pile with 1 teaspoon oil and 1 teaspoon vinegar. Top with a lime slice and sprinkle with some serrano slices. Roast the vegetables in the oven for 20 minutes, or until they are soft and lightly browned around the edges.

Place one piece of black cod, skin side down, on each vegetable pile, and drizzle 1 tablespoon Soy Caramel Sauce on each piece of fish. Roast for another 8 to 10 minutes, or until a press of the finger reveals a sliding away, ever so gently, of the fish into the beginning of individual flakes; the internal temperature of the fish should reach 135°F. Serve with rice and the remaining ¼ cup sauce.

jerry's black cod
with shiso-cucumber salad and carrot vinaigrette

SERVES 4

For the black cod:
1 pound black cod fillet, skinned,‡ bones removed, cut into 4 equal portions
1 tablespoon soy sauce
½ tablespoon sugar

For the carrot vinaigrette:
¾ cup carrot juice
2 tablespoons small-diced shallot
1 teaspoon grated fresh peeled ginger
1½ tablespoons lemon juice
Scant ¼ teaspoon fine sea salt
¼ cup peanut oil or high-quality vegetable oil

For the shiso-cucumber salad:
3 tablespoons seasoned rice wine vinegar
1 tablespoon lemon juice
2 teaspoons grated fresh peeled ginger
1 teaspoon minced serrano chile
2 tablespoons minced red onion
1½ tablespoons chopped fresh shiso (or substitute mint or cilantro)
1 English cucumber or 2 Persian cucumbers, halved lengthwise, deseeded, and sliced into thin half-moons

For garnish:
2 fresh shiso leaves, sliced into very thin strips

PAIRING: First choice: Kabinett riesling; second, Alsatian pinot gris.

A great recipe is based on three things: the use of high-quality seasonal ingredients; a perfect balance of sweet, spicy, salty, bitter, and sour; and sourcing it from a great chef you begged to contribute to your book. This one comes from the former chef of The Herbfarm Restaurant and the owner of Poppy and Lionhead in Seattle, Jerry Traunfeld. This is a winner of a dish that I adapted only slightly, and it fires on all fronts. Thanks, Jerry!

To prepare the black cod, toss the fillets with the soy sauce and sugar in a mixing bowl or ziplock bag. Marinate the fish in the refrigerator for about 2 hours.

To prepare the vinaigrette, in a small saucepan over medium-high heat, combine the carrot juice, shallot, ginger, lemon juice, and salt, and cook until the liquid boils down to one-third of the amount you started with, about 10 minutes. Cool. Pour the carrot reduction into a blender and, with the motor running, slowly pour in the oil. Set aside.

To prepare the salad, in a medium bowl, combine the vinegar, lemon juice, ginger, chile, red onion, and shiso. Let the dressing sit for 30 minutes to mellow the onion and meld the flavors. Toss the cucumber with the dressing.

Preheat the oven to 325°F.

Transfer the fish to a baking sheet, discarding the marinade. Bake for 10 to 12 minutes, or until a small amount of liquid collects at the bottom of the fillets and the fish flakes easily when nudged with your finger; the internal temperature of the fish should reach 135°F.

Put small mounds of the shiso-cucumber salad on each of 4 plates. Prop a fish fillet on each. Drizzle about 1 tablespoon of the carrot vinaigrette alongside the fish. Garnish with the shiso.

‡ Go to GoodFishBook.com for a demonstration of how to remove the skin from a fillet.

sake-steamed black cod

with ginger and sesame

SERVES 4

1 pound black cod fillet, skin on,
    cut into 4 equal portions
⅛ teaspoon fine sea salt
Freshly ground black
    pepper (optional)
1 cup sake
1 cup water
1 tablespoon soy sauce
1 tablespoon grated fresh
    peeled ginger
2 teaspoons plus ¼ teaspoon
    toasted sesame oil, divided
8 ounces (about 4 cups)
    fresh spinach
¼ cup thinly sliced radishes
1 tablespoon plus 2 teaspoons
    seasoned rice wine vinegar,
    divided
1 tablespoon sesame seeds
½ teaspoon sugar

PAIRING: First choice is
Junmai-shu sake; second,
gewürztraminer.

Black cod is an extremely rich fish, full of good omega-3 fatty acids, and therefore kind to novice cooks, as it is hard to overcook. I developed this recipe to downplay the black cod's natural fattiness for a night when you want a lighter meal. The fish and spinach are steamed and served with the sake-infused steaming liquid and a quick radish-and-sesame pickle.

Season the black cod with the salt and pepper to taste.

Add the sake, water, soy sauce, ginger, and 2 teaspoons of the oil to a pot with a steamer insert. (You could also use your pasta pot and insert.) Bring to a boil over high heat and then reduce the heat to a simmer. Simmer for 5 minutes to reduce the liquid and concentrate the flavor. Add the spinach to the steamer insert (making sure the bottom of the insert isn't in the steaming liquid), cover the pot, and steam the spinach until it wilts, 2 to 3 minutes. Remove the spinach and set it aside to cool. Remove the pot from the heat, leaving the sake broth in the pot.

In a small bowl, mix the radishes with 1 tablespoon of the vinegar. Let the radishes marinate until you are ready to serve.

Squeeze all of the liquid out of the spinach with your hands, and chop it into bite-size pieces. In a small sauté pan, toast the sesame seeds over medium-high heat until lightly browned and fragrant, about 3 minutes. Reserve 1 teaspoon for garnish. Grind the rest of the sesame seeds with the sugar in a spice grinder or mortar and pestle. Transfer to a small bowl and stir in 1 tablespoon of the sake broth, the remaining 2 teaspoons vinegar, a pinch of salt, and the remaining ¼ teaspoon oil. Toss the spinach with this dressing. Place the spinach in a deep, wide serving bowl and cover to keep warm. Set aside.

Bring the sake broth back to a boil over high heat. Place the black cod pieces on the steamer insert and place in the pot. Reduce the heat to maintain a simmer. Cover the pot and steam the fish until a press of the finger reveals a sliding away, ever so gently, of the fish into the beginning of individual flakes; the internal temperature of the fish should reach 135°F.

To serve, top the spinach with the steamed black cod. Pour some of the sake broth over the fish and around the spinach. Squeeze the rice wine vinegar from the radishes and discard. Mix the radishes with the reserved teaspoon of sesame seeds. Garnish the fish with the radish-sesame pickle.

tataki's "faux-nagi"

SERVES 4

For the black cod:
1 pound black cod fillet, skin
  on, bones removed (or use
  a tail piece)
¼ teaspoon fine sea salt

For the sauce:
¼ cup low-sodium or regular
  soy sauce
¼ cup sugar
1½ tablespoons sake
1½ tablespoons mirin
½ cup dried bonito flakes* (also
  known as *katsuobushi*)
2 tablespoons water

For the marinade:
2 tablespoons sake
2 pieces kombu*

For serving:
1 teaspoon potato starch**
1 tablespoon water
2 tablespoons sesame seeds
1½ cups cooked and seasoned
  sushi rice
1 sheet nori, cut into ½-by-
  3-inch strips (optional)

I'll be honest with you. When I first learned that unagi was an unsustainable choice I went to the closest sushi bar and buried this new knowledge in thirty pieces of unagi nigiri. When I came down from my soy-soaked eel high, I felt like I was ready to go without. But I wasn't too happy about it. Until along came chefs Raymond Ho and Kin Lui at San Francisco's Tataki Sushi and Sake Bar, who developed this dish, which I adapted ever so slightly for this book. This brilliant dish takes its cue from the buttery richness of eel and, in my opinion, does it one better, with a more consistent texture and better flavor.

To prepare the black cod, season the fillet with the salt. Wrap in plastic wrap and refrigerate for 15 to 20 minutes. In the meantime, prepare the sauce.

To prepare the sauce, mix all of its ingredients in a small saucepan. Bring to a boil over high heat, reduce the heat to medium, and simmer gently for about 10 minutes. Strain through a fine-mesh sieve and discard the bonito flakes. Set aside.

To marinate the black cod, remove the fillet from the refrigerator and unwrap. Rinse the salt off with very cold water. Blot the fish dry with a paper towel. Wet a new paper towel with the sake and use this towel to moisten the kombu. Sandwich the fillet between the two pieces of sake-moistened kombu. Rewrap the fillet in plastic wrap and refrigerate for 30 to 40 minutes. Unwrap, remove the kombu (to prevent too strong a flavor), and return the fillet to the refrigerator in a bowl, covered with plastic wrap.

When you are ready to serve, reheat the sauce. Mix the potato starch with the water. Add half of this mixture to the sauce and wait until it thickens, stirring constantly, 2 to 3 minutes. Add more if necessary to thicken the sauce to the consistency of jam. Toast the sesame seeds in a dry skillet over medium-high heat until lightly brown and fragrant.

* Bonito flakes and kombu can be found in most large supermarkets, every Asian market, or online.

**Potato starch can be found in Asian markets or natural food stores. Cornstarch can be used in its place, though potato starch has slightly better "holding" power when you boil a sauce.

PAIRING: First choice is Junmai-shu sake; second, Oregon pinot gris.

Slice the fillet into ¼-inch rectangular slices (as you would for nigiri). Lightly char one side of the fish with a small butane torch (or sear very briefly in a hot saucepan). Paint sauce on the fish with a small pastry brush. Sprinkle with the sesame seeds.

You can serve this dish one of two ways: Form nigiri by molding the rice into logs, laying the fish slices over the rice, and wrapping the narrow middles with nori "belts." Brush the tops of the nigiri with more sauce. Alternatively, spoon the rice onto 4 plates, lay the fish slices on top of the rice, and drizzle sauce over the fish.

Freshwater eel (unagi) farming is problematic because the eels are captured from the wild as juveniles, before they have a chance to reproduce; they're then raised and sold from Asian farms. This type of aquaculture is known as "ranching," and it is particularly unsustainable. Eel populations have declined by estimates of as much as 95 percent. Furthermore, eel often escape from their "ranches" and transfer diseases to an already threatened wild population. If you need another reason not to eat them, freshwater eel are often contaminated with PCBs.

rainbow trout

I went trout fishing for the first time a few summers ago, though the use of the word "trout" might be a tad bit generous. Technically I caught more trees, shrubs, and other anglers' lines than I did trout. My wife, April, is the angler in our household. She grew up in Eastern Oregon, in a small town called La Grande. Her first trout-fishing trip was at five years old. As the only girl with two older brothers, she was being given a reprieve from icky "girl" activities, like playing house and dressing up dolls.

Her older brother played patient and bemused teacher as she cast her first line onto her shirt. He laughed and detached the hook, pointed her shoulders in the right direction, and ducked as she sent her first successful cast into the lake. She stood back and acted as watchful sentry over that bobber, looking for any whisper of movement. Before too long that bobber disappeared under the water and then popped back up with a little dance. She tried to pull the fish in, but it appeared to have the upper hand. Her brother got the better of it and declared that trout to be, by far, the biggest catch of the whole trip.

For years afterward, April would beg her father to take her fishing. Father and daughter would set up their stools, place a forked stick in the ground, and lean their poles in the crook. They'd commune in silence ("Shh—the fish will hear us!" he'd warn her), staring out at the lake, a world of action beneath the illusion of stillness. April let me fish with her father's pole; we spent an entire day sharing the silence while I carefully baited the hook, cast the line just so, and then reeled in branch after branch after branch. April kindly didn't say a word.

WHAT MAKES THIS A GOOD FISH	Rainbow trout are native to the Pacific Northwest. Back in the day, native wild trout and oceangoing wild steelhead teemed in our rivers. These days, hatchery-stocked trout outcompete wild stock and have contributed to wild steelhead being listed as an endangered species. It's good, therefore, to be aware of sustainable substitutes for native wild species, such as farmed rainbow trout.

Idaho produces about three-quarters of the farmed trout sold in the United States. Farmed trout is a sustainable choice for several reasons: 1) It is farmed in raceways, a form of tank-based recirculating aquaculture systems, with few, if any, escapement problems. 2) Pesticide and antibiotic use is strictly regulated (though farmers do vaccinate their trout to prevent disease). 3) The feed conversion ratio for trout is relatively low, somewhere around 1 to 1.5 percent, meaning it takes anywhere from 1 to 1.5 pounds of feed to produce 1 pound of usable protein. 4) Water is partially treated before leaving the raceways, which limits pollution to neighboring areas.

One more thing to keep in mind with farmed fish in general: you are what you eat, and by extension, you are what your fish ate. We all need to put pressure on fish farmers to feed their fish healthy food.

BY ANY OTHER NAME	Rainbow trout (*Oncorhynchus mykiss*) are also known as silver trout and sometimes golden trout (although golden trout are technically a subspecies). To confuse matters further, outside the United States, trout can be farmed in the ocean in saltwater pens or cages and marketed as "steelhead" or "salmon-trout." The flesh of these trout is reddish, as opposed to that of rainbows, which is white. This type of farming incurs the same sorts of significant environmental problems as offshore salmon farming (see page 20).

SEASON	Year-round.

BUYING TIPS	Look for trout that have glistening skin with eyes that are bright and are not sunken. When pressed gently, the flesh should bounce back. It should smell good or neutral. Trout don't need to be scaled. Fishmongers are happy to remove the head, butterfly the trout, or fillet it for you.
QUESTIONS TO ASK BEFORE YOU PULL OUT YOUR WALLET	Where does it come from? Trout is raised on every continent but Antarctica. Buy domestic trout from as close to your home as you can. If you see wild steelhead being sold, please consider giving it a break and not buying it.
CARING FOR YOUR GOOD FISH	If you're not going to use your trout right away, put it in the coldest part of your fridge or place the package in a colander over a bowl and put some ice on top of it to keep it at its best. Thaw frozen trout according to How to Safely Thaw Frozen Fish on page 18.
HOW THIS TYPE OF SEAFOOD IS RAISED OR HARVESTED	Rainbow trout seed is purchased from hatcheries or grown directly on the farm, and fry are placed in concrete or earthen troughs called raceways in which fresh water continuously flows.
SUSTAINABLE SUBSTITUTES	Farmed arctic char is a great replacement for farmed rainbow trout. A second choice would be pink, keta, coho, or sockeye salmon.

cast-iron rainbow trout

SERVES 4

½ ounce (½ cup) dried wild
   mushrooms, or 3 ounces
   (1 cup) fresh wild mushrooms
2 (1-pound) whole rainbow
   trout, filleted‡; heads, tails,
   and ribs removed
½ teaspoon fine sea salt
¼ teaspoon freshly ground
   black pepper
¼ cup all-purpose flour, for
   dusting the fillets
3 strips bacon, cut into small
   dice (about ½ cup)
High-heat vegetable oil,
   for frying
¼ cup small whole fresh
   sage leaves
½ cup dry white wine

‡ Go to GoodFishBook.com for
a demonstration of how to fillet
a fish.

PAIRING: First choice is
Oregon pinot noir; second,
white Burgundy.

I learned how to make this dish when I cooked at La Spiga in
Seattle. I loved its simplicity and earthy flavors: nutty trout, woodsy
mushrooms (chanterelles are amazing in this recipe), smoky bacon,
piney sage, and bright wine. Serve the trout right from the skillet—
the residual heat retained in the iron keeps the dish warm.

Preheat the oven to 200°F.

If using dried wild mushrooms, I recommend a 5-minute soak
in warm water followed by some agitation with your hands to
release any grit or dirt. Pull the mushrooms up and out of the
warm water and then soak them in enough boiling water to cover
for 10 minutes to rehydrate. Both soaking liquids can be poured
through a fine-mesh sieve to get rid of grit and then used as
mushroom stock. If using fresh mushrooms, remove any grit by
gently brushing or washing them, then cut into bite-size pieces.

Season the trout fillets with the salt and pepper. Dust them with
the flour on both sides, shaking off any excess.

Heat a cast-iron skillet over medium heat. Add the bacon and
cook until its fat is rendered and the bacon is crisp, 7 to 8 minutes. Transfer the bacon with a slotted spoon to a paper-towel-
lined plate and set aside. Increase the heat to high. When the
pan is very hot, add the trout fillets, skin side up, reduce the heat
to medium-high, and cook for about 2 minutes. Flip and cook
for another 2 to 3 minutes, or until the internal temperature
of the fish reaches 125 to 130°F. Transfer the fillets to an oven-
proof platter and keep them warm in the oven while you fry the
remaining fish (add oil, 1 tablespoon at a time, if the pan is dry).

When you've removed the last piece of fish, add 1 tablespoon oil to
the pan. When the oil is hot, add the mushrooms and sauté for 3 to
4 minutes, or until lightly browned. Add the sage leaves and cook
for another minute. Add the bacon back to the pan, then add the
wine, scraping the bottom of the pan to release any stuck-on bits,
and cook for another 1 to 2 minutes. Taste for seasoning, then pour
the mushroom mixture over the fillets. Serve immediately.

pan-fried trout
with dilly beans

SERVES 4

For the vegetables:
1 pound fingerling potatoes, halved lengthwise
½ pound carrots, cut into large dice (about 1 cup)
1½ teaspoons extra-virgin olive oil
¼ teaspoon fine sea salt
¼ teaspoon freshly ground black pepper
5 sprigs fresh lemon thyme (optional)

For the trout:
2 (1-pound) whole rainbow trout, filleted,‡ heads, tails, and ribs removed
½ teaspoon fine sea salt
¼ teaspoon freshly ground black pepper
2 teaspoons unsalted butter
2 teaspoons high-heat vegetable oil
¼ cup dry white vermouth

For the coriander-lemon butter sauce:
2 tablespoons unsalted butter
1 teaspoon lemon zest
1 teaspoon whole coriander seeds, freshly ground in a spice grinder

For serving:
Dilly Beans (recipe follows)

I'm not sure what it is about trout, but it just loves potatoes and lemon and butter more passionately than other fish. The nuttiness of trout and butter left to bubble and brown in a cast-iron pan is just goodness writ large. If you are the plan-ahead sort, the dilly beans can be made up to a week ahead and the vegetables can be roasted the day before and just reheated. Then all you have to do the day of is spend ten minutes pan-frying the trout and making a simple sauce. The dilly beans offer a perfect brightness to cut the richness of the sauce.

Preheat the oven to 400°F.

To prepare the vegetables, place the potatoes and carrots on a parchment-lined baking sheet. Toss them with the olive oil, salt, and pepper and spread them out on the pan, placing the potatoes cut side down. Tuck the lemon thyme sprigs in and around the vegetables. Roast on the middle rack of the oven, uncovered, for 35 minutes, or until the vegetables are caramelized and tender. Discard the thyme sprigs. Keep the vegetables warm.

To prepare the trout, season the fillets with the salt and pepper. Heat a large heavy sauté pan over high heat. Once hot, reduce the heat to medium-high. Add half of the butter and vegetable oil, and cook 2 fillets, skin side up, for about 2 minutes. Flip and cook for another 2 to 3 minutes, until the internal temperature of the fish reaches 125 to 130°F. Transfer to a platter and cover loosely with aluminum foil while you cook the other 2 fillets, using the remaining butter and oil. Transfer the fillets to the platter, turn off the heat, wait 1 minute for the pan to cool, and then add the vermouth, stirring to loosen any bits clinging to the pan. Then make the butter sauce in the same pan.

‡ Go to GoodFishBook.com for a demonstration of how to fillet a fish.

PAIRING: First choice is sauvignon blanc; second, Chablis.

To prepare the sauce, add all of its ingredients to the pan and swirl them around just until you can smell the coriander, about 30 seconds. Pour over the trout fillets and serve with the roasted vegetables and Dilly Beans.

SERVES 4

½ pound green beans, trimmed
1 cup white vinegar or apple cider vinegar
1 cup water
1 tablespoon sugar
1 tablespoon kosher salt
½ teaspoon whole coriander seeds
½ teaspoon whole black peppercorns
1 bay leaf

DILLY BEANS

Place the green beans in a shallow heatproof container.

In a medium saucepan, combine the vinegar, water, sugar, salt, coriander seeds, peppercorns, and bay leaf, and bring to a boil over high heat. Reduce the heat to medium and simmer for 5 minutes. Pour the hot vinegar mixture over the green beans, making sure the beans are fully submerged.

After the beans and vinegar have cooled, cover the container and refrigerate for at least 24 hours (the flavor improves after 48 hours). The beans will keep in the refrigerator for up to 10 days.

quinoa cakes

with smoked trout and chive sour cream

MAKES APPROXIMATELY
32 (1-INCH) CAKES

⅔ cup quinoa, rinsed and drained

1⅓ cups water

½ teaspoon fine sea salt

¼ cup minced shallots

1 teaspoon extra-virgin olive oil

¼ cup all-purpose flour*

¼ cup feta cheese (I like Israeli
   or French sheep feta)

¼ cup chopped fresh
   Italian parsley

1 egg

1 egg yolk

⅛ teaspoon freshly ground
   black pepper

High-heat vegetable oil,
   for frying

¼ cup plain whole-fat Greek-
   style yogurt or sour cream

2 tablespoons thinly sliced
   fresh chives (reserve chive
   tips for garnish)

4 ounces smoked trout (or
   substitute with smoked salmon
   or smoked char; see page 163
   for instructions on how to
   smoke fish at home)

*Gluten-free? Rice flour is a
great substitute for the all-
purpose flour in this recipe.

PAIRING: First choice is
vinho verde; second,
champagne or cava.

Quinoa is the grain that makes you feel wholesome just pronounc-ing it correctly. It's fun to say—try it with me: keen-WAAAAA. It cooks up in fifteen minutes and has more protein than any other grain. It's easy to find good-quality smoked trout in most markets. This recipe is great as an appetizer but also makes for an unusual brunch if you make the cakes bigger and then poach or fry an egg and put that on top.

Add the quinoa, water, and salt to a medium saucepan. Bring to a boil over high heat. Cover, reduce the heat to medium-low, and simmer gently until the quinoa has absorbed the water, 12 to 15 minutes. Spread the quinoa out on a baking sheet to cool. While it cools, cook the shallots with the olive oil in a small skillet over medium-high heat for 5 minutes, or until the shallots have softened. In a large bowl, gently mix the cooled quinoa with the cooked shallots, flour, feta, parsley, egg, and egg yolk. Season with the pepper.

Heat a large heavy skillet over medium heat and add 2 table-spoons vegetable oil. Lightly wet your hands. Scoop out a small amount of the quinoa mixture, press it lightly into a ball, and then flatten it into a cake. Repeat with the remaining quinoa. Fry the cakes until the bottoms are golden brown and crunchy, 1 to 2 minutes per side. Drain on a paper-towel-lined plate. Fry addi-tional batches as needed.

In a small bowl, combine the yogurt and chives. Season to taste with salt. Place a small piece of smoked trout on each quinoa cake and garnish with a dollop of chive cream and a chive tip.

smoked trout mousse
with radish and cucumber quick pickle

MAKES ABOUT 1 CUP

For the radish and cucumber quick pickle:

¼ cup julienned radish

¼ cup small-diced cucumber

1 tablespoon snipped fresh chives

1 tablespoon seasoned rice wine vinegar

For the mousse:

8 to 10 ounces smoked trout,* skinned, broken into pieces

4 ounces cream cheese

1½ tablespoons lemon juice

½ teaspoon minced fresh lemon thyme, or ½ teaspoon minced fresh thyme and 1 teaspoon lemon zest

¼ to ½ teaspoon fine sea salt (depending on the saltiness of the trout)

⅛ teaspoon cayenne

¼ cup heavy cream

Freshly ground black pepper

*Look for quality smoked trout in the refrigerated section of your local market, or smoke your own by following the instructions on page 163.

PAIRING: First choice is champagne; second, Chablis.

I have a selection of recipes on hand that I informally call "What the hell do I bring to the potluck?" recipes. They are designed to step in when time betrays you and you'd like to show up to your friend's home looking good with the least amount of effort expended. This recipe takes fifteen minutes tops, and you can garnish it with flair and drama at your friend's home by loudly kvetching about slaving over a hot stove for hours, even if you haven't.

To prepare the quick pickle, in a small bowl, mix all of its ingredients and let sit for 30 minutes.

To prepare the mousse, add the smoked trout, cream cheese, lemon juice, lemon thyme, salt, and cayenne to a food processor and blend well, for at least 2 to 3 minutes. In a medium bowl, whip the cream into soft peaks using either an electric mixer or a whisk, and fold it into the mousse to lighten it. Season to taste with salt and black pepper.

Serve the mousse on crackers or toast. Or if you suddenly find yourself with extra time, you could make smoked-trout deviled eggs (hard-boil some eggs and mix the mousse with the cooked egg yolk). Garnish the mousse with a small amount of the quick pickle.

albacore tuna

I stared blankly at my friend, trying to look knowledgeable. She asked me if I wanted to go in on buying whole local albacore tuna and wondered if I would teach her how to fillet it, which, admittedly, I had never done before. The fish were coming in whole and ungutted off a local boat. "Sure," I told her, "I'd love to," and then I hurried off to spend an hour on YouTube, where I found numerous people with wildly different techniques for filleting whole tuna. I picked up a few tips and then sharpened my knives. I pantomimed my attack strategy, looking more like a demented ninja with an inadequate sword than a seasoned albacore filleter.

The day came, and I met my friends at Fishermen's Terminal, where we selected whole fish directly off the boat. On a hot August afternoon we set up a makeshift albacore-processing line. We all took a turn practicing the techniques of gutting, cleaning, skinning, and filleting. It was messy work and "fragrant" at that. (Gutting fish carries with it a certain special value-added olfactory experience.) I saved a few heads for crab bait, and we buried the bones and tails in the yard, deep enough so the dogs wouldn't find this special treat. The loins, four beautiful rosy pink cuts per fish, were vacuum sealed in bags marked for our different freezers and packed on ice in coolers. We toasted our stinky, messy selves with a cold, crisp beer, while flies buzzed over our heads, mistaking us for dead fish. And really, who could blame them?

WHAT MAKES THIS A GOOD FISH	I encourage you to seek out Pacific Coast troll (or pole)-caught and line-caught albacore tuna. There are several reasons why we should support this fishery: 1) It has low bycatch levels because the fish are caught individually and inspected one by one. 2) It has low mercury levels because it targets younger albacore. 3) Pacific albacore stocks are not depleted the way they are in the North Atlantic and other regions. A second option would be Hawaiian-caught long-line albacore. The United States has better bycatch regulations in place than long-line fisheries worldwide (though this method is still not ideal).
BY ANY OTHER NAME	Albacore tuna (*Thunnus alalunga*) is also called tombo (in Hawaii you might see it called tombo ahi), longfin tunny, or, in Japan, *shiro maguro* or *bin'naga maguro*.
SEASON	June to October.
BUYING TIPS	Albacore tuna is very soft when raw and firms up as it cooks. Treat it gently when raw to prevent bruising and tearing. The meat of fresh albacore should be bright, from a white-pink to deeper pink color, and have no blood spots/bruising. The texture will be soft and oily. Whole albacore shouldn't have dents or dings in the skin (a sign of poor handling).

QUESTIONS TO ASK BEFORE YOU PULL OUT YOUR WALLET	Where is this tuna from? Look for US Pacific Coast albacore. How was it caught? Prioritize troll- or line-caught. As a second choice, look for Hawaiian long-line caught.
CARING FOR YOUR GOOD FISH	If you're not going to use your albacore right away, put it in the coldest part of your fridge or place the package in a colander over a bowl and put some ice on top of it to keep it at its best. Thaw frozen albacore according to How to Safely Thaw Frozen Fish on page 18.
HOW THIS TYPE OF SEAFOOD IS RAISED OR HARVESTED	Albacore is a highly migratory species, meaning it travels great distances in the open ocean throughout its lifecycle. Fishermen often travel hundreds of miles offshore to catch albacore. Consequently, when fishermen find a school of albacore, bait is often thrown over the side to keep the school close by as the tuna are caught one by one with hooks and lines.
SUSTAINABLE SUBSTITUTES	Use another meaty firm or semi-firm fish; wahoo, mahi-mahi, halibut, or salmon come to mind.

albacore parcels
with mint-pistachio pesto

SERVES 4

For the mint-pistachio pesto:
¾ cup shelled pistachios
¼ cup sliced almonds
½ cup extra-virgin olive oil
⅛ teaspoon red pepper flakes
½ cup packed fresh mint leaves
¼ teaspoon fine sea salt

For the tuna:
1 tablespoon extra-virgin olive
   oil, plus additional for brushing
   the parchment
½ small red onion, cored and
   sliced into thin half-moons
   (about ½ cup)
½ teaspoon fine sea salt, divided
⅛ teaspoon freshly ground
   black pepper
Parchment paper or
   aluminum foil
1 pound albacore loin, cut into
   4 equal portions
1 cup cherry tomatoes, halved

PAIRING: First choice is albariño;
second, arneis.

I learned how to make a version of the mint-pistachio pesto from watching a Martha Stewart show, and it has become part of my regular rotation: tossed into pasta salads, served alongside grilled fish, or conveyed to my mouth by any means necessary—it's that good. Next time you go car camping, make this recipe in foil parcels. Keep them on ice until you get to your destination, then grill them over a strong fire.

....

Preheat the oven to 350°F.

To prepare the pesto, spread the pistachios out on a baking sheet and add the almonds at the far end. Toast in the oven for 4 minutes, then check to see if the nuts are lightly brown. If not, roast them for another minute or two. Leave the oven on.

When the nuts are toasted, transfer them to the bowl of a food processor, along with the oil, red pepper flakes, mint, and salt. Pulse into a chunky or smooth pesto: your choice. Set aside.

To prepare the tuna, heat a large sauté pan over medium-high heat. Add the oil and then the onion and ¼ teaspoon of the salt and sauté for about 8 to 9 minutes, or until the onions are lightly browned. Divide into 4 equal portions and set aside.

Increase the oven temperature to 450°F.

Cut 4 (18-inch) lengths of parchment paper (or you can make this in foil parcels, crinkling the edges to keep the liquids in). Fold each piece of parchment in half and trace a large, fat half-heart shape on each one. Cut out the shapes.

Open the parchment papers and brush one side of each heart lightly with oil. Lay a tuna steak on each oiled section and top with the remaining ¼ teaspoon salt and the pepper, followed by 2 tablespoons of mint-pistachio pesto, ¼ cup of the cherry tomatoes, and a quarter of the sautéed red onions. Fold the other

CONTINUED

half of the parchment over the fish and, starting at the top of the paper, make a small fold to crease the 2 sides together. Locate the midpoint of your fold and make another fold that starts there. Repeat, continuing around the whole outer edge of the paper. When you get to the end, tuck what's left securely under the parcel. The idea is to trap the steam, so look at all your creases and make sure no steam can escape. Place the parchment parcels on a baking sheet and cook for 5 to 7 minutes. Check the internal temperature by pushing a thermometer probe through the parchment and into the center of the fish. Remove the packets from the oven when the fish reaches 110 to 115°F for rare to medium-rare.

To serve, place one parcel on each plate and let your guests open them at the table. (Scissors or knives may be needed for parchment parcels; foil is easy to open without.)

albacore niçoise

SERVES 4

8 plum tomatoes, halved

2 tablespoons extra-virgin
olive oil

1 tablespoon balsamic vinegar

¼ teaspoon fine sea salt

⅛ teaspoon freshly ground
black pepper

5 sprigs lemon thyme or
regular thyme

¾ pound fingerling potatoes,
halved, or 1 large Yukon
Gold potato, skin on, cut into
large dice

1 tablespoon kosher salt

1 (6-ounce) can troll-caught
albacore in extra-virgin olive
oil, drained, 1 tablespoon of
the oil reserved

1 teaspoon Dijon mustard

Juice of 1 lemon (about
3 tablespoons), divided

Leaves from 1 head butter
lettuce

⅓ cup nicoise olives

¼ pound Dilly Beans (page 195)

4 hard-boiled eggs, halved

4 pieces toasted crusty bread

PAIRING: First choice is vinho
verde; second, muscadet.

Salade niçoise is a traditional salad that originated in Nice, France. It is a "composed" salad, meaning a dish where you can show your guests your personality type. Anal types will place each ingredient in efficient, color-coordinated piles, most likely not touching each other. Laissez-faire types will have everything piled randomly on the platter. I leave this up to you and your therapist.

. . . .

Preheat the oven to 300°F.

In a medium bowl, toss the tomatoes with the oil, balsamic vinegar, sea salt, and pepper. Transfer the tomatoes to a baking sheet lined with parchment paper, tucking the lemon thyme sprigs under the tomatoes. Bake for 45 to 60 minutes, or until the tomatoes are semidried and lightly caramelized.

Meanwhile, place the potatoes and kosher salt in a small pot, cover with water, and bring to a boil over high heat. Cook until the potatoes are tender, about 10 minutes. Drain the potatoes and put them in a small bowl. Add the reserved tuna oil, mustard, and 1 teaspoon of the lemon juice, reserving the remainder to dress the salad. Mix well and set aside.

On a platter, according to your nature, arrange the lettuce, tuna, potatoes, slow-roasted tomatoes, olives, Dilly Beans, and eggs. Drizzle the remaining lemon juice and oil over the salad. Serve with the toasted bread drizzled with more oil.

olive oil–poached albacore steaks

with caper–blood orange sauce

SERVES 4

2 cups plus 1 tablespoon
extra-virgin olive oil, divided

1 pound albacore loin, cut into
4 (1-inch) steaks

2 blood or navel oranges

½ small red onion, cored and
sliced into thin half-moons
(about ½ cup)

⅛ teaspoon fine sea salt

1 teaspoon minced
fresh rosemary

⅛ teaspoon red pepper flakes

1 tablespoon red wine vinegar

2 tablespoons dry white
vermouth or dry white wine

¼ cup mild green olives (such
as Castelvetrano), pitted and
sliced into thin strips

1½ tablespoons chopped capers

¼ cup chopped fresh
Italian parsley

¼ cup shelled pistachios,
for garnish

2 cups arugula

PAIRING: First choice is albariño;
second, Oregon pinot gris.

I think one reason people shy away from oil-poached anything is that they probably have an evolutionarily hard-wired fear of that much hot oil. It's probably a self-protection thing, but let me gently walk you through a decidedly safe preparation. The oil never gets very hot in this recipe—precisely why the tuna ends up moist and succulent. Another reason people shy away from oil poaching is because they think they need to throw away the oil when they are done. Not true! Strain it, refrigerate it, and use it for cooking. It will keep for months in the refrigerator. Now that I've soothed your fears, proceed gaily forward into a world of meltingly tender tuna with fruity and piquant olives, blood oranges, and a wisp of chile-induced heat, felt just for a moment at the back of the throat, to remind you that you're still very much alive.

. . . .

In a medium, deep saucepan over medium-low heat, heat 2 cups of the oil until it registers 230°F on an instant-read thermometer. Add the tuna steaks, two at a time, and cook for 3 to 5 minutes (don't adjust the heat—it's OK if the temperature drops): 3 minutes for rare (110°F), 4 minutes for medium-rare (115°F). Remove the steaks from the oil with tongs and transfer to a paper-towel-lined plate. Return the oil to 230°F and cook the remaining steaks. Reserve and set aside the poaching oil while you prepare the sauce.

Zest the blood oranges to yield ½ teaspoon zest. Then juice the oranges to yield ¼ cup juice, and cut the remaining flesh into small dice to yield ½ cup.

CONTINUED

In a medium sauté pan over medium-high heat, add the remaining 1 tablespoon oil. When the oil is hot, add the onions and salt. Sauté for 6 to 7 minutes, or until the onions are soft, then add the blood orange juice and zest, rosemary, red pepper flakes, red wine vinegar, vermouth, olives, and capers, and sauté for another minute or so. Add the parsley and blood orange pieces, stir well, and taste for seasoning. Keep warm.

Toast the pistachios in a small skillet over high heat, stirring occasionally, until lightly browned, about 5 minutes.

To serve, place some arugula on each of 4 plates. Drizzle a few teaspoons of the reserved poaching oil over the arugula and sprinkle with a touch of salt. Top with an albacore steak (sliced, if desired) and spoon the caper–blood orange sauce over the top. Garnish with the toasted pistachios.

seared albacore

with ratatouille and caramelized figs

SERVES 4

For the ratatouille:

1 tablespoon extra-virgin olive
   oil, divided

1 tablespoon high-heat
   vegetable oil, divided

1 small eggplant, cut into
   small dice

¼ teaspoon plus ⅛ teaspoon
   fine sea salt, divided

1 medium zucchini, cut into
   small dice

1 red pepper, cut into small dice

1 medium Walla Walla or other
   sweet onion, cored and sliced
   into thin half-moons

1 tablespoon minced
   fresh parsley

1 teaspoon minced fresh thyme

1 teaspoon minced
   fresh oregano

1 teaspoon minced
   fresh rosemary

⅛ teaspoon freshly ground
   black pepper

For the tuna:

1 pound albacore loin, cut into
   4 equal portions

¼ teaspoon fine sea salt

⅛ teaspoon freshly ground
   black pepper

2 tablespoons high-heat
   vegetable oil, divided

6 fresh figs, halved

1 cup cherry tomatoes, halved

August is a time of such intense, overflowing bounty that we are literally buried in produce. In times of extreme fecundity, I make recipes that include, at the minimum, 56,782 pounds of produce. This seems to be the best strategy to stay ahead of nature. If I'm not making gazpacho, I'm making this ratatouille. Caramelize some fresh figs and serve with a medium-rare albacore steak, ratatouille, and a red-wine-and-balsamic reduction and you only have 56,781 pounds of produce left to eat.

To prepare the ratatouille, heat a large sauté pan over medium-high heat. Add 1 teaspoon each of the olive oil and vegetable oil. Add the eggplant and ⅛ teaspoon of the salt, and sauté for 7 to 8 minutes, or until the eggplant is lightly browned and soft. Transfer to a large bowl. Add another 1 teaspoon each of the olive oil and vegetable oil, and sauté the zucchini with ⅛ teaspoon of the salt in the same fashion. Add it to the eggplant. Repeat the process one last time with the oil, red pepper, onion, and salt. Stir the cooked vegetables together; add the parsley, thyme, oregano, rosemary, and pepper. Taste and add more salt if necessary.

To prepare the tuna, heat a large skillet over high heat. Season the albacore steaks with the salt and pepper. Add 1 tablespoon of the vegetable oil to the skillet and, when it is hot, sear the tuna for about 2 minutes on each side for a juicy medium-rare; the internal temperature of the fish should reach 110 to 115°F. Transfer the steaks to a platter and cover lightly with aluminum foil to keep warm. Add the remaining 1 tablespoon oil and, when it is hot, sear the figs, cut side down, until they are brown, about 2 minutes. Flip them over, add the cherry tomatoes, and cook for another 3 to 4 minutes, or until the tomatoes are lightly charred. Transfer the figs and tomatoes to the platter with the albacore and place the skillet back over the heat to prepare the sauce.

CONTINUED

For the red-wine-and-balsamic sauce:

1 cup dry red wine

½ cup clam juice or chicken stock

3 tablespoons balsamic vinegar

PAIRING: First choice is red Burgundy; second, rosé.

SEARED ALBACORE, CONTINUED

To prepare the sauce, add the wine to the warm skillet you cooked the albacore and figs in. Reduce the wine by half, about 5 minutes. Add the clam juice and balsamic vinegar and reduce to a light syrup, about 3 minutes more.

To serve, on each of 4 plates, place an albacore steak with some figs and tomatoes and a heaping pile of ratatouille. Drizzle some of the pan sauce around the plate.

gin-and-tonic-cured albacore

with dandelion crackers and lime cream

For the gin-and-tonic-cured albacore:

2 teaspoons black peppercorns

1 teaspoon juniper berries

⅓ cup kosher salt

1 teaspoon lime zest

3 tablespoons light-brown sugar

1 tablespoon gin, divided

1½ pounds albacore loin, cut into a rectangular block no more than 1 inch thick (use trimmings to poach for *niçoise* salad or eat as sashimi)

For the lime cream:

⅓ cup cream cheese

⅛ teaspoon fine sea salt

¼ teaspoon lime zest

1½ tablespoons milk

For serving:

6 Dandelion Crackers (recipe follows), or store-bought high-quality thin crackers

---

PAIRING: First choice is sauvignon blanc; second, gin and tonic, naturally.

Before you think I'm encouraging you to dunk some tuna into a gin and tonic, I was merely inspired by the juniper, gin, and lime in one of my favorite adult beverages. Curing of the albacore is done much like you'd cure salmon for a traditional gravlax preparation. I hate to pick favorites, but this is one of my most cherished recipes in this book. It requires some advanced planning but not a lot of active work. You can make the lime cream the same day you cure the fish, the next day you can prepare the crackers and store them in an airtight container, and on the third day you can kick back with a gin and tonic and reap the rewards.

To prepare the albacore, grind the peppercorns, juniper berries, and kosher salt together in a spice grinder. Mix the ground spices with the lime zest and brown sugar in a small bowl. Place a piece of plastic wrap on the counter and spread half of the peppercorn mixture onto the plastic. Sprinkle with ½ tablespoon of the gin, then lay the fillet on top of that. Sprinkle the tuna with the remaining ½ tablespoon gin and then spread the rest of the peppercorn mixture on top of the tuna. Wrap tightly, place in a dish that will hold any juices that may escape, position a few heavy cans on top of the fillet to weigh it down, and place in the refrigerator.

Every day, for 3 days, flip the wrapped fillet. At the end of the 3 days, wipe the majority of the cure off the albacore with a damp paper towel and slice the fish as thin as possible.

To prepare the cream, blend the cream cheese, salt, lime zest, and milk in the bowl of a food processor or by hand until well mixed.

There are a couple of ways to serve this dish. You can lay the albacore slices on a platter, place the Dandelion Crackers in a basket, and pass the lime cream around for people to assemble as they wish. Alternatively, you can break the Dandelion Crackers into bite-size pieces, place an albacore slice on top, and garnish with a small dollop of lime cream.

¾ cup semolina flour

¾ cup all-purpose flour, plus
   additional for dusting the
   baking sheet

1 teaspoon fine sea salt

1 tablespoon sugar

½ cup warm water

2 tablespoons extra-virgin
   olive oil, plus additional for
   brushing crackers

⅓ cup dandelion petals, pansies,
   or nasturtiums (or a mixture)*

Cornmeal, for dusting the
   baking sheets (optional)

Coarse sea salt, for sprinkling
   the crackers

---

*Dandelions are easy to find—
the trick is making sure they
are clean. If you know where to
find a lawn full of dandelions,
you should determine before
picking them whether they have
been sprayed with weed killer or
other chemicals, or by animals.
Pansies and nasturtiums are
pretty easy to grow at home,
and many large supermarkets
are starting to sell little boxes of
edible flowers.

DANDELION CRACKERS

In a medium bowl, whisk together the flours, fine sea salt,
and sugar. Add the water, oil, and dandelion petals. In a stand
mixer with a dough hook attachment, add the dough and mix
at medium speed for 5 to 7 minutes. (If the dough doesn't come
together into a loose ball, add more water 1 tablespoon at a
time.) Alternatively, knead by hand on a floured countertop.
The dough should be just a bit tacky: not too dry, not too sticky
to work with. If you need to add a bit more water (or flour) to
achieve this, do so.

Shape the dough into a large ball and divide into 6 equal portions.
Gently rub each piece with a bit of oil, shape into a small ball, and
place on a plate. Cover with a clean dishtowel or plastic wrap and
let rest at room temperature for 30 minutes to 1 hour. While the
dough is resting, preheat the oven to 425°F. Place a pizza stone, if
you have one, in the oven.

When the dough is ready, flatten the dough balls. Using a rolling
pin or a pasta machine, shape them into flat strips. Pull the
dough out a bit thinner by hand (the way you might pull pizza
dough). You can also leave the cracker dough in long strips or cut
it into whatever shape you like at this point.

Set the crackers on baking sheets dusted with flour or cornmeal, poking each with the tines of a fork to prevent puffing.
Brush them with oil, and sprinkle with coarse sea salt. If you
are using a pizza stone, transfer the crackers directly onto it
and bake in batches. If you don't have a pizza stone, bake the
crackers on the baking sheets. Bake until deeply golden, about
10 minutes, and let cool before eating. The crackers will crisp
as they cool.

arctic char

Arctic char is the smart, well-dressed girl in the corner of the room who's quiet and subtle and doesn't hit you over the head with her confidence, yet everyone in the room (especially her) knows she's got it all going on. Sure, the sexy salmon gets all the attention with her flashy red dress, but that's so very (yawn) predictable. When I was first introduced to arctic char, I was drawn in by her gorgeous pink and white dots—her playful summer skirt like a party dress from the '50s.

Arctic char is a chameleon, both a freshwater fish and a saltwater fish. She keeps you guessing. She's tough and can survive in deep, frigid lakes. She can sometimes leave you cold but never bored. Arctic char used to be elusive—a rare fish in the wild—but she's increasingly available down home and local on the farm. Salmon may be sexy, but that char, she's coy and special and dependable: she's the marrying kind.

WHAT MAKES THIS A GOOD FISH	An elusive and beautiful species that is similar to salmon and trout, arctic char was the dominant species in the Arctic for centuries and a significant food of the Inuit. Arctic char is farmed in land-based closed systems where escape is rare.
BY ANY OTHER NAME	Arctic char (sometimes spelled "charr") (*Salvelinus alpinus*) is also called *iwana* and alpine char.
SEASON	Year-round.
BUYING TIPS	Arctic char has thin skin and tiny scales that do not need to be removed. Make sure the skin glistens and the flesh bounces back when you gently press on it.
QUESTIONS TO ASK BEFORE YOU PULL OUT YOUR WALLET	Arctic char is one of the most sustainably farmed fish out there. Where did it come from? Try to buy fish grown as close to your home as possible. When was it harvested? As with all fish, you'll want to make sure it hasn't been sitting around for very long (unless it's properly frozen). Up to five days from harvest is my usual window, but the nose always knows.
CARING FOR YOUR GOOD FISH	If you're not going to use your char right away, put it in the coldest part of your fridge or place the package in a colander over a bowl and put some ice on top of it to keep it at its best. Thaw frozen char according to How to Safely Thaw Frozen Fish on page 18.
HOW THIS TYPE OF SEAFOOD IS RAISED OR HARVESTED	Arctic char is farmed in a highly controlled environment (think high-tech aquariums) where the water is cleaned, filtered, and then recycled back through the system; this recirculated water is replenished only when too much water has been lost through evaporation.
SUSTAINABLE SUBSTITUTES	Coho, pink, or keta salmon or farmed rainbow trout are excellent substitutes for arctic char. In fact, feel free to use all the recipes in the trout and char chapters interchangeably.

pan-fried char

with crispy mustard crust

SERVES 4

1 tablespoon lemon juice

1 tablespoon Dijon mustard

¼ teaspoon brown
   mustard seeds

1 pound arctic char fillet,
   skinned, pin bones removed,‡
   cut into 4 equal portions

½ cup panko

¼ cup finely chopped fresh
   Italian parsley

½ tablespoon plus 1 teaspoon
   freshly grated lemon zest
   (from 1 large lemon), divided

½ teaspoon fine sea salt, divided

Scant ⅛ teaspoon cayenne

2 tablespoons unsalted butter,
   at room temperature

1 tablespoon high-heat
   vegetable oil

---

‡ Go to GoodFishBook.com
for a demonstration of how to
remove the skin and pin bones
from a fillet.

PAIRING: First choice is sauvignon
blanc; second, Chablis.

As much as chefs love fancy recipes, the simplest ones inevitably get the most radio play. This dish goes wonderfully with some simple steamed broccoli or broccolini. If for some weird reason you have leftovers from this dinner, run out and get a good baguette or ciabatta roll and smear it with an herb mayonnaise or some leftover lemon butter, some lovely butter lettuce, and a slice of beefsteak tomato. You will have yourself one fabulous fish sandwich.

....

In a small bowl, combine the lemon juice, mustard, and mustard seeds. Brush this mixture on both sides of the char fillets. In another small bowl, combine the panko, parsley, ½ tablespoon of the lemon zest, ¼ teaspoon of the salt, and cayenne. Transfer the panko mixture to a plate and coat the char fillets with the crumbs on both sides.

In a small bowl, mix the butter with the remaining 1 teaspoon lemon zest and the remaining ¼ teaspoon salt. Set aside.

Heat a large skillet over high heat. Add the oil and, when it is hot, gently slide the fillets into the pan, skin side up. Cook for 3 to 4 minutes, or until it has browned a bit. Flip and cook until the internal temperature reaches 125 to 130°F.

To serve, place ½ tablespoon lemon butter on top of each piece of char.

char *with grilled romaine, grapes, and balsamic vinegar*

SERVES 4

High-heat vegetable oil,
   for oiling the grill
3 tablespoons extra-virgin
   olive oil, divided
1 bunch romaine lettuce,
   cut through the core into
   4 equal portions
1 pound arctic char fillet, pin
   bones removed,‡ cut into
   4 equal portions
½ teaspoon fine sea salt
⅛ teaspoon freshly ground
   black pepper
4 slices good crusty bread
½ small red onion, cored and
   sliced into paper-thin half-
   moons (about ½ cup)
½ cup halved and seeded wine
   or tart table grapes
¼ cup balsamic vinegar

‡ Go to GoodFishBook.com
for a demonstration of how to
remove pin bones from a fillet.

PAIRING: First choice is Soave
Classico; second, vernaccia.

I remember the first time someone told me about a grilled romaine salad. I believe I turned my nose up at the thought. I couldn't get past the idea of cooked warm lettuce. Blech. Luckily, I will try anything once, and I'm so glad I did. Now a whole world has opened up, and that world includes smoking greens like escarole and frisée (see Smoked Sardines with Piquillo Pepper Sauce on page 291). This is a very simple recipe for a late-summer or early-fall evening.

Preheat a grill over high heat. Oil the grate with vegetable oil.

With your hands, rub 1 tablespoon of the olive oil all over the romaine sections and the char. Season the char and romaine with the salt and pepper. Grill the romaine until it is wilted and slightly charred, 5 to 7 minutes, turning as needed. Transfer to a plate and set aside. Grill the char fillets, skin side up, for 3 to 4 minutes, or until it has browned a bit. Flip and cook until the internal temperature of the fish reaches 125 to 130°F. Transfer to a plate, cover, and set aside. Grill the bread and set aside.

Heat a sauté pan over medium-high heat and add the remaining 2 tablespoons olive oil. Add the red onions and sauté for 5 to 7 minutes, or until the onions are starting to brown. Add the grapes and balsamic vinegar, and cook until the vinegar evaporates, 2 to 3 minutes.

Spoon the onion-grape mixture over the grilled fish and romaine, and serve with the grilled bread.

char with roasted cauliflower

and apple-vanilla vinaigrette

SERVES 4

For the vegetables:
1 head cauliflower, stemmed
½ small red onion, cored and
  sliced into thin half-moons
  (about ½ cup)
1 teaspoon extra-virgin olive oil
¼ teaspoon fine sea salt
¼ teaspoon freshly ground
  black pepper
¼ cup chopped fresh
  Italian parsley

For the cauliflower puree:
1 tablespoon kosher salt
Reserved cauliflower half
2 tablespoons whole milk
Fine sea salt

**For the apple-vanilla
  vinaigrette:**
¼ cup apple juice or cider
¼ cup clam juice
½ vanilla bean, sliced
  lengthwise down the middle,
  seeds scraped
¼ cup dry white vermouth
2 tablespoons apple
  cider vinegar
3 tablespoons extra-virgin
  olive oil

One night at a restaurant, I was served a single scallop with a butter sauce made with vanilla bean. I remember staring at the little flecks of vanilla seed and secretly dragging my finger through the sauce, thinking that I would have never thought vanilla would pair so well with seafood. But it really worked. When developing recipes for this book, I found that the sweetness of the vanilla needs to hang on something to keep the dish from becoming cloying—and that is where an earthy hook comes in here with the cauliflower. This dish demands a chilly fall evening when cauliflower is in season and the apple cider is flowing.

To prepare the vegetables, preheat the oven to 400°F.

Line a baking sheet with parchment paper. Cut the head of cauliflower in half. Cut one of the halves into ¼-inch slices (reserving the other half for the puree). Spread the cauliflower slices and onion on the baking sheet. Drizzle with the oil and mix to coat it well, then sprinkle the salt and pepper over the top. Roast in the oven for 20 minutes, or until the cauliflower browns on one side. Remove from the oven and toss with the parsley. Set aside and keep warm.

To prepare the cauliflower puree, bring a medium pot of water to a boil over high heat. Add the kosher salt and the reserved cauliflower half and cook until tender, 10 to 15 minutes. Drain the cauliflower, chop it coarsely, and puree it and the milk in a food processor or blender until very smooth. Taste the puree and season with ¼ teaspoon sea salt, adding more if necessary. Transfer the puree to a bowl, cover with foil, and keep warm.

CONTINUED

For the arctic char:

1 pound arctic char fillet, skin on, cut into 4 equal portions

¼ teaspoon fine sea salt

1 tablespoon high-heat vegetable oil

Herb Oil (page 100), for serving (optional)

PAIRING: First choice is Alsatian pinot gris; second, Savennières.

To prepare the vinaigrette, add the apple juice, clam juice, vanilla bean and seeds, vermouth, and apple cider vinegar to a small saucepan. Bring to a boil over high heat, then reduce the heat to a simmer and cook until the liquid reduces to 3 tablespoons, about 10 minutes. Discard the vanilla bean. Transfer the liquid to a blender and, with the motor running, stream in the olive oil. Taste and add salt if necessary.

To prepare the char, season both sides of the fillets with salt. Heat a large skillet over high heat. Add the vegetable oil and, when it is hot, carefully place the fillets skin side down in the pan. Cook for about 3 minutes, or until the skin is crispy. Carefully flip the fish over and cook for another 2 minutes, or until the internal temperature of the fish reaches 125 to 130°F. Remove the skillet from the heat.

Place a large spoonful of cauliflower puree on each of 4 plates, and top with a piece of char, crispy skin side up. Distribute the roasted vegetables over and around the fish, then drizzle the vinaigrette all around the plate. Drizzle with Herb Oil and serve.

char katsu

with ponzu sauce and cucumber-hijiki salad

SERVES 4

For the ponzu sauce:
1½ cups water
⅓ ounce (about ¾ cup) dried
    katsuobushi (bonito flakes)
⅓ cup soy sauce
¼ cup freshly squeezed citrus
    juice (a mixture of lemon-lime
    and even grapefruit is nice;
    use yuzu if you can find it)
1 tablespoon seasoned rice
    wine vinegar

For the char katsu:
1 pound arctic char fillet,
    skinned,‡ cut into 4 equal
    portions
¼ teaspoon fine sea salt
⅛ teaspoon freshly ground
    black pepper
2 tablespoons all-purpose flour
1 egg, beaten
½ cup panko
¼ cup high-heat vegetable oil
Cucumber-Hijiki Salad
    (recipe follows)
Cooked rice, for serving

───────────────

‡ Go to GoodFishBook.com
for a demonstration of how to
remove the skin from a fillet.

───────────────

PAIRING: First choice is
dry riesling; second, Junmai-
shu sake.

I was lucky enough to go to the Seattle Culinary Academy where one of my favorite instructors was K. G. Miyata, a champion ice carver in his native Japan, and as far as I'm concerned, the fastest hands with a knife ever. I got what many other culinary school grads don't: a really nice background in Japanese cuisine and sushi making. This recipe goes out to you, chef K. G.

To prepare the ponzu sauce, put the water in a deep pot and heat over medium-high heat. Just before the water boils, add the bonito flakes and turn off the heat. Skim off any foam that rises to the surface. Let the bonito sit in the water for 10 minutes. Strain the stock into a small bowl through a coffee filter or tea towel. Discard the bonito flakes.

Take ⅓ cup of the stock (save the rest for use in soups or marinades) and mix it with the soy sauce, citrus juice, and rice wine vinegar in a medium bowl. Set aside.

To prepare the char katsu, season the char fillets with the salt and pepper. Set up a plate with the fish, a plate with the flour, a bowl for the egg, a plate for the panko, and a final plate for the coated fillets. Using one hand for wet ingredients and one hand for dry, bread the fillets by patting them into the flour and tapping off the excess, dipping them into the egg and letting the excess run off, and, finally, coating them in the panko.

Heat a large sauté pan over medium-high heat. Add the vegetable oil and, when it is hot, fry the fish fillets until brown on both sides, about 4 minutes each side; the internal temperature of the fish should reach 125 to 130°F. This is casual, family-friendly food. Place the fillets on a platter with a small bowl of ponzu sauce and a spoon. Pass the Cucumber-Hijiki Salad and rice separately.

1 English cucumber or 2 Persian
cucumbers, halved lengthwise,
deseeded, and sliced into thin
half-moons

2 tablespoons hijiki,* rehydrated
in hot water for 10 minutes
and strained

2 tablespoons chopped
fresh mint

1 tablespoon orange zest
(from ½ orange)

3 tablespoons seasoned rice
wine vinegar

1½ tablespoons toasted
sesame oil

1 teaspoon chile oil

Fine sea salt

CUCUMBER-HIJIKI SALAD

In a large bowl, combine the cucumber, hijiki, and mint. In a
separate small bowl, whisk together the orange zest, rice wine
vinegar, and oils; toss with the salad. Let the salad sit at room
temperature for about 30 minutes before serving. Taste for salt
and adjust seasoning as needed.

---

*Hijiki is a brown-black sea vegetable that grows on rocky
coastlines around Japan, China, and Korea. It is sold dehydrated
in large supermarkets and natural food stores.

lingcod

1:34 am, on deadline to finish chapter, fall asleep watching a video of a huge lingcod refusing to let go of a smaller hooked fish and being pulled aboard, its intellectual capabilities not quite as impressive as its voracious appetite . . . . zzzzz—

I receive an invitation to the annual Pacific Coast Fish office party. I don my best wetsuit, check my hair in the mirror, and dive in. What a scene meets me at the door! Everyone is talking about shrimp and salmon and tuna and how desirable they are, blabbity-blah-blah, everyone's favorites and all. Meanwhile Ling is over there in the dark corner, mottled brown hoodie pulled over his head. "Buckethead" they call him. Popular creatures can be so cruel. Shy and never the most handsome guy, Ling stays hidden until he gets hungry and can't help himself. Waving his jazz hand–like fins wildly at his sides, he lunges his big clunky head toward the snack table and grabs an entire octopus along with part of the table in his mouth as all the fish shriek—who is that *monster*? He won't let go of the octopus as security drags him out of the room. At the door, he waves his fin goodbye as he stuffs a cocky salmon in his mouth, shutting him up forever. The tuna and shrimp are silenced, cowering behind what's left of the table. Revenge of the Ling.

I wake up in a cold sweat, remembering my dream. I grab a pencil and notepad and jot down: Ling—develop recipes worthy of this magnificent creature; also, sleep with the light on.

WHAT MAKES THIS A GOOD FISH	As with salmon, there was a time when lingcod was overfished, but in the United States we've gotten better at protecting our fish and chips. The lingcod fishery in Alaska is carefully managed, and no fishing is allowed during spawning and nesting times. Minimum sizes for catch in both the Alaska and US West Coast lingcod fisheries have helped to protect younger fish, which reach maturity at two years old. This assures the juvenile lingcod can take part in spawning the next generation before they become dinner. Interesting fact: lingcod females tend to travel great distances in their lifetime while lingcod males move very little from where they are born. After spawning, the lingcod dads stay at home guarding the nest until the eggs hatch.
BY ANY OTHER NAME	Lingcod (*Ophiodon elongatus*) is neither ling nor cod, but a member of the greenling family. It's commonly called ling or cod because it resembles those fish. Other possible names are cultus cod, blue cod, bluefish, green cod, buffalo cod, greenling, white cod, and buckethead.
SEASON	Year-round.
BUYING TIPS	Lingcod is a fish with the blues—about 20 percent of the fish will have flesh with a blueish tint. Don't be worried, and scoop it up if you see it. The old-timers swear this is the best lingcod you will ever eat; once cooked it will be a lovely white. Otherwise look for general signs of quality and freshness: a light press on the flesh snaps back into shape, either no smell or a light ocean-breeze smell, and no pooling water around the fish in its packaging.

QUESTIONS TO ASK BEFORE YOU PULL OUT YOUR WALLET

Was the lingcod caught with hook and line gear (handline, jig, bottom long-line)? Look for lingcod caught this way for the best quality and the least potential damage to the habitat.

....

CARING FOR YOUR GOOD FISH

If you're not going to use your lingcod right away, put it in the coldest part of your fridge or place the package in a colander over a bowl and put some ice on top of it to keep it at its best. Thaw frozen lingcod according to How to Safely Thaw Frozen Fish on page 18.

....

HOW THIS TYPE OF SEAFOOD IS RAISED OR HARVESTED

Lingcod are by caught by handline, jig, bottom long-line (all hook and line gear types), and trawl gear. US West Coast trawl lingcod are now considered sustainable by many sources due to fisheries management changes and the fleet's use of better-designed nets that reduce bycatch. My preference is for hook and line–caught fish as they are more gently handled on the boat.

....

SUSTAINABLE SUBSTITUTES

Lingcod has a dense, substantial texture. Halibut would be a good stand in. Also look for coho salmon as a possible substitute.

lingcod bouillabaisse

with piquillo peppers

SERVES 4

For the piquillo rouille:
2 egg yolks
2 medium or 3 small piquillo
  peppers, drained
2 tablespoons lemon juice
1 teaspoon sherry vinegar
  (preferably Arvum Gran
  Reserva)
¼ teaspoon fine sea salt
⅛ teaspoon saffron threads
Pinch of cayenne
½ cup extra-virgin olive oil

For the bouillabaisse:
1 tablespoon high-heat
  vegetable oil
1 pound lingcod fillet, skinned,‡
  bones removed, cut into
  4 equal portions
¼ teaspoon fine sea salt
¼ cup extra-virgin olive oil
1 medium fennel bulb, cored,
  thinly sliced crosswise, fronds
  reserved for garnish
½ cup small diced yellow onion
⅛ teaspoon saffron threads
2 (8-ounce) bottles clam juice
½ cup dry white wine or dry
  white vermouth
1½ cups tomato sauce
2 tablespoons Pernod
10 peppadew peppers, drained
  and quartered
Very finely grated zest of
  1 orange
1 pound mussels, scrubbed
  and debearded‡

Traditionally, making bouillabaisse is a two- to three-day affair, as it is paramount that you must first procure a boat. Once secured, you must actually catch some local fish. Then you need to harvest some shellfish. Next, *oui, oui,* all the way home—quick! quick!—and make a kickass seafood stock. Strain that. Add vegetables and then strain those because the broth must be very refined, even though the origins of this soup are pretty humble. Still with me? No? Great, do it the way I've written, using a few "cheater" ingredients (clam juice and tomato sauce) that nonetheless produce a delightfully aromatic and legit approximation of this classic seafood stew from the port city of Marseilles in Provence. Both piquillo and peppadew peppers are available in jars or in the bulk antipasti areas of nice grocery stores.

To make the rouille, in a blender or food processor, puree all of its ingredients except the olive oil until smooth. Add the olive oil in a very slow drizzle, until a mayonnaise-like consistency is reached. Taste and adjust seasoning.

To make the bouillabaisse, in a medium skillet over high heat, add the vegetable oil. Sprinkle the salt over the lingcod and slide the fish into the pan, serving side down (the prettier inside of the fillets). Reduce the heat to medium and cook the lingcod until it develops a nice brown crust on one side, 3 to 4 minutes. Immediately remove the lingcod from the pan. Add the olive oil to the pan along with the fennel and onion. Sauté, stirring occasionally, until lightly browned, about 10 minutes.

Meanwhile, in a small bowl, combine the saffron threads with 1 tablespoon of the clam juice to let it bloom (flavor and color released) for about 2 minutes. Add the white wine to the pan with the vegetables and let reduce until the pan looks dry. Add the clam juice, saffron with liquid, tomato sauce, Pernod, peppadews,

CONTINUED

For serving:

8 toasted baguette slices

———————————————

‡ Go to GoodFishBook.com
for a demonstration of how to
debeard and clean mussels and
how to remove the skin from
a fillet.

———————————————

PAIRING: First choice is Spanish
rosé; second, albariño.

and orange zest. Stir and bring the mixture to a boil over high
heat. Reduce to a simmer and cook until the fennel has softened,
about 10 minutes.

Add the mussels to the pan and simmer until they open. (Any
mussels that do not open can be cooked longer or discarded.)
Reduce the heat to low and add the lingcod pieces, seared side up,
along with any juices from the resting dish. Continue to simmer
until the cod is cooked through; the internal temperature of the
fish should reach 125 to 130°F.

To serve, spread some of the rouille on the baguette slices. Serve
the bouillabaisse, drizzled with olive oil and garnished with fennel fronds, with the rouille-coated toasts.

lingcod with crispy chickpeas
and quick-pickled apricots

SERVES 4

For the crispy chickpeas:
½ teaspoon coriander seeds
¼ teaspoon cayenne
Heaping ¼ teaspoon fine
  sea salt
1 (15-ounce) can chickpeas
  (not unsalted), drained
2 tablespoons unsalted
  butter, melted

For the chickpea puree:
1 (15-ounce) can chickpeas,
  scant ½ cup liquid reserved
  (drain any excess)
1½ tablespoons tahini
1½ tablespoons freshly
  squeezed lemon juice
1 tablespoon extra-virgin
  olive oil
¾ teaspoons fine sea salt
Pinch of cayenne

For the quick-pickled apricots:
¼ cup dried apricots, cut into
  very small ⅛-inch dice
1 tablespoon freshly squeezed
  lemon juice

For the pistachio-herb garnish:
2 tablespoons unsalted butter
¼ cup pistachios,
  roughly chopped
¼ cup fresh Italian parsley
  leaves, roughly chopped
¼ cup fresh mint leaves,
  roughly chopped
1 teaspoon lemon zest
⅛ teaspoon fine sea salt

This dish appears more complicated than it actually is in practice. You could even use store-bought hummus, but did you know it only takes ten minutes to make really great homemade hummus? Now that you know this, is there a certain part of you wondering why you are buying it? Have I shamed you? I didn't mean to. I meant to make you feel guilty. Is that the same as shaming? I'm not sure. I'm not asking you to cook your own beans, just whiz stuff up in a blender. So yeah, make your own damn hummus. Love you, mean it!

To make the crispy chickpeas, preheat the oven to 425°F. Grind the coriander seeds, cayenne, and salt in a spice grinder until fine. In a medium bowl, toss the chickpeas with the butter and then the spice mixture. Spread the chickpeas on a baking sheet and roast in the oven until crispy and dried out, about 15 minutes.

To make the chickpea puree, combine all its ingredients (including the reserved bean liquid) in a blender and blend very well. Transfer to a small bowl.

To make the pickled apricots and herb garnish, in a small bowl, mix the apricots with the lemon juice and set aside. In a small skillet over medium heat, melt the butter and allow it to cook until it smells nutty, 2 to 3 minutes. Add the pistachios and cook for another 2 to 3 minutes, or until the nuts darken a bit. Transfer to a small bowl, let cool, and then stir in the parsley, mint, lemon zest, and salt. Set aside.

To prepare the fish, in a medium skillet over high heat, add the vegetable oil. Sprinkle the salt over the lingcod and slide the fillets into the pan. Reduce the heat to medium and cook until the fish is brown on one side, 3 to 4 minutes. Flip and cook until the internal temperature of the fish reaches 125 to 130°F. Remove the fish to a plate and cover lightly with a piece of foil.

CONTINUED

For the lingcod:

2 tablespoons high-heat
　vegetable oil

1 pound lingcod fillet, skinned,‡
　bones removed, cut into
　4 equal portions

¼ teaspoon fine sea salt

½ cup plain whole-fat
　Greek-style yogurt

For serving:

1 tablespoon sumac (optional)

_____

PAIRING: First choice is albariño;
second, grüner veltliner.

Liquid will pool around the fillets as they rest. Drain off this liquid and add it to the yogurt.

To serve, spoon about 2 tablespoons greek yogurt onto each of 4 plates. Spoon about 2 tablespoons chickpea puree next to the yogurt dollop. (You'll have leftover puree.) Plate the fish and top with the apricots and herb garnish. Sprinkle the plate with some crispy chickpeas and the sumac.

_____

‡ Go to GoodFishBook.com for a demonstration of how to remove the skin from a fillet.

lingcod

with citrus and arbequina olives

SERVES 4

1 pound lingcod fillet, skinned,‡
    bones removed, cut into
    4 equal portions
1 teaspoon chipotle chile powder
1 teaspoon fine sea salt, divided
3 tablespoons high-heat
    vegetable oil, divided
1 pound fingerling potatoes,
    halved lengthwise
1 medium shallot, thinly sliced
    (about ½ cup)
¼ cup dry white vermouth
16 ounces canned or jarred
    whole tomatoes
1 (16-ounce) jar roasted red
    peppers, drained, cut into thin
    julienne strips
1 orange, cut into supremes*
¼ cup arbequina olives
2 tablespoons fruity Spanish
    extra-virgin olive oil, plus more
    for garnish
Baguette slices, toasted
Your favorite hot sauce (optional)

---

*Don't know how to supreme
citrus fruit? Learn how by
watching the video at
bit.ly/2qw6LwA.

---

‡ Go to GoodFishBook.com
for a demonstration of how to
remove the skin from a fillet.

PAIRING: First choice is white
Bordeaux; second, viognier.

This dish is easy one-pot, one-pan cooking, as the potatoes are doing their thing in the oven while you're busy with the lingcod on the stovetop. Everything is done together. Line your pan with parchment paper and then compost it at the end. Use your bread to mop up the juices in the pot. Have a dog? Let her prewash the dishes, making cleanup a breeze. Remember to tell your diners that there are pits in the olives. Lawsuits really get in the way of a friendship.

....

Preheat the oven to 400°F.

Sprinkle the lingcod with the chile powder and ¼ teaspoon of the salt. In a medium skillet over high heat, add 2 tablespoons of the vegetable oil. Slide the fillets into the pan, serving side down (the prettier inside of the fillets). Reduce the heat to medium and cook the lingcod until it develops a nice brown crust on one side, 3 to 4 minutes. Immediately remove the fillets from the pan and set aside.

Add the fingerling potatoes to the hot pan with the remaining 1 tablespoon vegetable oil and sprinkle with ½ teaspoon of the salt. Fry them, turning occasionally, until browned. Transfer the potatoes to a baking sheet and finish cooking in the oven until they are easily pierced by a knife, 5 to 10 minutes.

Meanwhile, add the shallot to the pan with the remaining ¼ teaspoon of the salt and cook until the shallot slices start to brown, 6 to 8 minutes. Deglaze the pan with the vermouth and simmer until it has evaporated. Add the tomatoes with juice to the pan along with the red peppers, orange, olives, and olive oil. Simmer until the tomato juice mixture has reduced by half. Return the lingcod to the pan and finish cooking them for 2 to 3 minutes, or until the internal temperature of the fish reaches 125 to 130°F.

Plate the lingcod in 4 shallow bowls along with some of the potatoes. Pour some tomato sauce around and over them. Drizzle with a bit of hot sauce and more olive oil. Serve with the toasted baguette.

lingcod and spot prawn paella

with charred lemons

SERVES 4

1 lemon

3 teaspoons high-heat vegetable oil, divided

½ pound spot prawns

¼ cup dry white vermouth or dry white wine

1 quart homemade or store-bought fish stock or paella base (I love Aneto Cooking Base for Seafood Paella)

½ teaspoon saffron threads, bloomed in 1 tablespoon warm water

1 pound lingcod fillet, skinned,‡ bones removed, cut into 4 equal portions

¼ teaspoon plus ⅛ teaspoon fine sea salt, divided

¼ cup extra-virgin olive oil, plus additional for serving

1 stalk celery, cut into small dice

½ yellow onion, cut into small dice

3 dried nora chiles (available from MarxPantry.com), destemmed and crumbled, with seeds, or substitute ½ teaspoon red pepper flakes

½ teaspoon sweet pimenton

½ teaspoon spicy pimenton

1½ cups Bomba Valencia rice

½ pound manila clams, scrubbed

½ cup frozen peas

I'm not going to lie to you. Making paella well takes practice. Doing it over live fire takes years of practice. So let's start with an easier version, one where you can do it in a smaller paella pan on your stovetop. The hardest part of paella is having the rice come out perfectly done, with a *socarrat* on the bottom (that's the lovely crunchy rice crust that is the mark of a well done paella) while no other component is overdone (in this case, the lingcod, shrimp, and mussels). Follow my directions carefully, especially the part where I tell you to stop stirring. You need to let the rice be in contact with the bottom of the pan after a certain point, totally undisturbed, so it can develop its crust. The heat needs to be perfect so it doesn't burn. Look for a nice gentle bubbling of the liquid and let your nose help guide you. If you smell even the slightest hint of burning, turn the heat down. Most importantly, if it's not exactly the way you hoped for the first time you try this recipe, try, try again. It took me at least ten times of making paella to get it right. Even the mistakes are delicious, so keep at it.

....

Cut a small portion off the ends of the lemon and discard. Cut the rest of the lemon into ¼-inch-thick slices. Heat a medium sauté pan over high heat. Add 1 teaspoon of the vegetable oil and lay the lemon slices in the pan to char them, flipping as needed, until well blackened in the center. Remove them to a plate. Turn off the heat but leave the skillet.

Peel the shells off the prawns, leaving the tails attached. Devein the prawns and set aside. Put the shells in the skillet and turn the heat to high. Toast the shells until they darken and smell aromatic, 3 to 4 minutes. Deglaze the pan with the vermouth. Transfer the toasted shells and any liquid to a deep pot. Add the stock or paella base. Bring to a boil over high heat, then reduce to a gentle simmer and infuse the stock with the shell flavor for 20 minutes. Strain the shells out of the stock and return the stock to the pot. Add the bloomed saffron threads with liquid and keep warm.

‡ Go to GoodFishBook.com for a demonstration of how to remove the skin from a fillet

PAIRING: First choice is albariño; second, Cava.

Add the remaining 2 teaspoons vegetable oil to a 12-inch paella pan over high heat. Sprinkle the lingcod with ¼ teaspoon of the salt and slide the fillets into the pan, serving side down (the prettier non-skin side of the fillets). Reduce the heat to medium and cook the lingcod until it develops a nice brown crust on one side, 3 to 4 minutes. Immediately remove the lingcod from the pan and set aside.

Add the olive oil to the paella pan. Add the celery and onion along with the nora chiles, both pimentons, and remaining ⅛ teaspoon salt. Cook, stirring, for 7 minutes. Add the rice and stir it into the vegetable mixture to coat it with the oil and lightly toast it. Pour in the infused paella base. Stir the rice to evenly distribute it around the pan. *This is the last time you will stir the paella.* Bring the liquid to a boil over high heat, then reduce the heat to a simmer. Simmer the paella until the rice starts to poke out of the top of the broth around the edges of the pan, about 10 minutes (though this can vary depending on your stove).

Push the clams into the rice until they're about half submerged. Be careful not to disturb the bottom layer of the rice. Cook for 5 to 7 minutes, or until the clams are just beginning to open. Sprinkle the peas evenly across the top. Lay the shrimp in the pan, again submerging them most of the way up their sides. Tuck the lingcod pieces into the rice, submerging only the uncooked side. Carefully shove any clams that are slow to open farther down into the rice. Cover the pan for 2 to 3 minutes to make sure the shrimp get cooked on the top. Continue to cook, lid off, just until the liquid is absorbed and the rice is tender. Be careful not to overcook the shrimp. Lay the charred lemon slices over the top and drizzle with some additional olive oil. Serve the paella in the pan, family-style. Pass extra salt at the table.

pacific cod

When I was choosing which sustainable fish to include in this book, I have to admit that I knew Pacific cod was a great choice, sustainability-wise, but I just couldn't get too excited about it from a culinary perspective. I didn't include it in the first edition of *Good Fish*, and I regretted that because, as a fish, Pacific cod is as good as the recipe that's developed for it—meaning, what I suffered from was a lack of imagination when it came to this mild white fish. Where wild salmon and oysters demand attention and special accommodations for their unique and bold flavors, Pacific cod puts its head down and gets the work done and doesn't care if you think it's not that interesting. I'm humbled to admit that I overlooked you, Pacific cod, and I'm making up for it now. And *shh*, it's still one of the cheapest wild fish out there. Go git it before that changes.

WHAT MAKES THIS A GOOD FISH	Pacific cod is common from Alaska to California. Most of the catch is from Alaska, a robust commercial fishery that has been putting fish on dinner plates since the early nineteenth century. Some of the sustainable management practices for the cod fishery include using at-sea observers who look for bycatch, restricting fish to certain areas, enforcing annual catch limits based on best-available science, and limiting the number of fishing permits.
BY ANY OTHER NAME	Pacific cod (*Gadus macrocephalus*) is also called P-cod, Alaska cod, cod, gray cod, grayfish, true cod, and, in Japan, *tara*.
SEASON	Year-round.
BUYING TIPS	Look for firm, opaque white flesh. If you see fresh Pacific cod, chances are it came from a US West Coast source. Frozen or previously frozen Pacific cod will most likely be from Alaska. Frozen Pacific cod can be a great value for a versatile fish to have on standby in your home freezer.
QUESTIONS TO ASK BEFORE YOU PULL OUT YOUR WALLET	Is this Pacific or Atlantic cod? Go with our local favorite, Pacific cod, as Atlantic cod is facing some challenges. If you are on the Eastern Seaboard there are sustainable options for Atlantic cod, but you'll need to consult with the local experts (fishermen and fishmongers) to learn where to find them.
CARING FOR YOUR GOOD FISH	If you're not going to use your Pacific cod right away, put it in the coldest part of your fridge or place the package in a colander over a bowl and put some ice on top of it to keep it at its best. Thaw frozen Pacific cod according to How to Safely Thaw Frozen Fish on page 18.
HOW THIS TYPE OF SEAFOOD IS RAISED OR HARVESTED	Pacific cod is caught with pots, jigs, bottom long-lines, and bottom trawl. My personal preference is for long-line, pot, or jig-caught fish. The Pacific cod trawl fishery has worked hard to reduce bycatch and the impacts of their fishing gear by restricting the footprint of their fishing areas. For these reasons, trawl-caught Pacific cod is considered sustainable by many sources.
SUSTAINABLE SUBSTITUTES	Pacific cod is a lean, moderately dense fish and great as a blank slate to bigger, bold flavors. Substitute with lingcod, or pink or keta salmon.

cod and squid okonomiyaki

SERVES 4

For the dashi:

10 to 15 grams (⅓ to ½ ounce)
  kombu (kelp)
4 cups water
20 grams (0.8 ounce)
  katsuobushi (bonito flakes)

For the batter:

2 eggs, lightly beaten
¾ cup cake flour
1 teaspoon toasted sesame oil
½ pound Pacific cod fillet,
  skinned,‡ bones removed, cut
  into small dice
½ pound squid tubes and
  tentacles, cleaned and cut into
  ¼-inch rings‡
4 packed cups thinly shredded
  red and green cabbage
1 cup finely grated peeled
  mountain potato (*yamaimo*)
½ cup drained pickled ginger
  (either white or pink), minced
½ cup *katsuobushi* (the small
  shavings), plus additional
  for garnish
1 teaspoon fine sea salt
½ cup *tenkasu* (tempura bits)
High-heat vegetable oil,
  for frying
1 small bottle *okonomiyaki*
  sauce (preferably Otafuku
  brand)

Okonomiyaki (pronounced oh-ko-no-me-ya-key) roughly translates to "grilled how you like it." It's a Japanese savory pancake that's not really a pancake at all, save for the fact that, yes, there are eggs and flour in the recipe and it's round. One of the most famous dishes from Osaka (the other one being *takoyaki*, or octopus balls), *okonomiyaki* is messy, gooey, and savory street food that is especially satisfying when you're pounding beers. You can put all kinds of things in *okonomiyaki*, but I find the seafood ones to be the best. If you want to really gild the lily here, lay some strips of bacon down in the pan before adding the batter.

....

To make the dashi, in a medium saucepan, combine the water and kombu. Bring to a boil over medium heat. When you start to see bubbles form around the kombu, remove it to a cutting board. Finely julienne half of the kombu and use as an add-in for the okonomiyaki batter, if desired. Add the *katsuobushi* to the water, return to a boil, and let simmer for 2 minutes. Turn off the heat and let the dashi sit for 5 minutes before straining it through a fine-mesh sieve. Set the dashi aside to cool before proceeding with the batter. Dashi can be stored in the refrigerator for up to 1 week or in the freezer for 2 to 3 months.

To make the batter, in a large bowl, combine the eggs with the cake flour, ¾ cup of the cooled dashi, and sesame oil. Whisk to blend well. Stir in the cod, squid, cabbage, mountain potato, pickled ginger, *katsuobushi*, and salt. Let the batter rest for 20 minutes.

CONTINUED

For serving:

1 small bottle Japanese-style mayonnaise (preferably Kewpie), for garnish

Aonori (a type of nori flakes), for garnish

---

‡ Go to GoodFishBook.com for a demonstration of how to remove the skin and from a fillet and how to clean and cut up a squid.

PAIRING: First choice is Asahi Super Dry beer; second, Junmai-shu sake.

Preheat a skillet over medium-high heat. Just before cooking, stir the *tenkasu* into the batter. Add 2 tablespoons vegetable oil to the skillet for each pancake. Increase the heat to high. Pour a 6-ounce ladleful of the batter into the skillet. Flatten it out a little. Use a spatula to help form the edges into a circle. Reduce the heat to medium-low, then cover the pan. Let the pancake brown on the bottom. When it's well browned, 8 to 10 minutes, flip the pancake and drizzle the top with 2 tablespoons of the *okonomiyaki* sauce. Continue to cook until the other side is browned and the pancake is cooked through (about 15 minutes total, though larger ones may take longer). Serve the pancakes drizzled with about 2 tablespoons mayonnaise, more *okonomiyaki* sauce to taste, and plenty of *aonori* and additional *katsuobushi*.

pacific cod and mussels

*with crispy potatoes and warm olive oil
and bay broth*

SERVES 4

For the crispy potatoes:

1 pound small red potatoes
(approximately 2 inches
in diameter)

4 tablespoons extra-virgin olive
oil, divided

½ teaspoon fine sea salt

1 teaspoon minced fresh
rosemary

For the cod and mussels:

¼ cup extra-virgin olive oil, plus
additional for garnish

½ cup thinly sliced shallots

½ teaspoon fine sea salt

4 canned whole tomatoes
(preferably Muir Glen
fire-roasted)

12 Castelvetrano olives

4 dried bay leaves

⅛ teaspoon red pepper flakes

½ cup dry white wine or dry
white vermouth

1 pound mussels, scrubbed and
debearded‡

1 pound Pacific cod fillet,
skinned,‡ bones removed, cut
into large cubes

1 lemon, cut into wedges,
for garnish

This is West Coast winter comfort food. Feel free to interchange clams for mussels in this recipe as both play well with the cod. When serving, remind your guests there are pits in the olives and not to eat the bay leaves (unless they're into that, and then who am I to judge?). Remind me to tell you about the time my six-year-old nephew gagged on a bay leaf at an Italian restaurant on my birthday when I was sitting next to him. Probably better to save that story for when you're not perusing a cookbook.

Preheat the oven to 450°F.

To make the crispy potatoes, spread the potatoes on a baking sheet, then toss with 2 tablespoons of the oil and the salt. Roast them until just tender, 30 to 40 minutes. Use a cup or mug to press the potatoes down on the pan, flattening them until they are about ¾ inch thick. The skins will split, but don't squish them so hard that the potatoes lose too much of their shape. Drizzle the remaining 2 tablespoons oil over the potatoes. Stir well and roast again until they are browned on the bottom, about 20 minutes. Sprinkle the rosemary over the top. Stir well, flipping the potatoes over, and return the potatoes to the oven until browned on the second side, another 10 to 15 minutes. Ideally the potatoes are crispy on the outside and fluffy and moist in the center.

To prepare the cod and mussels, in a wide sauté pan with tall sides or a short, wide pot over medium-high heat, heat the oil. Add the shallots and salt and cook for 6 to 7 minutes, or until soft. Add the tomatoes (breaking them up as they go in the pan), olives, bay leaves, and red pepper flakes. Cook for about 5 minutes, or until

‡ Go to GoodFishBook.com for a demonstration of how to remove the skin from a fillet and how to debeard and clean mussels.

PAIRING: First choice is albariño; second, verdicchio.

the tomatoes have started to break down a bit. Deglaze the pan with the wine and cook until most of the wine has evaporated. Add the mussels, cover the pan, and cook until they open, about 5 minutes. Reduce the heat to medium and add the cod, gently stirring the fish into the sauce. Cover the pan and let the fish gently cook for 2 to 3 minutes. Turn off the heat, keeping the pan covered for a minute or two.

Place a large scoop of the "stew" in each serving bowl, tuck a few crispy potatoes in on the side, and then drizzle the dish with olive oil. Give each guest a lemon wedge to squeeze over their bowl at the table.

thai fish cakes

with cucumber-chile sauce

MAKES 30 SMALL CAKES

For the cucumber-chile sauce:

1 small cucumber (or ½ English cucumber), deseeded, cut into small dice

1 serrano chile (seeds and membranes removed for less heat), minced

¼ cup very finely diced red bell pepper

¼ cup minced cilantro, plus additional for garnish

¼ cup minced Thai basil, plus additional for garnish

¼ cup seasoned rice wine vinegar

2 tablespoons chopped toasted peanuts

1½ tablespoons fish sauce

2 teaspoons sugar

For the fish cakes:

1½ pounds Pacific cod fillet, skinned,‡ bones removed, cut into large cubes

4 ounces Thai red curry paste

2 egg whites

2 teaspoons sugar

2 teaspoons fish sauce

1 quart high-heat peanut or safflower oil

8 lime leaves, cut into very thin ribbons

PAIRING: Only choice is Singha or other pilsner.

Say you had a pound or two of various scraps of cod, none big enough to serve as a fillet. Say you're enamored with Thai cuisine and you have these scraps and some chiles, cilantro, and—of course—fish sauce, because you buy it in bulk. Now say you stop by a market and grab some lime leaves (major markets carry them). Well, I'd say you were on your way to a pretty terrific appetizer. Serve the cakes with jasmine rice or wrap them in lettuce leaves, tucking in some extra sprigs of cilantro and Thai basil.

....

To make the cucumber-chile sauce, combine all its ingredients together in a medium bowl. Set aside while you make the fish cakes.

To make the fish cakes, put the cod into a food processor and process until it becomes a paste. Transfer the paste to a stand mixer with the paddle attachment (use a bigger bowl than you think you need) and add the curry paste, egg whites, sugar, and fish sauce. Beat the fish mixture at medium-high speed for at least 5 full minutes, scraping down the sides of the bowl from time to time. The goal here is to create a very sticky texture, which translates into the desired bouncy texture of the cakes.

Meanwhile, in a medium pot, heat the oil to 350°F.

While the oil is heating, fill a medium bowl with water. You will need to wet your hands and form the fish cakes into loose approximations of balls approximately 2 inches in diameter and about ½ inch thick—don't worry too much about the shape as the ugly ones are just as delicious as the perfectly round ones. Fry the cakes in three batches, making sure the oil returns to 350°F before you add the next batch. When the cakes are uniformly dark brown, remove them to a paper-towel-lined tray.

Serve the fish cakes right away with the cucumber-chile sauce and garnish with the lime leaves.

---

‡ Go to GoodFishBook.com for a demonstration of how to remove the skin from a fillet

jamaican cod run down
with boiled green bananas

SERVES 4

For the boiled green bananas:
1 tablespoon kosher salt
4 green (unripe) bananas, ½ inch
  of each end trimmed off
1 teaspoon lemon juice

For the run down:
1 tablespoon coconut oil
½ cup small-diced yellow onion
2 bay leaves
1 tablespoon minced
  fresh thyme
1 teaspoon smoked paprika
½ teaspoon smoked sea salt
1 (14-ounce) can full-fat
  coconut milk
1 (14-ounce) can whole
  tomatoes (preferably Muir
  Glen fire-roasted), pureed in
  a blender
1 red bell pepper, cut into long
  ¼-inch strips
2 serrano chiles(seeds and
  membranes removed for
  less heat), minced, or 1 whole
  scotch bonnet (if you really
  like heat)
2 limes: 1 juiced and 1 cut into
  wedges, for garnish
2 teaspoons fish sauce
1 teaspoon white wine vinegar
  or distilled white vinegar
1 to 2 teaspoons sugar
1 pound Pacific cod fillet,
  skinned,‡ bones removed, cut
  into large dice

One of my caregivers when I was a little girl was a Jamaican woman named Louise. I distinctly remember eating my first-ever plantain that she fried in a skillet for us. It was baffling to a white suburban kid from New Jersey to watch her cooking a "banana," and I was so picky then that I can't say I really appreciated the Jamaican fare of rice and beans and fried fish that she would sometimes make for us. Run down (often pronounced *run dun*) is a traditional stew made in Jamaica; mackerel is often used, though salt cod is also common. Theories abound as to the origin of the name, but some say it's because the fish falls apart into tiny pieces "running down" the plate. Another name for the dish is Fling-Me-Far. Your guess is as good as mine as to the origin. When I made this recently and took a bite, I felt like I was tasting a long-forgotten memory of home.

....

To make the boiled bananas, bring a medium pot of water to a boil over high heat and add the salt. Make a shallow slit just through the skin on two sides of each banana to make it easier to peel. Boil the bananas in their skin for 7 to 8 minutes. Pull them out of the water—the peel should come off easily. Return the bananas to the water along with the lemon juice (to prevent browning), and boil the bananas for another 5 minutes, or until they are tender. Cut each banana in half crosswise. Keep warm.

While the bananas cook, start preparing the run down. Heat the coconut oil in a large sauté pan or a wide, shallow pot over medium heat. Add the onion, bay leaves, thyme, paprika, and salt and cook for 6 to 7 minutes, or until the onions soften and become opaque. Add the coconut milk, increase the heat to medium-high, and simmer the mixture until you see oil separate and appear on the top of the coconut milk in thin rivulets, about 10 minutes. Add the pureed tomatoes, bell pepper, serranos, lime juice, fish sauce, vinegar, and sugar and simmer for 10 minutes.

‡ Go to GoodFishBook.com for a demonstration of how to remove the skin from a fillet.

PAIRING: First and only choice is Red Stripe Jamaican lager.

Increase the heat to high and add the cod pieces, pushing them into the sauce. Turn off the heat, cover the pan, and poach the fish for 5 minutes. (Remove the pot from the burner if you have an electric stove.) Taste and adjust the seasoning, adding more fish sauce, lime juice, or vinegar to taste.

Serve the bananas alongside a heaping ladleful of the run down. If desired, you can sear the bananas first in a little coconut oil over medium-high heat to caramelize them a bit.

mahi-mahi

I remember when I first learned that the name of Hawaii's state fish was the humuhumunukunukuapua'a. My theory is that Hawaiians repeat their words because the ignorant white man refused to listen. "What's that fish you say?" "Mahi." "What??" "Mahi!" "Sorry, didn't catch that." "MAHIMAHI!!" I later learned that Hawaii's state fish translates to "trigger fish with a snout like a pig," which has to be the funniest description of a fish ever. This got me thinking more about mahi-mahi and hoping for some equally funny meaning. Turns out it means "strong strong," and if you've ever fished for it and had it run your line all the way down, you'll be in agreement. Mahi-mahi is a gorgeous fish in striking yellows and blues, with a prominent forehead where a few fillets are hiding. It's good eating, though perhaps not as good eating to Hawaiians as wahoo (or "ono"), which translates to—wait for it—"good to eat."

WHAT MAKES THIS A GOOD FISH	Mahi-mahi reach maturity at the young age of four to five months. These fish are biological overachievers and spawn year-round with females releasing anywhere from forty thousand to one million eggs at a time. These two factors combine to make mahi-mahi a resilient fish that shows all signs of being able to withstand fishing pressure. But on the home front, make sure to eat a variety of fish so your personal appetite's impact is spread over a whole ocean of delicious seafood.
BY ANY OTHER NAME	The name mahi-mahi (*Coryphaena hippurus*) in Hawaiian means "strong strong" and refers to its reputation as a great swimmer. They are also known as dorado, dolphin, dolphinfish, and, in Japan, *shiira*.
SEASON	You will see fresh mahi-mahi on the market year-round but not always from a sustainable source. Make sure the mahi-mahi you purchase comes from the Pacific Ocean and was US caught. Peak Hawaiian mahi-mahi season is March through May and again from September through November. Also, prices will vary dramatically depending on the time of year; for this reason frozen mahi-mahi will most likely offer you a quality product at a more consistent price point.
BUYING TIPS	Fresh mahi-mahi is sold as fillets as well as beheaded and gutted. Frozen mahi-mahi is available as either skin-on or skinless boneless fillets or portions. The flesh will be pale pink and turn a lovely white when cooked.

QUESTIONS TO ASK BEFORE YOU PULL OUT YOUR WALLET

Where is it from? Mahi-mahi can be found in the Pacific, Atlantic, and Indian oceans as well as the Mediterranean and Caribbean seas. Mahi-mahi from US fisheries are a sustainable catch. Other than the long-line fishery from Ecuador and some Eastern Pacific seine fisheries that don't use fish-aggregating devices, it is best to stay away from imported mahi-mahi, as not all countries manage their fisheries to sustainable levels.

CARING FOR YOUR GOOD FISH

If you're not going to use your mahi-mahi right away, put it in the coldest part of your fridge or place the package in a colander over a bowl and put some ice on top of it to keep it at its best. Thaw frozen mahi-mahi according to How to Safely Thaw Frozen Fish on page 18.

HOW THIS TYPE OF SEAFOOD IS RAISED OR HARVESTED

Mahi-mahi live in deep waters and travel great distances in their up to seven-year lifetime. Mahi-mahi from US fisheries are caught in several ways: troll, pole, or long-line. As these fish are caught out to sea, the long-lines used to fish for them must float in the water column (not rest on the ocean floor as is the case for halibut and black cod). As a result, other species of fish and animals can be attracted to the baited hooks floating in the water, and bycatch can be a problem if precautions are not taken. US fishermen are making great efforts to limit bycatch, such as using circle hooks that allow easier release of unintended catch.

SUSTAINABLE SUBSTITUTES

Mahi-mahi is steak-like and semi-rich with good moisture content. Substitute with lingcod, halibut, albacore, or coho salmon.

mahi-mahi red curry

with thai basil and lime leaves

SERVES 4

1 tablespoon virgin coconut oil

1 cup small-diced red onion
 (about ½ large red onion)

¼ teaspoon fine sea salt

1 teaspoon grated fresh peeled
 turmeric, or ¼ teaspoon
 ground turmeric

1 teaspoon grated fresh
 peeled ginger

¼ cup dry white vermouth or
 white wine

1 red bell pepper, sliced
 lengthwise into ⅓-inch strips

6 lime leaves

3 tablespoons Thai red
 curry paste

1 (14-ounce) can full-fat
 coconut milk

1 (8-ounce) bottle clam juice

½ cup unsalted whole cashews

1 teaspoon lime juice

½ teaspoon fish sauce

1 pound mahi-mahi fillet,
 skinned,‡ cut into ½-inch cubes

1 bunch Thai basil leaves,
 roughly chopped, for garnish

Jasmine rice, for serving

---

‡ Go to GoodFishBook.com
for a demonstration of how to
remove the skin from a fillet.

PAIRING: First choice is Kabinett
riesling; second, Singha beer.

I was equally wooed and traumatized by Thailand when I traveled there way back when. Wooed by the cuisine that strikes the perfect balance between hot, spicy, sweet, and sour, punctuated by the pungency of fish sauce and the burning in my lungs from lethal chiles hitting hot woks. Wooed by the people who were just as friendly to foreigners as the country's promotional materials promised. But I was traumatized by the monkeys, the mamas clutching their little babies, lips curled around their teeth as they followed me in the town of Songkhla and mugged me for my mango. Back in Seattle, my friend Kabian loves to cook Thai food as much as I do. Her stepmother is Thai and taught her some dishes familiar to Americans, such as *gai krapow* (Thai basil chicken), and some unfamiliar, such as sun-dried beef served with sticky rice. When Kabian and her wife, Liz, brought home their new baby, Graycen, from the hospital, I developed this recipe and brought it over, along with a pot of jasmine rice. I literally spooned it into Liz's mouth as she fed her four-day-old baby, too busy to feed herself.

....

In a medium pot over medium-high heat, melt the coconut oil. Add the onion and salt and cook for 5 to 7 minutes, or until soft. Add the turmeric and ginger and sauté for another minute or two. Deglaze the pan with the vermouth and scrape the bottom of the pot to release any brown bits. Add the bell pepper, lime leaves, and curry paste and sauté for 2 to 3 minutes. Add the coconut milk. Bring to a boil over high heat, then reduce to a gentle simmer and cook, uncovered, for 10 minutes. Add the clam juice, cashews, lime juice, and fish sauce and return to a boil. Add the mahi-mahi, tucking the fish under the liquid. Remove the pot from the heat, cover, and set a timer for 5 minutes. Remove the lid, garnish with the basil leaves, and serve.

mahi-mahi

with fried basil, avocado, and tomato salad

SERVES 4

For the avocado mash:

1 avocado

1 serrano chile (seeds and
  membranes removed for less
  heat), minced

2 tablespoons roughly
  chopped cilantro

1 tablespoon lime juice

½ teaspoon fine sea salt

¼ teaspoon Tabasco or other
  hot sauce

For the tomato-basil salad:

1 avocado

1 cup cherry tomatoes,
  quartered

10 large fresh basil leaves, cut
  chiffonade (about ¼ cup)

2 tablespoons extra-virgin
  olive oil

1 teaspoon white wine vinegar

¼ teaspoon fine sea salt

**For the fried basil and
  mahi-mahi:**

1 cup high-heat vegetable oil

¾ bunch fresh basil leaves

½ cup thinly sliced shallots

1 pound mahi-mahi fillet,
  skinned,‡ bones removed, cut
  into 4 equal portions

I'm not really a fan of food and equipment fads, even though sometimes I fall victim to them. I'm guilty of having used "deconstructed" in a recipe title or two. And here's where the rubber meets the road, because this dish is kind of a fish taco that has been, you know—don't make me say it—reorganized into its various parts to form a version of itself that might make you think FISH TACO! but if it were on a restaurant menu you'd pay four times the cost of a fish taco. (And that's how you skirt around using the word "deconstructed.") Be sure to save the flavorful oil used to fry the basil and shallot; strain it and store in the refrigerator to use in stir-fries or when searing fish or steaks.

To make the avocado mash, in a small bowl, mash up the avocado. Add the serrano, cilantro, lime juice, salt, and Tabasco and mix well. Set aside.

To make the tomato-basil salad, cut the avocado into small dice. Place in a small bowl along with the tomatoes, basil, olive oil, vinegar, and salt. Mix well and set aside.

To prepare the fried basil and mahi-mahi, in a small saucepan, heat the vegetable oil to 350°F. Line a plate with paper towels and set it nearby. Place the basil leaves in the pot (they will sizzle and splatter oil a bit, so be careful) and fry until they darken and crisp up, 2 to 3 minutes. Using a strainer, remove the leaves to the paper towels. Return the oil to 350°F and add the shallots to the pot; fry until golden brown, 3 to 4 minutes. Remove to the paper towels.

¼ teaspoon plus ⅛ teaspoon
  fine sea salt, divided
1 ear of corn, shucked (or
  substitute with ¾ cup frozen
  corn kernels)
1 large heirloom tomato, cut
  crosswise into ½-inch slices

---

‡ Go to GoodFishBook.com
for a demonstration of how to
remove the skin from a fillet.

PAIRING: First choice is albariño;
second, Mexican lager.

Season the mahi-mahi with ¼ teaspoon of the sea salt. Transfer 1 tablespoon of the basil-infused oil from the saucepan to a large skillet and place over high heat. Add the corn cob and char it until brown in places, rotating it every 15 seconds. Remove it from the pan and set aside. Slide the fillets into the pan, reduce the heat to medium-high, and cook until the bottoms are nicely browned, 3 to 4 minutes. Flip and cook until the internal temperature of the fish reaches 130°F, 3 to 4 minutes more. Remove to a plate

Cut the corn kernels from the cob, let cool for a minute, and then mix them into the tomato-basil salad. Spoon some avocado mash onto each plate, then place the fish on top. Season the tomato slices with the remaining ⅛ teaspoon salt. Place one piece on each plate. Top the fish with the tomato-basil salad and then garnish with the fried basil and shallots.

mahi-mahi

with south indian spiced mango

SERVES 4

1 pound slightly underripe
   mango (2 cups), cut into
   ⅓-inch strips
1¼ teaspoons fine sea
   salt, divided
3 tablespoons virgin coconut oil
2 tablespoons fennel seeds
2 tablespoons cumin seeds
2 teaspoons brown
   mustard seeds
2 teaspoons turmeric powder
1 to 2 teaspoons red pepper
   flakes, depending on your
   heat tolerance
1 tablespoon high-heat
   vegetable oil or refined
   coconut oil
1 pound mahi-mahi fillet,
   skinned,‡ cut into 4 equal
   portions

─────────────────

‡ Go to GoodFishBook.com
for a demonstration of how to
remove the skin from a fillet.

─────────────────

PAIRING: First choice is pinot
blanc; second, grüner veltliner.

This is a simple weeknight dinner with few ingredients and huge, bold flavor. If you can choose one underripe mango and one ripe one, the mixture of tart green mango with a perfumed ripe one adds even more complexity to the dish. Unless you're Indian, the amount of spices will seem like a lot. Go with it: the magic of the dish depends on it. When you get a perfect bite of luscious mahi-mahi with the sweet, tart mango and then crunch through a bit of the toasty seeds, a bit of bright fennel here, a touch of earthiness from the cumin there—the long, slow burn of the chiles in your throat—you'll understand what I'm talking about. Serve with basmati rice (and make it more interesting by using half water/half coconut milk when you cook your rice).

In a medium bowl, toss the mango with 1 teaspoon of the salt and set aside for 10 minutes.

Meanwhile, in a large skillet over medium heat, heat the coconut oil for 20 seconds or so. Add the fennel, cumin, and mustard seeds and stir until the seeds pop and the spices are fragrant, about 1 minute. Remove the pan from the heat and stir in the turmeric and red pepper flakes. Taste the mango; if it's too salty, rinse it off and drain. Pour the hot oil over the mango, stirring to distribute the spices.

In a medium skillet over high heat, add the vegetable oil. Season the mahi-mahi with the remaining ¼ teaspoon salt and slide the fillets into the pan. Reduce the heat to medium and cook the fish until brown on the bottom. Flip and cook until the internal temperature reaches 125 to 130°F.

Serve the fish with the mango pickle spooned over the top.

mahi-mahi

with tostones, black beans, and tabasco honey

SERVES 4

For the black beans:
1 (25-ounce) can black beans
  (not unsalted), ¼ cup liquid
  reserved (drain any excess)
½ (14-ounce) can full-fat
  coconut milk
1 teaspoon fish sauce
2 bay leaves
1 serrano chile, halved
  lengthwise, stem end
  intact (optional)

For the Tabasco honey:
2 tablespoons honey
2 tablespoons water
½ teaspoon Tabasco
⅛ teaspoon fish sauce

For the plantains:
⅓ cup high-heat vegetable oil
4 green plantains (just starting
  to get spots), peeled, cut into
  1-inch pieces
¼ teaspoon fine sea salt
1 lime, cut into wedges

For the mahi-mahi:
1 pound mahi-mahi fillet,
  skinned,‡ bones removed, cut
  into 4 (4-ounce) fillets
¼ teaspoon fine sea salt
¼ cup chopped tomatoes,
  for garnish

Have you ever waited for a plantain to ripen? It's like watching paint dry. Except this paint will dry long after the other ingredients you bought for the recipe are rotten. This is why, I believe, wise cooks invented the tostone using a technique to make something rather inedible—an unripe plantain—rather delicious. It requires pan-frying an unripe plantain, squishing it, and then pan-frying again, and it's fun to make. Feel free to substitute the plantains with the green bananas on page 252. Or you could even go sweet and just fry some regular semi-ripe bananas in oil to serve with this dish. If you do that, leave off the Tabasco honey and simply hit the dish with straight Tabasco or whatever hot sauce you prefer.

To make the beans, in a medium saucepan over medium-high heat, combine the beans and reserved bean liquid, coconut milk, fish sauce, bay leaves, and serrano. Bring to a boil over high heat, then reduce to a simmer for 15 minutes. You want the beans to remain a little saucy. Add more coconut milk, if necessary. Remove the bay leaves and serrano before serving.

To make the Tabasco honey, in a small bowl, mix together all its ingredients and set aside.

To make the plantains, in a medium skillet over medium-high heat, heat the oil. After a minute, place the plantains in the oil and fry on both sides for approximately 3 minutes per side. Remove the plantains from the pan and place them all together on a cutting board. Set a plate over them and press down to flatten them. They should be about ⅓ inch thick. Return the plantains to the skillet and fry for 1 minute on each side. Season with the salt and squeeze some lime over them. Set aside but leave the skillet on the heat.

‡ Go to GoodFishBook.com
for a demonstration of how to
remove the skin from a fillet.

PAIRING: First choice is
Schnickelfritz Bavarian
Weissbier (from Urban Chestnut
Brewing Company, if you can
find it); second, hefeweizen with
an orange.

To prepare the mahi-mahi, season the fish with the salt. Slide the fillets into the skillet and reduce the heat to medium-high. Cook the mahi-mahi until the bottom is nicely browned, 3 to 4 minutes. Flip and cook until the internal temperature of the fish reaches 125 to 130°F. Remove to a plate.

To serve, spoon some beans onto each plate. Set the fish on top, the tostones to the side, and garnish with the tomatoes and a drizzle of Tabasco honey.

wahoo (ono)

I asked my colorful Scottish friend, Gill, if she wouldn't mind testing one of my wahoo recipes, and she informed me that the fish guy at the market said: "Wahoo also goes by the name of *ono*. When the quality is great we say 'Wahoooo!' and if it's dodgy, we say 'Oh NO!'" It's such a dumb Dad thing to say, but now I can't stop thinking Wahoooo! Oh NOOO! each time I write about this fish. I am sharing this throw-away story with you so that you can have it work its way deep into your psyche, informing your purchasing decisions and getting me a kickback on the increase in wahoo sales and a lock on wahoo futures. I don't even know what that means. I'm sure it's legal. Who's that at the door? Oh NOOOOOO!

WHAT MAKES THIS A GOOD FISH	A member of the mackerel family, wahoo swim the Pacific, Atlantic, and Indian oceans. In US waters, wahoo are caught with hook and line gear types that have little impact on the ocean habitat. While we have much to learn about wahoo, sustainability experts consider the population to be resilient. Mahi-mahi, another delicious sustainable fish, and wahoo are often caught together. Fun fact: "Don't bite off more than you can chew" does not apply to wahoo, as it is believed that a wahoo is able to eat fish larger than itself by using its sharp teeth to slash them into snack-size pieces. Wahoo does have more mercury than the other fish recommended in this book, so enjoy it as an occasional meal; adults should have no more than two servings a month, children under twelve no more than one per month.
BY ANY OTHER NAME	Wahoo (*Acanthocybium solandri*) can be found under many names, including Pacific ono, kingfish, peto, guarapucu, thazard bâtard, Pacific kingfish, and, in Japan, *kamasu-sawara*.
SEASON	Year-round, but peak season is May through October.
BUYING TIPS	Wahoo has about the same shelf life as sardines and other omega-3 rich silver fish, which is shorter than other fish; use it the same day or next day and pay close attention when purchasing it. Ask to smell it.
QUESTIONS TO ASK BEFORE YOU PULL OUT YOUR WALLET	Where was this fish caught? Feel good buying this fish as long as it comes from a US fishery. Be aware that wahoo from other countries may not be sustainably caught.

CARING FOR YOUR GOOD FISH	If you're not going to use your wahoo right away, put it in the coldest part of your fridge or throw the package in a colander over a bowl and put some ice on top of it to keep it at its best. Thaw frozen wahoo according to How to Safely Thaw Frozen Fish on page 18.

HOW THIS TYPE OF SEAFOOD IS RAISED OR HARVESTED	Wahoo from US fisheries are caught in several ways: troll, pole, or long-line. As these fish are caught offshore, the long-lines used to catch them must float in the water column (not rest on the seafloor as is the case for halibut and black cod). As a result, other species of fish and animals can be attracted to the baited hooks floating in the water, and bycatch can be a problem if precautions are not taken. US fishermen are making great efforts to limit bycatch and getting better each year. While long-line-caught wahoo is a sustainable option, wahoo landed by trolling or pole fishing tend to have less impact since the fish are landed live, one at a time, and unintended catch can be released when caught.

SUSTAINABLE SUBSTITUTES	Wahoo is steak-like and mild and has a dense texture. Albacore is a perfect substitute. Halibut would be my second choice.

wahoo *with orange-chile caramel and blackened broccolini*

SERVES 4

For the orange-chile caramel:
¼ cup orange juice
¼ cup sake
1 teaspoon soy sauce
1 teaspoon red wine vinegar
1 teaspoon Dijon mustard
1 teaspoon honey
1 teaspoon orange zest
½ teaspoon fish sauce
½ teaspoon chipotle
  chile powder
¼ teaspoon red pepper flakes
4 tablespoons (½ stick) cold
  unsalted butter

For the blackened broccolini:
2 bunches broccolini,
  ends trimmed
1 large naval orange, peel cut
  off, flesh cut crosswise into
  4 (½-inch) slices
1 tablespoon toasted sesame oil
2 teaspoons fish sauce
¼ teaspoon fine sea salt

For the wahoo:
1 pound wahoo fillet, skinned,[†]
  bones removed, cut into
  4 equal portions

[‡] Go to GoodFishBook.com
for a demonstration of how to
remove the skin from a fillet.

PAIRING: First choice is Kabinett
riesling; second, New Zealand
sauvignon blanc.

Wahoo is such a meaty, dense fish that it goes really well with a rich sauce. If you've made the soy caramel on page 71, you'll recognize the sauce here as its lightly spicy citrusy cousin. As with the soy caramel, you can make the sauce reduction and store it in the refrigerator for up to a week before you need it. Reheat gently, add a tablespoon of water to thin it a bit, and then finish it with the butter when the fish is ready. The blackened broccolini is a great, quick side to have at the ready for many of the dishes in this book.

Preheat the oven to 450°F.

To make the orange-chile caramel, in a small saucepan, combine all its ingredients except for the butter. Bring to a boil over high heat, then reduce to a simmer and cook until reduced by half, 6 to 8 minutes. Set aside.

To make the blackened broccolini, on a large baking sheet lined with parchment paper, spread out the broccolini and orange slices. Drizzle the oil and fish sauce over the top and toss well. Sprinkle with the salt. Remove the oranges to a plate and transfer the pan with broccolini to the oven. Forget about it (or set a timer for 15 minutes). When you remember to check on it, the broccolini should ideally be a bit blackened, charred around the edges. Turns out it tastes great partially incinerated. Seriously.

Meanwhile, return the caramel reduction to the stove over low heat. Whisk in the butter, 1 tablespoon at a time, until the sauce has thickened and developed great body.

To prepare the wahoo, lay the reserved oranges over the broccolini and top each orange slice with a piece of fish. Drizzle half of the caramel over the fish and bake until the internal temperature of the fish reaches 125°F. Check after 6 minutes and keep checking every 2 minutes after that. Serve each guest a wahoo fillet, orange slice, and side of broccolini. Pass extra sauce at the table.

wahoo *with grilled pineapple and poblano pepper salsa*

SERVES 4

For the soy glaze:
2 tablespoons packed dark
  brown sugar
1 tablespoon soy sauce
  (I recommend Yamasa brand)
2 teaspoons lime juice
2 teaspoons high-heat
  vegetable oil
¼ teaspoon red pepper flakes

4 fresh pineapple rings,
  cut ½ inch thick, core cut out
  with a small ring mold
  (or paring knife)

For the poblano pepper salsa:
1 charred poblano pepper,
  seeded, cut into small dice
½ cup chopped fresh tomato
½ avocado, cut into medium
  dice (optional)
2 tablespoons minced
  fresh cilantro
1 tablespoon minced red onion
2 tablespoons extra-virgin
  olive oil
1 teaspoon red wine vinegar
¼ teaspoon fine sea salt

For the wahoo:
1 pound wahoo fillet, skinned,‡
  cut into 4 equal portions
¼ teaspoon fine sea salt
1 tablespoon refined coconut oil
  or high-heat vegetable oil

_____

PAIRING: First choice is New
Zealand sauvignon blanc;
second, mojito.

If you live in Hawaii, this dish can be on your semi-regular rotation (see the information about mercury content on page 268). Wahoo, pineapple, avocado: check, check, check. If, however, you live in the Pacific Northwet (not a typo), buy the heavy-duty SAD light and crank it up, invite your vitamin D–deficient friends over for dinner, and serve this dish while you all plan your vacation to Hawaii because *oh my god, Becky*, you need a little sunshine in your life. Serve with rice cooked with coconut milk in place of the water and mojitos. Scatter copies of *The Ultimate Kauai Guidebook* around the room.

....

Preheat the oven to 325°F. Line a baking sheet with parchment paper and set aside.

To make the soy glaze, combine all its ingredients in a medium bowl. Add the pineapple rings and toss them around. Let them sit in the marinade while you prepare the salsa.

To make the poblano pepper salsa, in a medium bowl, mix together all its ingredients. Taste and adjust the seasoning as needed.

To prepare the wahoo, season it with the salt. Add the coconut oil to a large sauté pan over high heat. Slide the fillets into the pan and reduce the heat to medium-high. Cook the fish until brown on the bottom, 3 to 4 minutes. Immediately remove the fillets from the pan. Remove the pineapple from the marinade, letting any excess drip back into bowl. Sear the pineapple in the pan until it chars a little, about 2 minutes on each side.

Lay the pineapple slices on the baking sheet. Top each one with a piece of fish. Drizzle the marinade over the top. Put the baking sheet in the oven and cook until the internal temperature of the fish reaches 125°F. (Check after about 5 minutes.) Serve with the salsa spooned on top.

_____

‡ Go to GoodFishBook.com for a demonstration of how to remove the skin from a fillet.

wahoo torta

with pickled jalapeños and tomatoes

SERVES 4

For the pickled jalapeños and tomatoes:
½ cup water
½ cup white wine vinegar
2 tablespoons sugar
2 teaspoons kosher salt
2 jalapeños, cut into
  ¼-inch slices
1 cup whole cherry tomatoes

For the slaw:
2 cups equal parts finely
  shredded green and
  red cabbage
1 teaspoon fine sea salt
½ cup chopped cilantro leaves
  and stems
1 tablespoon lime juice

For the spicy mayo:
¼ cup mayonnaise
¼ cup sour cream
2 teaspoons sriracha or other
  hot sauce

For the seared green onions:
1 teaspoon high-heat
  vegetable oil
1 bunch green onions, trimmed,
  halved crosswise
Scant ⅛ teaspoon fine sea salt

I had my first torta on a busy corner in Mexico City, marginally lost and hungry enough to buy something so caloric it should have come with a warning. I lost count at five different kinds of meats shoved into that beast of a sandwich. It was a messy, humbling experience and, no joke, bigger than the circumference of my head. Not wanting to be a quitter, it took me about an hour to finish it completely. I didn't eat dinner that night or breakfast the next day. Tortas haven't taken off in America the way tacos have, but I'm sure that will soon change. There are no recognized rules with tortas—just as there seems to be no other parameter to a sandwich other than squishing stuff between bread—though the inclusion of refried beans, avocado, and pickled jalapeños seem to pop up more often than not. This is my version of a torta—hold the beans—fishwich-style.

....

To make the pickled jalapeños and tomatoes, in a medium saucepan over high heat, combine the water, vinegar, sugar, and salt and bring to a boil over high heat. Add the jalapeños and tomatoes, reduce the heat to medium, and simmer gently for 5 minutes. Turn off the heat and let them sit for 10 minutes. Strain the jalapeños and tomatoes and set aside. (You can reserve the pickling liquid in the refrigerator and use again.)

To make the slaw, in a large bowl, toss the cabbage with the salt and let it sit for 15 minutes. Rinse the cabbage (to get rid of most of the saltiness) and then squeeze it really well to drain. Put the cabbage in a bowl and mix in the cilantro and lime juice. Set aside.

To make the spicy mayo, combine all its ingredients in a small bowl and mix well. Set aside.

For the battered wahoo:

4 cups high-heat vegetable oil

½ cup plus 1 tablespoon all-purpose flour, divided

1 teaspoon baking powder

½ teaspoon fine sea salt

½ teaspoon smoked paprika

4 ounces beer, such as Tecate or other light beer

½ pound wahoo fillet, skinned,[‡] bones removed, cut into thin ¾-inch tall pieces, for faster frying

For serving:

4 Mexican bolillo or ciabatta rolls (hollowed out to make them less bready)

1 lime, cut into wedges

[‡] Go to GoodFishBook.com for a demonstration of how to remove the skin from a fillet.

PAIRING: First choice is Tecate or other Mexican light beer; second, Torrontés.

To make the seared green onions, in a skillet over high heat, add the oil and then the green onions. Sprinkle with the salt. Cook, tossing occasionally, until charred all around. Set aside.

To prepare the battered wahoo, heat the oil in a pot to 365°F. Meanwhile, in a medium mixing bowl, whisk together ½ cup of the flour, the baking powder, salt, and paprika. Add the beer and whisk well. Dredge the wahoo fillets with the remaining 1 tablespoon flour and then dip them into the batter.

Carefully add the fish to the pot and deep-fry for 1 to 2 minutes. Flip and cook the second side for 2 to 3 minutes more, or until the batter is well browned. Drain the fish on a paper towel–lined plate.

To assemble and serve, spoon one-quarter of the slaw into the base of each roll. Add jalapeños and tomatoes to taste, then the fish and a dollop of the spicy mayo. Top with the green onions. Serve each torta with a wedge of lime. Cut it in half or quarters if you're a quitter.

wahoo *with coriander-and-cardamon-spiced coconut sauce*

For the coriander curry blend:
¼ cup coriander seeds
2 tablespoons cumin seeds
10 green cardamom pods
3 whole cloves
1 cinnamon stick, broken into
  smaller pieces
1 teaspoon brown
  mustard seeds
1 teaspoon fennel seeds
½ teaspoon fenugreek seeds
¼ teaspoon red pepper flakes

**For the wahoo and
  coconut sauce:**
1 pound wahoo fillet, skinned,‡
  bones removed, cut into
  4 equal portions
¼ teaspoon plus ⅛ teaspoon
  fine sea salt, divided
1 tablespoon refined coconut oil
¼ cup dry white vermouth
1 (14-ounce) can full-fat
  coconut milk
1 teaspoon finely grated fresh
  peeled turmeric, or
  ¼ teaspoon ground turmeric
¼ teaspoon freshly ground
  black pepper
1 tablespoon lime juice
1 teaspoon fish sauce
½ teaspoon honey

PAIRING: First choice is Kabinett
riesling; second, albariño.

This is another one of those recipes that appears more difficult than it is due to the length of the ingredient list (I promise!). I imagine that even in thirty-minute Indian dinner cookbooks, the ingredients still trail down the page. There is something so sensual about working with these spices—make sure to stop and smell each one as you measure them out. Serve the curry with bread or rice to enjoy the sauce as well as the "crack" salad (minus the prawns) on page 88.

To make the coriander curry blend, add all of its ingredients to a spice grinder and grind to a fine powder. Reserve ¼ cup plus ½ teaspoon of the spice blend. (Package up the rest in an airtight container for another day.)

To prepare the wahoo and coconut sauce, rub the wahoo pieces with the reserved ¼ cup of the spice blend and then season with ¼ teaspoon of the salt.

In a large sauté pan over high heat, melt the coconut oil. Slide the fillets into the pan and reduce the heat to medium-high. Cook the fish until brown on the bottom, 3 to 4 minutes. Immediately remove from the pan and set aside.

Add the reserved ½ teaspoon spice blend to the pan and quickly stir it to toast the spices. Deglaze the pan with the vermouth. Add the coconut milk, turmeric, and pepper and simmer until the sauce reduces by half. Add the lime juice, fish sauce, honey, and the remaining ⅛ teaspoon salt. Taste and adjust the seasoning as needed. Bring the sauce to a boil over high heat. Return the wahoo to the pan, uncooked side down. Turn off the heat, cover the pan, and let the residual heat finish cooking the fish; the internal temperature should reach 125°F.

Serve the fish over the coconut sauce and dip your bread or fingers into the sauce.

‡ Go to GoodFishBook.com for a demonstration of how to remove the skin from a fillet.

LITTLEFISH & EGGS

sardines & herring

When the last large sardine cannery in the United States, Maine's Stinson Seafood, shut its doors in 2010 after 135 years of operation, our country's culinary relationship with the sardine was threatened, but it did not die. In the last few years there has been a resurgence in the collective attention on little silver fish. Lots of the excited talk circles around their healthful qualities—how they are high in protein and omega-3 fatty acids, and extremely low in mercury and other pollutants. That's all good news, but what gets me excited about these little silver fish is their big, incomparable flavor. I consider sardines and herring (and their little silver sisters and brothers) to be the fish lover's fish and the spiritual and culinary opposite of tilapia (a fish with all the gastronomic draw of a dish towel). Little silver fish lovers across the world UNITE!

| **WHAT MAKES THIS A GOOD FISH** | Sardine and herring fisheries are well managed and the harvests levels are set well below the limit marine researchers say is sustainable. Though be aware: due to ocean conditions and fluctuations in water temperature, forage fish such as sardines (and anchovies) experience natural boom and bust cycles at forty- to sixty-year cycles. So, if for any reason sardines are not available, substitute herring. If your fishmonger doesn't have herring, try mackerel, anchovy, or smelt. Forage fish are your flexible friends who are up for whatever you want to have for dinner. |

| **BY ANY OTHER NAME** | Pacific herring (*Clupea pallasii*) is known in Japan as *nishin*; Pacific sardines (*Sardinops sagax*) are also called pilchards or *iwashi* in Japanese. |

| **SEASON** | The season depends on when the various sardine stocks travel up the Pacific Coast, but generally, prime season is January through August (with some fresh sardines still available into October). Of course, canned are available year-round. At the time of publication, the sardine fishery was closed to allow the fish to recover. Until the fishery is open again, use herring or other little silver fish. Pacific herring from California are harvested late winter to early spring. The Alaska herring fishery is much larger, and herring are harvested in different regions at different times of year with the exception of summer months. |

| **BUYING TIPS** | You can sometimes find quality frozen Pacific sardines and herring year-round at Asian markets and specialty shops. Fresh Pacific sardines and herring are incredible and knock-your-socks-off delicious but hard to find. Fresh sardines are delicate little flowers and don't have the shelf life of other, sturdier species. You'll want really, really freshly caught sardines: three days out of the water max—maybe four if they were handled very well. |

You may seasonally see "roe on kelp." This is Pacific herring roe that has adhered to kelp fronds and been harvested for sale. The Japanese call it *komochi konbu* and *kazunoko konbu*. It is considered a delicacy. When buying spawn on kelp, ensure that the eggs appear fresh, translucent, and crunchy; the eggs covering one piece of kelp display a consistent color; the layer of eggs is strongly adhered to the kelp and not peeling off; and the product is appropriately packed in buckets with a brine solution or securely vacuum-packed with tight seals.

QUESTIONS TO ASK BEFORE YOU PULL OUT YOUR WALLET

Are these Pacific sardines or Pacific herring? Again, management around the world is not as strict as in the United States, so it's better—for many reasons—to buy domestic.

....

CARING FOR YOUR GOOD FISH

Because sardines and herring are especially perishable, keep them very, very cold and eat them the day you buy them. Thaw frozen little silver fish according to How to Safely Thaw Frozen Fish on page 18.

....

HOW THIS TYPE OF SEAFOOD IS RAISED OR HARVESTED

The nature of forage fish are to school tightly and swim in circles commonly called bait balls. Sardines are generally harvested by purse seining, which carries with it very little risk of bycatch. Gill-netting and midwater trawling are other ways sardines can be caught. Pacific herring are harvested by gill nets in California and purse seines in Alaska.

....

SUSTAINABLE SUBSTITUTES

Pacific herring and Pacific sardines are interchangeable. Pacific mackerel, jack mackerel, smelt, and anchovies are alternative options. Anchovies make a good stand-in, but keep in mind they are smaller, more intensely flavored, and when canned or tinned, much saltier.

dad's sardines on crackers
with caramelized onions

SERVES 6 TO 8 AS AN APPETIZER

1 (4-ounce) tin sardines, canned
   in extra-virgin olive oil
1 tablespoon dried
   Zante currants
1 tablespoon gin
½ cup small-diced red onion
¼ teaspoon fine sea salt
1 tablespoon extra-virgin
   olive oil
Freshly ground black pepper
Dijon mustard, for spreading
   on crackers
2 tablespoons finely chopped
   fresh Italian parsley

*You can learn the technique
for caramelizing onions by
watching a video demonstration
at bit.ly/2pytOrx.

PAIRING: First choice is
vermentino; second, rosé.

I was raised by a committee of loving folks consisting of the chair (my dad), co-chairs (my grandparents), and board members (my aunt and our "housekeeper" Louise, who did so much more than just keep house). Louise is Jamaican, and friends used to tell me that I had a slight Jamaican accent when I was a kid because she was one of my constant companions. Apparently, as the story goes, Louise misinterpreted a story my dad told her about a trip to England where he was served kippers for breakfast. I think she thought my dad wanted that, and so, occasionally, I'd be woken up by the smell of fish frying in a pan at six thirty a.m. Sometimes it would be sardines for breakfast. I don't think my dad had the heart to tell her he liked littlefish—but not with his morning coffee. This recipe goes out to Louise with love, wherever she may be (on earth or beyond), and to my dad, who raised me to be a good eater and stuck with me through the picky years.

Remove the sardines from the tin, discarding the oil, and place them in a bowl. Get the currants drunk by floating them in the gin.

In a small sauté pan over medium-high heat, caramelize the onions* by cooking them, along with the salt, in the oil. Keep cooking them until they get very soft and light brown. If they get too dry, add some water to prevent them from burning. It should take 15 to 20 minutes for the onions to get good and sweet.

OK, you're in the home stretch now—just mash up those sardines with a fork, add the drunk currants and the caramelized onions, and season generously with pepper. Eat the sardines on crackers with Dijon mustard and parsley. If you're really cool, you'll eat them for breakfast, like my dad did.

white bean and sardine salad
with fried eggs

SERVES 4

2 tablespoons red wine vinegar

¼ small red onion, cored and sliced into paper-thin half-moons (about ¼ cup)

⅛ teaspoon plus ¼ teaspoon fine sea salt, divided

1 (4-ounce) tin sardines, canned in extra-virgin olive oil

2 tablespoons sherry vinegar

2 cups bread cubes

3 tablespoons extra-virgin olive oil, divided

1 cup cooked white beans (canned is OK)

¼ cup chopped fresh Italian parsley

Freshly ground black pepper

4 eggs

Butter, for frying the eggs

¼ cup Parmigiano-Reggiano curls (made using a vegetable peeler)

PAIRING: First choice is verdicchio; second, vinho verde.

This recipe makes use of humble ingredients that can be picked up, last I checked, at a gas station. There is really nothing gourmet about them—in fact, for not much money, a tin of sardines, a can of beans, an egg, and some bread make for an extremely simple and healthful meal. I have prepared this recipe for sworn "sardine haters," and well, expect to hate no more.

Preheat the oven to 400°F.

In a small bowl, pour the red wine vinegar over the onions. Add ⅛ teaspoon of the salt. Mix well. Let them pickle at room temperature for at least 30 minutes (1 hour is better), stirring occasionally. When the onions are done, drain them, squeezing out any liquid and reserving it for other uses.

Remove the sardines from the tin, discarding the oil, and place them in a small bowl. Pour the sherry vinegar over the sardines and let them hang out for a bit while you make the croutons.

In a large bowl, toss the bread cubes with 2 tablespoons of the oil and the remaining ¼ teaspoon salt. Spread the croutons on a baking sheet and bake them in the oven for 10 to 12 minutes, or until they are crisp and lightly browned. Set aside.

Drain the sardines and pour the vinegar into a large bowl with the croutons, beans, and parsley, reserving the sardines. Add the remaining 1 tablespoon oil to the bowl. Taste and season with more salt as needed and pepper to taste. Place the salad on a platter.

Fry the eggs in a hot skillet with a little bit of butter, but leave the yolks runny. Top the salad with the pickled red onions, reserved sardines, fried eggs, and Parmigiano-Reggiano.

skillet herring

with fennel, currant, and pine nut salad

SERVES 4 AS AN APPETIZER OR LIGHT LUNCH

For the herring:
½ pound herring fillets
Zest and juice of
  1 medium lemon
  (you'll need 2 tablespoons
  juice), divided
⅛ teaspoon fine sea salt

For the fennel, currant, and pine nut salad:
1 tablespoon extra-virgin olive
  oil, plus additional for drizzling
½ cup thinly sliced shallots
⅛ teaspoon fine sea salt
2 tablespoons toasted pine nuts
½ medium fennel bulb, halved
  lengthwise, thinly shaved
  crosswise (preferably on a
  mandoline), fronds reserved
  for garnish
1 tablespoon Zante currants
¼ cup loosely packed fresh mint
  leaves, cut into thin ribbons
Freshly ground black pepper
1 tablespoon high-heat
  vegetable oil
Crusty artisan bread, for serving

PAIRING: First choice is arneis;
second, grüner veltliner.

There is a special place in my heart for this recipe. It started with an idea: Could I transport an eater to the Mediterranean with just a bite? One bite. I knew I needed a very fresh fish, a fish not normally cooked here in the United States, an underdog fish that deserved its day in the sun. I took the humble herring and started with a list of ingredients, crossing them off one by one until, hopefully, I distilled—in one bite—a sidewalk café baked in the sun and a Mediterranean breeze that makes you tuck your hair behind your ear and carries with it the faintest hint of the ocean.

To prepare the herring, place the fillets on a plate and drizzle 1 tablespoon of the lemon juice over them. Season with the salt. Set aside.

To prepare the salad, heat a medium sauté pan over medium-high heat. Add the olive oil and, when it is hot, add the shallots and salt and cook until lightly browned, about 7 minutes. Transfer the shallots to a large bowl, along with the pine nuts, fennel, currants, lemon zest, the remaining 1 tablespoon lemon juice, the mint, and pepper to taste. Mix well, taste, and adjust the seasoning as needed. Set aside.

Heat the vegetable oil in a large skillet over high heat. Once hot, gently slide the fillets into the pan, skin side up. Cook for 2 to 3 minutes, or until browned a bit. Flip and cook until the internal temperature of the fish reaches 125 to 130°F. Transfer to a plate.

To serve, place an equal portion of salad on 4 plates and top each with some herring. Drizzle about 1 teaspoon of olive oil over the top of each person's dish. Garnish with the fennel fronds and serve with the bread.

emmer pasta con le sarde

Pasta con le Sarde is a rustic Sicilian dish of pasta with sardine sauce. I've taken this classic dish and added a locally grown ancient Italian form of wheat (emmer, also known as farro) to make the pasta. I used to be one of those people who complained about whole-grain pastas. Dry! Like cardboard! Sucks all the moisture out of my face! I would say. Then one day I realized I was throwing out the proverbial whole-grain baby with the pasta water. I've found that making pastas with half all-purpose flour and half whole-grain flour happily walks the line between health, texture, and flavor. Emmer is enjoying a renaissance right now. I love how nutty and earthy it is—without it being so crunchy as to inspire me to dig out my old Birkenstocks.

....

To prepare the pasta, follow the directions for Homemade Fettuccine (page 36); except, for this recipe, I prefer a thicker noodle, so stop rolling the dough at the #5 or #6 setting. Bring a large pot of water to a boil over high heat and salt it heavily. While the water comes to a boil, make the topping and start the sauce.

To prepare the topping, heat a large skillet over medium-high heat. Add the oil and panko, and, stirring frequently, sauté the panko until it is golden brown, about 5 minutes. Transfer to a small bowl and mix thoroughly with the lemon zest, lemon juice, parsley, and salt. Set aside.

To prepare the sauce, wipe out your skillet and heat the oil over medium-high heat. Add the onions, garlic, celery, red pepper flakes, and salt. Sauté until the vegetables start to soften, about 7 minutes. Add the sardines, tomatoes, currants, and walnuts; cook, stirring occasionally, for another 5 minutes.

While the sauce cooks, make the pasta. Add the pasta to the boiling water, stir, and cook for about 3 minutes, or until it is a little bit under al dente. Drain through a colander, reserving ¼ cup pasta water.

SERVES 4

For the emmer pasta:
1 cup emmer flour*
1 cup all-purpose flour
3 large eggs
¼ teaspoon fine sea salt
1 tablespoon extra-virgin olive oil
1 tablespoon water

For the topping:
2 tablespoons extra-virgin olive oil
¼ cup panko
1 teaspoon lemon zest
1 tablespoon lemon juice
¼ cup minced fresh Italian parsley
⅛ teaspoon fine sea salt

For the sauce:
¼ cup extra-virgin olive oil, plus additional for drizzling (optional)
1 cup small-diced red onion
1 tablespoon minced garlic
½ cup small-diced celery
½ teaspoon red pepper flakes
¼ teaspoon fine sea salt
1 (4-ounce) tin sardines
1 (14-ounce) can tomatoes
1 teaspoon dried currants
⅓ cup roughly chopped toasted walnuts

---

*Bluebird Grain Farms, located in Washington's Methow Valley, mills their own flours. My favorite is their emmer flour. Order them online.

PAIRING: First choice is vermentino; second, Greco di Tufo.

Add the cooked pasta and reserved cooking water to the skillet with the sauce, reducing the heat to medium. Toss gently until the pasta has absorbed the sauce and is al dente, 3 to 4 minutes more.

Serve the pasta in bowls with the lemon-panko topping and a drizzle of olive oil.

WHAT IS A FORAGE FISH?

By Amy Grondin

Little silver fish are incredibly important to the marine food web. Sardines, herring, mackerel, anchovies, squid, and other small fish are collectively known as forage fish. Forage fish eat sunshine and turn it in to energy. Far-fetched? Not at all. The primary food forage fish eat is plankton—microscopic plants and animals. Mini sea plants need sun to grow just as plants on land do. When forage fish eat plankton, the "sunshine" stored in the plankton is absorbed by the fish and stored as fat or energy. As the old saying goes, the big fish eat the little fish. (We should add that the biggest fish eat the big fish.) This is how sunshine is transferred throughout the marine food web until a fish is caught and reaches our dinner plates. And this makes us part of the marine food web.

Forage fish are packed with nutrition, healthful oils, and incredible flavor. We used to eat lots of these fish, but somehow over the decades little fish fell off our menus. The Gen Xers and Millennials have not learned how to cook them nor developed a taste for their rich flesh. Today most of the forage fish caught in the United States are shipped overseas to other countries that still savor this catch. There is also another place little silver fish go.

When is the last time you saw a chicken, pig, or cow at the beach dive in the water to grab a fish and gobble it down? Never. That is the point. Before we started including fish in animal feed, it was not a part of land animals' diets. The fisheries that harvest forage fish for feed and other uses like fishmeal, fertilizer, and oil are known as reduction fisheries. These fisheries with massive harvests are putting pressure on forage fish populations. There are other options out there for animal feed. A better plan, one that is easier on the ocean, is for you to eat forage fish for dinner rather than eating the cow that ate the feed made from forage fish. You'll have a delicious meal and diversify the fish on your plate.

smoked sardines

with piquillo pepper sauce

SERVES 4

For the smoked sardines:

1 tablespoon extra-virgin
  olive oil
6 fresh sardines, head and tail
  on, butterflied and deboned‡
½ lemon
¼ teaspoon fine sea salt
½ cup apple wood or alder
  wood chips

For the vegetables:

1 teaspoon extra-virgin olive oil
1 bunch escarole or curly frisée,
  cut lengthwise into 4 equal
  portions, core left intact
¼ teaspoon fine sea
  salt, divided
2 plum tomatoes, halved
3 cups high-heat vegetable oil
¼ cup finely ground cornmeal
1 cup cauliflower florets (small
  ones—no bigger than 1 inch)
1 egg, beaten, mixed with
  ⅛ teaspoon Tabasco
2 tablespoons capers, drained
  and dried on paper towels

For the piquillo pepper sauce:

2 tablespoons extra-virgin
  olive oil
2 piquillo peppers
1 teaspoon sherry vinegar
¼ teaspoon cayenne
¼ teaspoon smoked paprika
¼ teaspoon fine sea salt

I love it when two heads are better than one in the kitchen. I was cooking with my dear friend Jet and mentioned I wanted to try smoking some sardines. Without skipping a beat, she said we should deep-fry cauliflower florets as a textural contrast. I suggested dipping the cauliflower in a cornmeal batter before frying, and she followed with an idea to serve the dish with a smoked tomato and piquillo pepper sauce to bring together all the flavors. There is simply no way I would have put these particular ideas together on my own; collaboration is the engine behind innovative recipes. This dish is like no other—I hope you enjoy it as much as we did.

To prepare the sardines, place the fillets on a baking sheet and drizzle the olive oil all over them. Squeeze the lemon on them. Toss to coat well. Sprinkle the salt over the fish inside and out.

Smoke the sardines according to the directions on page 163. Cook the sardines until the internal temperature reaches 125 to 130°F. When the sardines are done smoking, carefully transfer them to a plate, cover with aluminum foil, and keep warm.

To prepare the vegetables, put the escarole on a baking sheet, rub the olive oil all over it, season with ⅛ teaspoon of the salt, and smoke for about 4 minutes, or until the leaves lightly brown around the edges. Set aside. Smoke the plum tomatoes cut side up on the grate for a total of 5 minutes. Reserve the tomatoes to make the sauce.

Heat the vegetable oil in a medium saucepan over medium-high heat until it reaches 350°F. Season the cornmeal generously with the remaining ⅛ teaspoon salt. Set up a plate with the cauliflower, a bowl for the egg, a plate with the cornmeal, and a final plate for the coated cauliflower. With your hands, quickly dip the cauliflower florets into the beaten egg, and then coat with the cornmeal. Fry the cauliflower for 2 to 3 minutes, or until the

CONTINUED

‡ Go to GoodFishBook.com for a demonstration of how to butterfly and debone a sardine.

PAIRING: First choice is sparkling rosé; second, sauvignon blanc.

florets are browned and crisp-tender in the middle. Remove with a slotted spoon to a paper-towel-lined plate. Add the capers and fry just until they "bloom" open. (You'll see the sides wing out, and the capers will start to brown.) Set aside.

To prepare the sauce, add the olive oil, piquillo peppers, sherry vinegar, cayenne, smoked paprika, salt, and reserved smoked tomatoes to the bowl of a food processor. Puree until very smooth. Taste and adjust the seasoning as needed.

To serve, ladle some piquillo pepper sauce on each of 4 plates, lay some smoked escarole over the top, and place a smoked sardine on the escarole. Top with fried cauliflower pieces scattered on and around the fish. Garnish with the fried capers.

smoked herring on rye bread
with radishes, salted butter, and pickled onions

SERVES 4 AS AN APPETIZER

¼ red onion, cored and sliced
    into paper-thin half-moons
    (stem to root)
2 tablespoons red wine vinegar
⅛ teaspoon fine sea salt
1 (7-ounce) can smoked
    herring, drained
4 thin slices rye bread, toasted,
    each slice quartered
4 tablespoons high-quality
    salted butter, at room
    temperature
2 radishes, sliced paper-thin
    (preferably on a mandoline)
1 tablespoon capers
¼ cup tiny dill sprigs, for garnish

PAIRING: First choice is
Fino sherry; second, Italian
pinot grigio.

This is what you make when you think you have nothing to eat at home and then you surprise yourself by whipping out this very Scandinavian appetizer with what you thought just moments ago was *nothing* and now it's something fit for the kings and queens of Norway, or your Jewish great-aunt, or your salty neighbor who keeps promising to take you out on his boat. A perfect little appetizer for people who truly love fish—not those folks who say they like fish but who only eat shrimp and tilapia.

....

In a small bowl, combine the onion with the vinegar and salt. Mix well, cover, and refrigerate overnight or for a minimum of 2 hours. Drain the onions, reserving 1 tablespoon of the pickling liquid.

In a small bowl, mix the herring with the onions and reserved pickling liquid. Taste and season with more salt as needed.

On each toast quarter, spread some butter, arrange a few radish pieces, then some herring-onion mixture, and finally top with a few capers and dill sprigs.

sustainable caviar

I can't remember the occasion. The "occasion" seems less important than the way I chose to celebrate it. It was me. A spoon. A
glass of champagne. A tiny jar of caviar. But let's get serious—
unless you're fabulously wealthy, you and caviar are probably two
ships passing in the night. I once had the chance to try Osetra
caviar from the Caspian Sea, and it was remarkable. (I got a tip
from a friend that there was a place you could pay a small fee for
samples.) Years later I started learning more and more about seafood sustainability issues, and the thought of eating a generation
of wild sturgeon in one bite (and knowing that sturgeon was killed
for those eggs) took away my enjoyment.

I missed that little celebratory pop when your tongue presses
down on an egg against your teeth. I missed the flavor and the
occasion of sharing caviar (or eating it all by yourself). I learned all
about sustainably harvested caviar while at The Herbfarm. I tried
farmed white sturgeon caviar from California for the first time. On
my own, I experimented with *ikura* (keta salmon eggs from Alaska)
and trout eggs, and a whole new world of egg popping opened up
to me. Connoisseurs argue that the flavor is not the same as the
"real" thing (Caspian Sea sturgeon), and that even the word "caviar"
is reserved only for the eggs of the sturgeon. I argue that whether
you call it caviar or roe or eggs, there is plenty to be excited about
flavor-wise with sustainable "caviar."

WHAT MAKES THIS A GOOD FISH

Salmon roe comes from wild Alaska keta salmon, which are sustainably fished (see page 122 for an explanation of Alaska salmon's sustainability). Look for caviar from farmed trout and sturgeon (farmed in Idaho and California) so natural resources are not depleted to harvest the eggs. There are many sustainably farmed caviar options, but make sure to ask questions and purchase farmed caviar from places committed to supporting these issues.

BY ANY OTHER NAME

Keta salmon (*Oncorhynchus keta*) roe is known as *ikura* in sushi bars or to old salts as "bait." Rainbow trout (*Oncorhynchus mykiss*) roe is similar in color to salmon roe, but it has a smaller bead size. White sturgeon (*Acipenser transmontanus*) roe is farmed in California.

SEASON

Year-round for the types of caviar mentioned in this book.

BUYING TIPS

Look for eggs that are shiny, firm, and separate. They should have a fresh, light, briny smell.

QUESTIONS TO ASK BEFORE YOU PULL OUT YOUR WALLET

Purchase domestic fish eggs only to ensure their sustainability. The only wild caviar recommended for the Pacific Coast is salmon caviar (*ikura*). The others are all farmed: make sure to ask where they are from.

CARING FOR YOUR GOOD FISH

Keep your caviar very cold. I like to store it on an ice pack in a small cooler in the fridge. Unopened in your refrigerator, tinned caviar will last for two weeks, and vacuum-sealed jars will last for five to six weeks. Once the tins or jars are opened, they should be finished within two to three days. *Ikura* and trout roe can be frozen for later use. Farmed white sturgeon roe should not be frozen because the delicate texture will be compromised.

HOW THIS TYPE OF SEAFOOD IS RAISED OR HARVESTED

Wild salmon caviar is harvested from keta salmon returning in the fall. Farmed white sturgeon and trout roe are farmed in clean, artesian well water.

SUSTAINABLE SUBSTITUTES

Any of these sustainable types of roe can be substituted for one other in a pinch. I haven't tried it myself (yet), but be on the lookout for wild Alaskan herring roe—another option from a sustainable fishery.

caviar hash

SERVES 4

1 tablespoon unsalted butter

1 tablespoon extra-virgin
  olive oil

¾ pound russet or Yukon Gold
  potatoes, cut into medium
  dice (about 2 cups)

½ teaspoon fine sea salt,
  divided

2 cups arugula

4 eggs

1 tablespoon white wine vinegar

Freshly ground black pepper

Sour cream, for serving

1 ounce farmed white sturgeon
  or trout caviar

4 pieces good crusty
  bread, toasted

PAIRING: First choice is Chablis;
second, champagne.

This is the dish chefs eat when the work night is over and they're
hungry and tired and want something satisfying and quick (except
for the caviar part, because the customers got that). You will be
tempted to start throwing all sorts of things in with the potatoes,
but try to resist. The idea behind spending your hard-earned cash
on caviar is to be able to taste it. If you decide to make this without
the caviar, though, by all means fry up tons of onions and please
pass the Tabasco.

Heat a cast-iron or other skillet over medium-high heat. Add the
butter, oil (or, if you are lucky enough to have it, substitute with
duck fat), potatoes, and ¼ teaspoon of the salt. Once the potatoes
start browning on the bottom, 7 to 8 minutes, flip them over
with a thin-edged metal spatula (a fish spatula works well), carefully scraping along the bottom of the pan to release them without damaging that great crust. Keep cooking until the potatoes
are tender, about 5 minutes. Remove the pan from the heat, add
the arugula, and let it wilt among the potatoes. Set aside.

To poach the eggs, fill a medium bowl with ice water and set
aside. Crack each egg into an individual small cup. In a large
sauté pan over high heat, bring 3 inches of water to a boil. Add a
large pinch of salt and the white wine vinegar. Gently place each
egg into the simmering water. Reduce the heat to medium low.
Cook for 3 to 4 minutes, or until the whites are set but the yolks
are still soft. With a slotted spoon, transfer the eggs to the ice
water and place the bowl in the refrigerator until ready to serve.
(To reheat, place the eggs back into barely simmering water for
30 seconds.)

Season the poached eggs with the remaining ¼ teaspoon salt and
a few grinds of pepper. Serve each guest a scoop of potatoes and
arugula, then top with a poached egg, a dollop of sour cream, a
spoonful of caviar, and a piece of toast.

four-star duck eggs
with farmed white sturgeon caviar

**SERVES 4 AS AN
UNFORGETTABLE BRUNCH**

¼ cup heavy cream
6 duck eggs,* beaten
¼ teaspoon truffle salt**
1 tablespoon unsalted butter
1 ounce farmed white
   sturgeon caviar***
Fresh thyme leaves, for
   garnish (optional)

---

*If you can't find duck eggs, you
can approximate their richness
by using 6 chicken eggs plus
2 chicken yolks.

**Truffle salt can be found online
or at gourmet supermarkets

***Farmed white sturgeon caviar,
as well as the other types of roe
featured in this book, is available
online if you do not have access
to specialty food shops.

PAIRING: First choice is Chablis;
second, Sancerre.

This dish is so close to going whole hog that I might as well wrap it in gold leaf. I think I've used every luxury product there is in this recipe. The most significant aspect to get right is cooking the eggs perfectly, so follow these instructions carefully. It's an art, and it may take some discipline and perseverance to undo the way you've probably been making scrambled eggs your whole life. I can't wait for you to experience these soft, tiny, pillowy curds of golden goodness set off—just so—by the microscopic popping action of caviar beads between your teeth.

In a medium bowl, whisk the cream into the eggs, and season with the truffle salt. Let them rest for 10 minutes (this helps make for creamier eggs).

Heat a large nonstick pan over medium-high heat. Add the butter; let it bubble, then reduce the heat to medium-low. Pour in the beaten eggs, grab a wooden spoon, and start stirring. You will be tempted to increase the heat, but don't. If you keep stirring the eggs over a medium-low temperature, they will produce the creamiest, most delicious curds you've ever had. It should take about 10 minutes before they start to set into small curds, but they will still have lots of moisture. Look for a creamy, barely set appearance. Take the pan off the heat. Spoon the eggs into 4 bowls, top each with a spoonful of caviar, and garnish with the thyme.

potato and beet latkes

with horseradish sour cream and caviar

SERVES 4 TO 6 AS AN APPETIZER

¾ pound russet or Yukon Gold
  potatoes, grated using the
  largest holes of a box grater
  (about 2½ cups)
¼ cup grated peeled red beets
¼ cup grated peeled carrots
2 tablespoons grated onion
1 teaspoon fine sea salt
1 egg
¼ cup all-purpose flour
Freshly ground black pepper
High-heat vegetable oil, for
  pan-frying
½ cup sour cream
1 teaspoon prepared
  horseradish
4 ounces smoked trout, black
  cod, char, or salmon
1 ounce trout caviar or salmon
  eggs (*ikura*)
¼ cup fresh Italian parsley
  leaves or dill sprigs,
  for garnish

PAIRING: First choice is
champagne; second, muscadet.

I grew up in a pseudo-Jewish family, meaning we celebrated some of the holidays (the ones with the least amount of long-winded reading and fasting), and I was forced to go to temple until I was thirteen. My Jewish upbringing was less about religion and more about culture. Where there's culture, there's food, and frankly, in my family, it was always about the food. Latkes are a traditional dish served during Hanukkah. I came up with this dish by basically taking every food that appeared on our holiday table and putting it into one dish: grated beets reminded me of borscht, smoked fish reminded me of New York Jewish delis, horseradish reminded me of maror that we put on matzoh during Passover, and caviar reminded me of that time I caught my grandmother eating some out of a small jar while standing at the refrigerator when she thought no one was watching her.

In a large bowl, combine the potatoes, beets, carrots, and onion. Stir in the salt and let the vegetables sit for 10 minutes. (The salt will help bring out a lot of the moisture.) Over the sink, squeeze the vegetables with your hands to drain the liquid. Add the egg and flour and season with pepper to taste. Form a small amount into a tester latke (about 1 inch wide and flattened with your fingers so it is thin). Place some paper towels on a baking sheet.

Heat a medium cast-iron (or reliably nonstick) pan over medium-high heat. Add a tiny amount of oil and fry the tester latke until it is golden brown on both sides, about 5 minutes. Transfer to the baking sheet, and when the latke is cool, taste it for seasoning. Season the whole mixture if necessary with more salt. Form the rest of the latkes and fry them in batches in about ¼ cup oil, adding more as needed.

In a small bowl, mix the sour cream with the horseradish and set aside.

Top each latke with a small amount of smoked trout, a small dollop of horseradish cream, a little caviar, and parsley leaves. Serve immediately.

caviar on buttered brioche
with crème fraîche and chives

SERVES 6 TO 8 AS APPETIZER

½ cup warm water
(110°F to 120°F)

1 package active dry yeast

3 tablespoons sugar

6 extra-large eggs, at
room temperature

4¼ cups unbleached
all-purpose flour, plus
additional as needed

2½ teaspoons kosher salt

12 tablespoons (1½ sticks)
unsalted butter, at room
temperature

1 egg, beaten well with
1 tablespoon milk, for
egg wash

½ cup crème fraîche, whisked
to thicken

1 ounce farmed white
sturgeon caviar

1 tablespoon snipped chives,
for garnish

PAIRING: First choice is
champagne; second, Chablis.

You certainly don't have to make your own brioche for this recipe; you could just purchase some and proceed directly to using it as a caviar-distribution vehicle. But, truly, it's very easy to make and doesn't require any special skill (*shh*, don't tell French bakers I just said that). With that much butter and egg, it's a pretty forgiving recipe. If you happen to live near a farmers' market or know someone raising chickens, the bright orange of farm-grown eggs makes an especially golden brioche.

Preheat the bowl of a stand mixer by rinsing it with hot water. Combine the warm water, yeast, and sugar in the bowl. Mix with a wooden spoon and let rest for 5 minutes, or until the yeast and sugar dissolve. (The yeast should show signs of activity after 5 minutes by bubbling up—if not, start over with fresher yeast.) Add the eggs and, using the paddle attachment, beat on medium speed for 1 minute, or until well mixed. With the mixer on low speed, add 2 cups of the flour and the salt and mix for 5 minutes. With the mixer still on low, add 2¼ more cups of flour and mix for 5 more minutes. Scrape the dough into a large buttered bowl and cover with plastic wrap. Refrigerate overnight.

The next day, allow the dough to sit at room temperature for 1 hour. Meanwhile, grease a 9-by-5-inch loaf pan. Place the dough in the bowl of a stand mixer fitted with the dough hook, add the softened butter in chunks, and mix for 2 minutes, adding additional flour as needed to make a ball. Turn the dough out onto a lightly floured cutting board, then place it in the buttered loaf pan. Cover with a damp towel and set aside to rise at room temperature until doubled in volume, about 2 hours.

Preheat the oven to 350°F.

When the dough has risen, brush the top with the egg wash and bake for 30 minutes, or until the top springs back and it sounds slightly hollow when tapped. Turn the loaf out onto a wire rack to cool.

When cool, cut 4 thin (¼ inch or less) slices, remove the crusts, spread with butter, and cut each square into quarters. Preheat the broiler.

Place the brioche squares on a baking sheet and, watching carefully, broil on the middle rack until they crisp and brown lightly, 1 to 2 minutes. Remove, cool, and top each brioche square with some crème fraîche and caviar. Garnish with a sprinkle of chives.

celery root tart

with caramelized leeks and caviar

MAKES 4 SMALL OR
2 LARGE TARTS

For the tart dough:

2 cups all-purpose flour

1 cup (2 sticks) cold unsalted
butter, cut into ½-inch cubes

½ teaspoon fine sea salt

6 to 8 tablespoons ice water

1 egg, beaten well with
1 tablespoon water, for
egg wash

For the tart filling:

1 pound celery root (celeriac),
cut into medium dice

2 medium shallots, thinly sliced

2 teaspoons minced
fresh rosemary

2 tablespoons extra-virgin
olive oil

¼ teaspoon fine sea salt

1 egg, beaten

Cream, as needed for pureeing

2 tablespoons unsalted butter

1 medium leek, sliced into thin
rounds, white and light-green
parts only (about 2 cups)

For garnish:

¼ cup Parmigiano-Reggiano
curls, shaved with a peeler

1 ounce farmed white
sturgeon caviar

Learning how to make perfect pastry requires practice, but once the skills are attained, oh my goodness—you'll have the pleasure of watching your guests' eyes light up as flakes of pastry cascade from their smiling lips. I prefer all-butter doughs for their flavor, and I love how sweet and nutty celery root gets after it is roasted. I think, as of this writing, I've probably made and eaten at least a million of these tarts. Pull out the caviar for special occasions.

To prepare the dough, add the flour, butter, and salt to the bowl of a food processor. Pulse about 20 times, then check the consistency of the dough. The butter should be in pieces the size of small peas or large grains of rice. Keep pulsing as needed until the dough has reached that consistency, then transfer it to a large bowl.

Add 6 tablespoons of ice-cold water to the bowl and, with the fingers of one hand in a "claw" shape, mix the dough. Squeeze the dough in your hands: If it holds together, it's ready. If it's dry and does not hold together, add a tiny bit more water. Mix again with your hand. (You do not want to add too much water.)

When the dough is ready (it should be a bit crumbly), place it on some plastic wrap. Pull up the sides of the wrap, using it to help form the pastry into a disc. Cut the disc into quarters (or in half, for the larger tarts). Put each piece in plastic wrap and form them into rough discs. Chill in the refrigerator for 15 to 20 minutes.

Preheat the oven to 350°F.

Dust the counter and the dough with flour, and with a rolling pin, roll out each disc to ⅛-inch thickness. Using an 8-inch plate as a guide, cut the dough into circles. Crimp or fold in the edges of the tart shells, poke the bottoms all over with the tines of a fork, and place them on a baking sheet. Brush the edges with the egg wash. Chill for 15 minutes in the refrigerator.

‡ Go to GoodFishBook.com for a demonstration of how to make a quenelle.

PAIRING: First choice is champagne; second, muscadet.

Place the tart shells on the middle rack of the oven and bake for 15 to 20 minutes, or until nicely browned. You may want to rotate the pans top to bottom, front to back, midway through cooking. Lift the tart shells carefully and make sure the bottoms are lightly browned. Let cool.

Increase the oven temperature to 400°F.

To prepare the filling, in a medium bowl, combine the celery root, shallots, rosemary, oil, and salt. Transfer to a parchment-paper-lined baking sheet, and roast for 20 minutes, or until the celery root is soft.

Reduce the oven temperature to 350°F.

Transfer the mixture to a high-speed blender or food processor, add the egg, and puree, adding just enough cream (if needed) to facilitate the mixing process. Pulse for at least 3 minutes, or until the puree is very smooth.

To assemble the tarts, spread the filling onto the tart shells and bake in the oven for 5 minutes, or until the filling sets up. Meanwhile, in a medium sauté pan over medium heat, melt the butter and then add the leeks. Sauté until they are tender but not browned, about 8 minutes. When the celery root topping is nicely set, top the tarts with the leeks, then slice each one into 8 pieces and garnish with a Parmesan curl and a small quenelle (oval scoop) of caviar.‡

acknowledgments

Thank you, in no particular order, to my recipe testers, tasters and advisors: Carrie Kincaid, Heather Diller, Janet Beeby, Jen Warnick, Elaine Hackett, Courtney Nester, Holly Dinning Smith, David Mitchell, Gretta Graves, CJ Tomlinson, Ashlyn Forshner, Sana Jeweler, Shannon Romano, Gunilla Eriksson, Heather Weiner, Carma Gael, Caro Horsfall, Cindy Mix, Brett Andriesen, Kathleen Dickenson, Anne DeMelle, Alyssa Panning, Gill Dey, Rachel Belle Krampfner, Bud Wurtz, Laurie Robertson, Catherine Moon, Birgit and Lauri Jokela, Paola Albanesi, Melissa Poe, Lara Muffley, Werner Lew, Christine Dutton, Laurie Clark, Ivan Sucharski, Tele Aadsen, Joel Brady, Teresa Owens, Melinda Creed, Lucy Young, Victoria Staples Trimmer, Becky Ginn, Kim Allen, Maxine Williams, Marc Schermerhorn, David Wiley, Lorna Yee, Henry Lo, Derek Slager, Chris Nishiwaki, Larry Liang, Kristen Ramer Liang, Hans Giner, Elaine Mowery, Gordon King, Anna Berman, Shannon and Jason Mullett-Bowlsby, Michael Anderson, Shirley Abreu, Jenise Silva, Matthew Amster-Burton, John Tippett, Allison Day, Gregory Heller, Erika Garcia, Judy Niver, "Oyster Bill" Whitbeck, everyone at Mutual Fish, Nancy Harvey, Shauna James Ahern, Dan Ahern, Amy Duchene, Sue Skillman, Ryan Breske, Hsiao-Ching Chou, Rebekah Denn, Nancy Leson, Janis Martin, Emily Wines, Jake Kosseff, Doug Derham, Miki Tamura, Mona Memmer, Janis Fulton, Therese Ogle, Mimi Southwood, Ba Culbert and the staff at Tilikum Place Café, Susan Actor, Lisa Fisher, J. Christian Andrilla, Langdon Cook, Rocky Yeh, and the "Food Whores." A big sloppy kiss to Denise Anderson, the queen of recipe testers. Thanks to Elizabeth Wales, for sharing her expertise with me on the first edition. Jill Lightner, Jackie DeCicco, and Giselle Smith: you have all made me a better writer each time you edit my work.

They may not be aware of their membership, but the following people are all on my Seafood Advisory Committee; they are fishermen and renowned experts in their fields who have graciously donated their time to advise me on issues of seafood sustainability. Thank you to Jeremy Brown and Rich Childers for your expert review, and to Nick Furman of the Oregon

Dungeness Crab Commission. My eternal appreciation to Casson Trenor for your knowledge, passion, love of sushi, and quick pickup on the phone whenever I needed you; Jon Rowley, for inspiring me with all your love and appreciation for the inherent deliciousness of life; Rick Moonen, for being one of the most colorful advocates for the oceans I've ever had the pleasure of meeting—and an incredible chef, to boot; Hajime Sato, for following your heart and taking the huge risk of changing your business in favor of sustainable sushi; Jacqueline Church, for your support and long-standing commitment to sustainable seafood; and Marco Pinchot, for giving so freely of your time and knowledge in guiding our little rat pack on your shellfish-farming tours.

Jerry Traunfeld, I consider you my mentor, and it seems fitting that most of the first edition of this book was written at your restaurant, Poppy, while sitting at the bar drinking a Papi Delicious, tapping away at my computer, and eating some of the most extraordinarily prepared seafood dishes on the Pacific Coast. Thanks to all your staff at Poppy for taking such great care of me and April. Jeanette Smith and Ashlyn Forshner, my wing(wo)men, you two deserve a week's stay in a spa (yes, I'll rub your feet) for all the help and heart you contributed to this book—it wouldn't be half of what it is without your creativity, humor, and gentle guidance. Food adventures would not be the same without you both. Mark Malamud, Susan Hautala, and Jasper Malamud, you are my patrons, friends, family, clients, and guinea pigs—your kitchen has been my test kitchen for ten years and counting. This book is as much yours as it is mine.

Big-ups to my agent, Sharon Bowers, for being so easy to work with and at the ready to support me in whatever way I need. Thanks to the team at Sasquatch Books—especially my editors Susan Roxborough and Daniel Germain, copyeditor Rachelle Longé McGhee, production editor Em Gale, publisher Gary Luke, and designer Anna Goldstein (and Diane Sepanski and Lisa Gordanier for your work on the first edition)—who do all the largely behind-the-scenes work, without which these books wouldn't be made.

Clare Barboza, working with you has been like finding a missing limb that looks remarkably like a camera that takes both the shots I imagine in my head but can't produce and the shots I never had the vision to see in the first place. Some food-and-wine pairings are so sublime that the food makes an already good wine sing, and the wine makes an enjoyable dish unforgettable—and that is precisely how I think of my partnership with April Pogue. Sharing a life of food and wine with April makes everything better.

appendix a: a note on eating raw seafood

I'd like to clear up a few misconceptions. Some people are scared to eat sushi, or more accurately, raw fish. They are afraid it will make them sick. I can understand—I felt the same way when my oldest brother and sister-in-law first tried to tempt me with ruby-red slabs of tuna and meltingly tender bites of yellowtail. "I don't want to get sick," I protested, and they just shook their heads and said, "More for us!"

I'm not a microbiologist, but I would reckon that a warmish bowl of cooked rice left out for hours is more likely to make you sick than chilled raw fish in the cold case or a scallop crudo. One thing people don't realize is that the majority of fish you are served in the raw (with some exceptions) has been frozen before it gets to your plate. This is a good thing—not a sign of inferior quality. You want your fish to have been frozen if you eat it raw because deep-freezing kills parasites. This is especially important with salmon, which is prone to parasites. Please, for your own health and the health of your family, do not eat raw fresh salmon at home. And before you get the notion that you can just throw your salmon fillet in a home freezer for a few days before you eat it raw (or cure it), know this: a home freezer isn't kept cold enough to kill those parasites. If you are going to cure or prepare salmon sushi, buy high-quality fish that you know has been commercially frozen.

The following is taken directly from the Food and Drug Administration's website: "Freezing and storing at −4°F (−20°C) or below for 7 days (total time), or freezing at −31°F (−35°C) or below until solid and storing at −31°F (−35°C) or below for 15 hours, or freezing at −31°F (−35°C) or below until solid and storing at −4°F (−20°C) or below for 24 hours is sufficient to kill parasites. FDA's Food Code recommends these freezing conditions to retailers who provide fish intended for raw consumption." Another misconception? There is no legal definition of "sushi-grade." It is and always has been a marketing term.

While we are on the topic of misconceptions, "cooking" raw fish in acid, as when you make ceviche, does not eliminate parasitic contamination. It alters the protein, firming it up and changing the color of the fish, but it does not make it safe to eat. I use commercially frozen and then thawed fish when I make ceviche.

The truth is that cooking food is always the safest way to go. This applies to all foods, not just fish. These days, if you are still buying bagged commercial lettuce, you may want to cook that too. I jest, but not entirely. If you are immune compromised, pregnant, or very young, it's important to reduce your risks. Cooking food is a great way to do that. But for the rest of us, eating your fish raw shouldn't scare you—just take appropriate precautions.

It is actually illegal to serve raw fish in the United States unless it has first been frozen. The only exceptions to this rule are shellfish and tuna (as a deep-sea fish, tuna is exceptionally clean and free of parasites). Sushi bars don't advertise this fact because we Americans are pretty hung up on the idea that fresh fish is always superior. My thought is, unless you want to be sick, you'll reconsider this bias. Once you find out your fish has been in the deep freeze, eat it raw to your heart's content, keeping in mind that you still need to keep it cold and safe from cross-contamination, since you are not cooking it. Deliciousness awaits. Much to my brother's chagrin, he no longer gets the lion's share of the sushi.

appendix b: sustainable seafood resources

RECOMMENDED WEBSITES

Alaska Department of Fish and Game: www.adfg.state.ak.us
Alaska Seafood Marketing Institute: www.alaskaseafood.org
Environmental Defense Fund's Seafood Selector: www.seafood.edf.org
FishChoice: FishChoice.com
International Pacific Halibut Commission: www.iphc.washington.edu
Marine Stewardship Council: www.msc.org
Monterey Bay Aquarium's Seafood Watch: www.seafoodwatch.org
Ocean Portal: www.ocean.si.edu/ocean-acidification
Ocean Wise: www.oceanwise.ca
Pacific Fishery Management Council: www.pcouncil.org
Salmon-Safe: www.salmonsafe.org (Oregon); www.stewardshippartners
    .org/programs/salmon-safe-puget-sound (Washington)
Save Our Wild Salmon (SOS): www.wildsalmon.org
Seasonal Cornucopia: www.seasonalcornucopia.com
Seattle Aquarium: www.seattleaquarium.org

RECOMMENDED BOOKS

Bottomfeeder: How to Eat Ethically in a World of Vanishing Seafood
    by Taras Grescoe
*Crab: 50 Recipes with the Fresh Taste of the Sea from the Pacific, Atlantic &
    Gulf Coasts* and *Oysters: Recipes that Bring Home a Taste of the Sea* by
    Cynthia Nims
The Essential Oyster: A Salty Appreciation of Taste and Temptation
    by Rowan Jacobsen
*Fish Forever: The Definitive Guide to Understanding, Selecting, and Preparing
    Healthy, Delicious, and Environmentally Sustainable Seafood* by Paul Johnson
Fish Market: A Cookbook for Selecting and Preparing Seafood by Kathy Hunt
Fish Without a Doubt: The Cook's Essential Companion by Rick Moonen and
    Roy Finamore
Four Fish: The Future of the Last Wild Food by Paul Greenberg
The Joy of Oysters by Lori McKean and Bill Whitbeck
Salmon: Everything You Need to Know + 45 Recipes by Diane Morgan
Sustainable Sushi: A Guide to Saving the Oceans One Bite at a Time
    by Casson Trenor
Two If By Sea: Delicious Sustainable Seafood by Barton Seaver

index

Note: Photographs are indicated by *italics*.

A

albacore tuna, 13, 127, 201–215, 312
  Albacore Niçoise, 207
  Albacore Parcels with Mint-Pistachio Pesto, 204–206, *205*
  general discussion, 202–203
  Gin-and-Tonic-Cured Albacore with Dandelion Crackers and Lime Cream, 214–215
  Olive Oil–Poached Albacore Steaks with Caper–Blood Orange Sauce, *208*, 209–210
  Seared Albacore with Ratatouille and Caramelized Figs, 211–213, *212*
  See also fish, buying and handling
albumin, 141
anchovies, about, 283, 289
Anchovy-Almond Salsa Verde, 166
Apple-and-Chorizo Stuffing, 114
Apple-Vanilla Vinaigrette, *222*, 223–224
arctic char, 127, 217–227
  Char Katsu with Ponzu Sauce and Cucumber-Hijiki Salad, 226–227
  Char with Grilled Romaine, Grapes, and Balsamic Vinegar, 220, *221*
  Char with Roasted Cauliflower and Apple-Vanilla Vinaigrette, *222*, 223–224
  general discussion, 218
  Pan-Fried Char with Crispy Mustard Crust, 219
  Potato and Beet Latkes with Horseradish Sour Cream and Caviar, 302, *303*
  See also fish, buying and handling
Artichoke Soup, Oyster and, 57
Artichokes, Roasted Halibut with Radicchio-Pancetta Sauce, Peas, and, 159
Avocado Cream, 151
Avocado Herb Sauce, 72
Avocado Mash, 260

B

bacon, cooking in oven, how-to video for, 8
Bacon and Israeli Couscous, Mussels with, 48
Bacon-Cider Sauce, Dungeness Crab with, 76–77

Banana Leaf Salmon, Hajime's Steamed, 129
banana leaves, about, 129
Bananas with Jamaican Cod Run Down, Boiled Green, 252–253
Bean and Sardine Salad with Fried Eggs, White, 285
Beans, Dilly, 195
Beer, Steamers with, *32*, 33
Beet and Potato Latkes with Horseradish Sour Cream and Caviar, 302, *303*
Beurre Blanc, Tarragon, 104–105
black cod, 127, 177–187
  general discussion, 178–179
  Jerry's Black Cod with Shiso-Cucumber Salad and Carrot Vinaigrette, *182*, 183
  Potato and Beet Latkes with Horseradish Sour Cream and Caviar, 302, *303*
  Roasted Black Cod with Bok Choy and Soy Caramel Sauce, 180, *181*
  Sake-Steamed Black Cod with Ginger and Sesame, 184–185
  Tataki's "Faux-Nagi," 186–187
  See also fish, buying and handling
Bok Choy and Soy Caramel Sauce, Roasted Black Cod with, 180, *181*
bonito flakes, 187
Brioche with Crème Fraîche and Chives, Caviar on Buttered, 304–305
Broccolini, Blackened, 271
butter
  Coriander-Lemon Butter Sauce, 194–195
  Tarragon Beurre Blanc, 104–105
  Tomato-Espelette Butter, 51

C

calamari. *See* squid
Caramel, Orange-Chile, 271
Caramel Sauce, Soy, 71
Caramelized Figs, Seared Albacore with Ratatouille and, 211–213, *212*
Caramelized Leeks and Caviar, Celery Root Tart with, 306–307
Caramelized Onions, Dad's Sardines on Crackers with, 284
caramelizing scallops, tips for, 96
Carrot Cream, 99

Carrot Vinaigrette, 183
Carrots, Pickled, 99
Cashew Cream, 34
cast-iron skillets, 13
Cauliflower and Apple-Vanilla Vinaigrette, Char
    with Roasted, 222, 223–224
caviar, sustainable, 297–307
    Agedashi Salmon with Asparagus, Shiitakes,
        and Salmon Roe, 130, 131
    Caviar Hash, 299, 300
    Caviar on Buttered Brioche with Crème
        Fraîche and Chives, 304–305
    Celery Root Tart with Caramelized Leeks and
        Caviar, 306–307
    Four-Star Duck Eggs with Farmed White
        Sturgeon Caviar, 301
    general discussion, 298
    Potato and Beet Latkes with Horseradish Sour
        Cream and Caviar, 302, 303
    quenelles, how-to video for, 8
Celery Root Tart with Caramelized Leeks and
    Caviar, 306–307
char. See arctic char
Chickpeas, Crispy, 235
chile powder, ancho, 97
Chile Sauce and Herbs, Quick Squid with Red,
    110, 111
chile sauce, Thai sweet, 88
Chile-Cucumber Sauce, 250
Chile-Ginger Oil, Steamed Halibut with
    Sizzling, 160, 161
Chile-Orange Caramel, 271
chinook (king) salmon, 123, 137–155
Chorizo-and-Apple Stuffing, 114
Chowder, Razor Clam, 34
Chowder, Wild Salmon, with Fire-Roasted
    Tomatoes, 128
chum. See keta salmon
citrus, supreme, how-to video for, 238
Citrus and Arbequina Olives, Lingcod with,
    238, 239
clam juice, 9
clams, 15, 20, 27–39
    Fideos with Salmon, Clams, and Smoked
        Paprika, 153
    general discussion, 28–30
    Geoduck Crudo with Shiso Oil, 38, 39
    Homemade Fettuccine with Clams and
        Marjoram, 35–37
    Razor Clam Chowder, 34
    Steamers with Beer, 32, 33

Tamarind and Ginger Clams, 31
Coconut Curry with Charred Chiles and Lime,
    Halibut, 171–173, 172
Coconut Milk and Curry Leaves, Kerala Curry
    with, 134, 135
Coconut Pot Liquor and Sweet Potato Fries,
    Jerk-Spiced Salmon with, 137–139, 138
Coconut Sauce, Coriander-and-Cardamom-
    Spiced, with Wahoo, 276, 277
Coconut-Cucumber Soup with Dungeness Crab,
    Chilled, 73
cod. See black cod; lingcod; Pacific cod
Coffee-and-Spice-Rubbed Salmon Tacos with
    Charred Cabbage, Mango Salsa, and Avocado
    Cream, 150, 151–152
coho salmon, 123, 137–155
cooking and cleaning tools, 12, 13–15
cooking oil, high-heat, 9
cooking temperatures, 13, 127
Coriander-and-Lemon-Crusted Salmon with
    Poached Egg, Roasted Asparagus, and
    Hazelnuts, 144–145
Coriander-Lemon Butter Sauce, 194–195
Corn Soup, Summer Scallops with, 102 103
Couscous, Israeli, with Bacon and Mussels, 48
crab. See Dungeness crab
Crackers, Dad's Sardines on, with Caramelized
    Onions, 284
Crackers, Dandelion, 215
Croutons, Rye, 143
Crudo, Scallop, 94, 95
Crudo with Shiso Oil, Geoduck, 38, 39
cucumbers
    Chilled Cucumber-Coconut Soup with
        Dungeness Crab, 73
    Cucumber Quick Pickle, 198
    Cucumber-Chile Sauce, 250
    Cucumber-Hijiki Salad, 227
    Oysters on the Half Shell with Cucumber
        Sorbet, 60
    Shiso-Cucumber Salad, 182, 183
curry
    Halibut Coconut Curry with Charred Chiles
        and Lime, 171–173, 172
    Kerala Curry with Coconut Milk and Curry
        Leaves, 134, 135
    Mahi-Mahi Red Curry with Thai Basil and
        Lime Leaves, 258, 259
    Wahoo with Coriander-and-Cardamom-
        Spiced Coconut Sauce, 276, 277

D

Dandelion Crackers, 215
dandelions, harvesting, 215
dashi, 131, 245
deboning, how-to video for, 8
deboning tools, *12*, 14
dicing sizes, 9
Dilly Beans, 195
"dogs." *See* keta salmon
Duck Eggs with Farmed White Sturgeon Caviar, Four-Star, 301
Dungeness crab, 65–77
    Chilled Cucumber-Coconut Soup with Dungeness Crab, 73
    Dungeness Crab Mac and Cheese, *74*, 75
    Dungeness Crab Panzanella with Charred-Tomato Vinaigrette, 69
    Dungeness Crab with Bacon-Cider Sauce, 76–77
    general discussion, 66–68
    Newspaper Crab with Three Sauces, *70*, 71–72
    preparing and cooking, how-to video for, 8

E

Easiest Recipe in This Book, The, 132
Eastern oysters, 54
edamame, 62
eel, freshwater, 187
eggs
    Caviar Hash, 299, *300*
    Coriander-and-Lemon-Crusted Salmon with Poached Egg, Roasted Asparagus, and Hazelnuts, 144–145
    Four-Star Duck Eggs with Farmed White Sturgeon Caviar, 301
    Hangtown Fry, *58*, 59
    scrambling, how-to video for, 8
    White Bean and Sardine Salad with Fried Eggs, 285
Escabèche, Halibut, with Anchovy-Almond Salsa Verde, 166–167
European flats, 55

F

farmed *versus* wild fish, 19–21
Fennel, Currant, and Pine Nut Salad, 287
Fennel Two Ways, Grilled Sockeye Salmon with, 146, *147*
Fettuccine with Clams and Marjoram, Homemade, 35–37

Fideos with Salmon, Clams, and Smoked Paprika, 153
Figs, Caramelized, and Seared Albacore with Ratatouille, 211–213, *212*
filleting, how-to video for, 8
filleting knives, *12*, 14
fish, buying and handling, 313
    cooking tips, 126–127, 141
    farmed *versus* wild, 19–21
    fresh *versus* frozen, 17–18, 23
    "good fish" rules, 2
    how-to videos for, 8
    raw (sushi), 311–312
    smaller portions, more diversity, 21–22, 23
    thawing safely, 18
    tools for, *12*, 13–14
    wok-smoking, at home, 163
Fish Cakes with Cucumber-Chile Sauce, Thai, 250, *251*
fish eggs. *See* caviar, sustainable
fish sauce, 9
"flaking," 126–127
flour, emmer, 288
flour, gluten-free, 197
forage fish, 289
Fries, Sweet Potato, 137
frozen *versus* fresh fish, 17–18, 23
Fry, Hangtown, *58*, 59

G

galangal, 85
geoduck
    cleaning, how-to video for, 8
    general discussion, 28, 29, 30
    Geoduck Crudo with Shiso Oil, 38, *39*
Gin-and-Tonic-Cured Albacore with Dandelion Crackers and Lime Cream, 214–215
Ginger and Tamarind Clams, 31
gluten-free flour, 197
Gnocchi, Nettle, 164–165
Grapefruit and Mint. Pink Shrimp Salad with, 86, *87*
Green Goddess Sauce, 154
Greens, Grits, and Scallops, 97
Guinness Cream, Mussels with, 44

H

Hajime's Steamed Banana Leaf Salmon, 129
halibut. *See* Pacific halibut
Hangtown Fry, *58*, 59

Hash, Caviar, 299, *300*
Herb Avocado Sauce, 72
Herb Oil, 100, *101*
herring, 127, 281
   general discussion, 282–283, 289
   Skillet Herring with Fennel, Currant, and
     Pine Nut Salad, *286*, 287
   Smoked Herring on Rye Bread with Radishes,
     Salted Butter, and Pickled Onions, 294, *295*
Hijiki-Cucumber Salad, 227
Horseradish Sour Cream and Caviar, with
   Potato and Beet Latkes, 302, *303*
humpback ("humpies"). *See* pink salmon

I

ingredients and terms, 9–11

J

Jalapeños, Pickled, 274
Jamaican Cod Run Down with Boiled Green
   Bananas, 252–253
Japanese mint. *See* shiso
Jerk-Spiced Salmon with Coconut Pot Liquor
   and Sweet Potato Fries, 137–139, *138*
Jet's Oyster Succotash, 62, *63*

K

keta salmon, 123, 128–135
king (chinook) salmon, 123, 137–155
kitchen tools, *12*, 13–15
kombu, 187
Kumamoto oysters ("Kumos"), 54

L

Latkes, Potato and Beet, with Horseradish Sour
   Cream and Caviar, 302, *303*
Leeks, Caramelized, with Celery Root Tart and
   Caviar, 306–307
lemon juice, 10
Lemon Panko Sauce, 72
Lemon-Coriander Butter Sauce, 194–195
Lemongrass, Chile, and Basil, Wok-Seared Squid
   with, 113
Lemongrass and Shrimp Soup, Spicy, 84–85
Lemon-Thyme Sabayon, Oysters with, 61
Lime Cream, 214
Lime-Tequila Marinade, 169
lingcod, 127, 229–241

general discussion, 230–231
   Lingcod and Spot Prawn Paella with Charred
     Lemons, 240–241
   Lingcod Bouillabaisse with Piquillo Peppers,
     232, 233–234
   Lingcod with Citrus and Arbequina Olives,
     238, *239*
   Lingcod with Crispy Chickpeas and Quick-
     Pickled Apricots, 235–236
   See also fish, buying and handling
Linguine with Spot Prawns and Basil,
   Weeknight, *82*, 83

M

Mac and Cheese, Dungeness Crab, 74, 75
mackerel, 283, 289
mahi-mahi, 127, 255–265
   general discussion, 256–257
   Mahi-Mahi Red Curry with Thai Basil and
     Lime Leaves, 258, *259*
   Mahi-Mahi with Fried Basil, Avocado, and
     Tomato Salad, 260–261
   Mahi-Mahi with South Indian Spiced Mango,
     262, 263
   Mahi-Mahi with Tostones, Black Beans, and
     Tabasco Honey, 264–265
   See also fish, buying and handling
Mango, South Indian Spiced, with Mahi-Mahi,
   262, 263
Mango Salsa, 151
Mayo, Spicy, 274
Mint and Grapefruit, Pink Shrimp Salad with,
   86, *87*
Mint-Pistachio Pesto, 204
mirin, 10
Mousse, Smoked Trout, with Radish and
   Cucumber Quick Pickle, 198
mushrooms
   Agedashi Salmon with Asparagus, Shiitakes,
     and Salmon Roe, *130*, 131
   Cast-Iron Rainbow Trout, 192, *193*
   dried morels, rehydrating, 155
   Hajime's Steamed Banana Leaf Salmon, 129
   Oyster and Artichoke Soup, 57
   Roasted Salmon with Wild Mushrooms and
     Pinot Noir Sauce, 148–149
   Seared Salmon, Morels, and Peas with Green
     Goddess Sauce, 154–155
   Seared Salmon Tikka Masala, 140–141
   Smoked Halibut with Stinging Nettle Sauce
     and Nettle Gnocchi, 162–165

Tom Yum Goong (Spicy Shrimp and Lemongrass Soup), 84–85
mussels, 15, 20, 41–51
    general discussion, 42–43
    Mussels with Apple Cider and Thyme Glaze, 45
    Mussels with Bacon and Israeli Couscous, 48
    Mussels with Guinness Cream, 44
    Mussels with Pancetta and Vermouth, *46*, 47
    Mussels with Tomato-Espelette Butter, *50*, 51
    Pacific Cod and Mussels with Crispy Potatoes and Warm Olive Oil and Bay Broth, 248–249
    preparing and storing, how-to video for, 8

N

Nettle Sauce and Nettle Gnocchi, Smoked Halibut with Stinging, 162–165
nettles, foraging for, 162

O

Oil, Herb, 100, *101*
oil, vegetable, high-heat, 9
Okonomiyaki, Cod and Squid, 245–247, *246*
Olive Salad, 102
Olympia oysters ("olys"), 54
Onions, Caramelized, with Dad's Sardines on Crackers, 284
Onions, Pickled, 294
ono. *See* wahoo (ono)
orange, supreme, how-to video for, 238
Orange and Tamarind, Grilled Squid with, *116*, 117
Orange–Caper Sauce, Blood, 209–210
Orange-Chile Caramel, 271
oysters, 20, 53–63
    general discussion, 54–56
    Hangtown Fry, *58*, 59
    Jet's Oyster Succotash, 62, *63*
    Oyster and Artichoke Soup, 57
    Oysters on the Half Shell with Cucumber Sorbet, 60
    Oysters with Lemon-Thyme Sabayon, 61
    scrubbing and shucking, tools for, *12*, 15
    shucking, how-to video for, 8

P

Pacific cod, 127, 243–253
    Cod and Squid Okonomiyaki, 245–247, *246*
    general discussion, 244

Jamaican Cod Run Down with Boiled Green Bananas, 252–253
    Pacific Cod and Mussels with Crispy Potatoes and Warm Olive Oil and Bay Broth, 248–249
    Thai Fish Cakes with Cucumber-Chile Sauce, 250, *251*
    See also fish, buying and handling
Pacific halibut, 126–127, 157–175
    general discussion, 158
    Halibut Coconut Curry with Charred Chiles and Lime, 171–173, *172*
    Halibut Escabèche with Anchovy-Almond Salsa Verde, 166–167
    Halibut Tacos with Tequila-Lime Marinade and Red Cabbage Slaw, *168*, 169–170
    Halibut with Vanilla, Kumquat, and Ginger, 174, *175*
    Roasted Halibut with Radicchio-Pancetta Sauce, Peas, and Artichokes, 159
    Smoked Halibut with Stinging Nettle Sauce and Nettle Gnocchi, 162–165
    Steamed Halibut with Sizzling Chile-Ginger Oil, *160*, 161
    See also fish, buying and handling
Pacific oysters, 54
Paella with Charred Lemons, Lingcod and Spot Prawn, 240–241
Pancetta and Vermouth, Mussels with, *46*, 47
Pancetta-Radicchio Sauce, Peas, and Artichokes, with Roasted Halibut, 159
panko, about, 10
Panko Lemon Sauce, 72
Panzanella with Charred-Tomato Vinaigrette, Dungeness Crab, 69
pasta
    Dungeness Crab Mac and Cheese, *74*, 75
    Emmer Pasta con le Sarde, 288–289
    Fideos with Salmon, Clams, and Smoked Paprika, 153
    Homemade Fettuccine with Clams and Marjoram, 35–37
    Mussels with Bacon and Israeli Couscous, 48
    Smoked Halibut with Stinging Nettle Sauce and Nettle Gnocchi, 162–165
    Weeknight Linguine with Spot Prawns and Basil, *82*, 83
Pepper Rouille, Piquillo, 233
Pepper Salsa, Poblano, 272, *273*
Pepper Sauce, Piquillo, 291, 293
Pepper Sauce, Sherry, 114
Peppers, Squid with Chickpeas, Potatoes, and Piquillo, 112

perilla. *See* shiso
Pesto, Mint-Pistachio, 204
pickles
    Dilly Beans, 195
    Pickled Carrots, 99
    Pickled Jalapeños and Tomatoes, 274
    Pickled Mustard Seeds, 143
    Pickled Onions, 294
    Quick-Pickled Apricots, 235
    Radish and Cucumber Quick Pickle, 198
    Radish-and-Sesame Pickle, 184–185
pink salmon, 123, 128–135
Pinot Noir Sauce, 148
Pistachio-Mint Pesto, 204
Ponzu Sauce, 226
potato starch, 187
potatoes
    Albacore Niçoise, 207
    Caviar Hash, 299, *300*
    Nettle Gnocchi, 164–165
    Pacific Cod and Mussels with Crispy Potatoes and Warm Olive Oil and Bay Broth, 248–249
    Pan-Fried Trout with Dilly Beans, 194–195
    Potato and Beet Latkes with Horseradish Sour Cream and Caviar, 302, *303*
    Razor Clam Chowder, 34
    Squid with Chickpeas, Potatoes, and Piquillo Peppers, 112
    Wild Salmon Chowder with Fire-Roasted Tomatoes, 128
prawns. *See* shrimp

Q
quenelles, how-to video for, 8
Quinoa Cakes with Smoked Trout and Chive Sour Cream, *196*, 197

R
Radicchio-Pancetta Sauce, Peas, and Artichokes, Roasted Halibut with, 159
Radish and Cucumber Quick Pickle, 198
Radish-and-Sesame Pickle, 184–185
rainbow trout, 127, 189–198
    Cast-Iron Rainbow Trout, 192, *193*
    general discussion, 190–191
    Pan-Fried Trout with Dilly Beans, 194–195
    Potato and Beet Latkes with Horseradish Sour Cream and Caviar, 302, *303*
    Quinoa Cakes with Smoked Trout and Chive Sour Cream, *196*, 197

Smoked Trout Mousse with Radish and Cucumber Quick Pickle, 198
See also caviar, sustainable; fish, buying and handling
Ratatouille and Caramelized Figs, with Seared Albacore, 211–213, *212*
raw seafood, 311–312
recipe ingredients and terms, 9–11
recipes, difficulty levels of, 7
rice wine vinegar, seasoned, 11
roe. *See* caviar, sustainable

S
sake, about, 10
Sake-Steamed Black Cod with Ginger and Sesame, 184–185
salads
    Albacore Niçoise, 207
    Char with Grilled Romaine, Grapes, and Balsamic Vinegar, 220, *221*
    Cucumber-Hijiki Salad, 227
    Dungeness Crab Panzanella with Charred-Tomato Vinaigrette, 69
    Fennel, Currant, and Pine Nut Salad, 287
    Grilled Salmon with Watercress Salad, Rye Croutons, and Buttermilk Dressing, *142*, 143
    Grilled Sockeye Salmon with Fennel Two Ways, *146*, 147
    Grilled Spot Prawns with "Crack" Salad, 88, *89*
    Olive Salad, 102
    Pink Shrimp Salad with Grapefruit and Mint, 86, *87*
    Red Cabbage Slaw, 169
    Shiso-Cucumber Salad, *182*, 183
    Tomato-Basil Salad, 260
    White Bean and Sardine Salad with Fried Eggs, 285
salmon, wild, 20–21, 121–155
    Agedashi Salmon with Asparagus, Shiitakes, and Salmon Roe, *130*, 131
    Coffee-and-Spice-Rubbed Salmon Tacos with Charred Cabbage, Mango Salsa, and Avocado Cream, *150*, 151–152
    cooking tips, 126–127, 141
    Coriander-and-Lemon-Crusted Salmon with Poached Egg, Roasted Asparagus, and Hazelnuts, 144–145
    Easiest Recipe in This Book, The, 132
    Fideos with Salmon, Clams, and Smoked Paprika, 153

general discussion, 122–127
Grilled Salmon with Watercress Salad,
    Rye Croutons, and Buttermilk Dressing,
    142, 143
Grilled Sockeye Salmon with Fennel Two
    Ways, 146, *147*
Hajime's Steamed Banana Leaf Salmon, 129
Jerk-Spiced Salmon with Coconut Pot Liquor
    and Sweet Potato Fries, 137–139, *138*
Kerala Curry with Coconut Milk and Curry
    Leaves, *134*, 135
Potato and Beet Latkes with Horseradish Sour
    Cream and Caviar, 302, *303*
Roasted Salmon with Wild Mushrooms and
    Pinot Noir Sauce, 148–149
Salmon in Spiced Tamarind Soup, 133
Seared Salmon, Morels, and Peas with Green
    Goddess Sauce, 154–155
Seared Salmon Tikka Masala, 140–141
Wild Salmon Chowder with Fire-Roasted
    Tomatoes, 128
See also caviar, sustainable; fish, buying and
    handling; sushi
salmonberry blossoms, 163
Salsa, Mango, 151
Salsa, Poblano Pepper, 272, *273*
Salsa Verde, Anchovy-Almond, 166
salt, types of, 10
sardines, 127, 281
    butterflying and deboning, how-to video for, 8
    Dad's Sardines on Crackers with Caramelized
        Onions, 284
    Emmer Pasta con le Sarde, 288–289
    general discussion, 282–283, 289
    Smoked Sardines with Piquillo Pepper Sauce,
        290, 291–293
    White Bean and Sardine Salad with Fried
        Eggs, 285
scalers, fish, *12*, 14
scallops, 91–105, 127
    general discussion, 92–93
    preparing and cooking, how-to video for, 8, 93
    Scallop Crudo, 94, *95*
    Scallops, Grits, and Greens, 97
    Scallops with Carrot Cream and Marjoram,
        98, 99–100
    Scallops with Tarragon Beurre Blanc, 104–105
    searing, tips for, 96
    Summer Scallops with Corn Soup, 102–103
scimitar (filleting) knives, *12*, 14
sea salt, 10
seafood, how-to videos for, 8

seafood, raw, 311–312
seafood sustainability basics, 2, 17–23, 313
    See also specific type of seafood
shellfish, 8, 20, 21–22, 23, 312
    See also specific type of shellfish
Sherry Pepper Sauce, 114
shiso, about, 11
Shiso Oil, Geoduck Crudo with, 38, *39*
Shiso-Cucumber Salad, *182*, 183
shrimp, 20, 21–22, 79–89
    deveining, how-to video for, 8
    general discussion, 80–81
    Grilled Spot Prawns with "Crack" Salad,
        88, *89*
    Lingcod and Spot Prawn Paella with Charred
        Lemons, 240–241
    Pink Shrimp Salad with Grapefruit and Mint,
        86, *87*
    Tom Yum Goong (Spicy Shrimp and
        Lemongrass Soup), 84–85
    Weeknight Linguine with Spot Prawns and
        Basil, *82*, 83
skillets, cast-iron, 13
skin removal, how-to video for, 8
Slaw, Red Cabbage, 169
smoked fish
    Potato and Beet Latkes with Horseradish Sour
        Cream and Caviar, 302, *303*
    Smoked Halibut with Stinging Nettle Sauce
        and Nettle Gnocchi, 162–165
    Smoked Herring on Rye Bread with Radishes,
        Salted Butter, and Pickled Onions, 294, *295*
    Smoked Sardines with Piquillo Pepper Sauce,
        290, 291–293
    Smoked Trout and Chive Sour Cream, Quinoa
        Cakes with, *196*, 197
    Smoked Trout Mousse with Radish and
        Cucumber Quick Pickle, 198
    wok-smoking technique for, 163
sockeye salmon, 123, 137–155
soups
    Chilled Cucumber-Coconut Soup with
        Dungeness Crab, 73
    Lingcod Bouillabaisse with Piquillo Peppers,
        232, 233–234
    Oyster and Artichoke Soup, 57
    Razor Clam Chowder, 34
    Salmon in Spiced Tamarind Soup, 133
    Summer Scallops with Corn Soup, 102–103
    Tom Yum Goong (Spicy Shrimp and
        Lemongrass Soup), 84–85

Wild Salmon Chowder with Fire-Roasted
Tomatoes, 128
Soy Caramel Sauce, 71
spatulas, fish, *12*, 14
spice grinders, 15
squid, 107–117
Chorizo-and-Apple-Stuffed Squid with Sherry
Pepper Sauce, 114
Cod and Squid Okonomiyaki, 245–247, *246*
cutting and cleaning, how-to video for, 8
general discussion, 108–109, 289
Grilled Squid with Tamarind and Orange,
116, 117
Quick Squid with Red Chile Sauce and Herbs,
110, *111*
Squid with Chickpeas, Potatoes, and Piquillo
Peppers, 112
Wok-Seared Squid with Lemongrass, Chile,
and Basil, 113
Steamers with Beer, *32*, 33
Stuffing, Apple-and-Chorizo, 114
Succotash, Jet's Oyster, 62, *63*
sushi, 311–312
sustainability. *See* seafood sustainability basics
Sweet Potato Fries, 137

T
Tabasco Honey, 264
Tacos, Coffee-and-Spice-Rubbed Salmon, with
Charred Cabbage, Mango Salsa, and Avocado
Cream, *150*, 151–152
Tacos, Halibut, with Tequila-Lime Marinade
and Red Cabbage Slaw, *168*, 169–170
tamarind, 11
Grilled Squid with Tamarind and Orange,
116, 117
Salmon in Spiced Tamarind Soup, 133
Tamarind and Ginger Clams, 31
Tarragon Beurre Blanc, 104–105
Tart, Caramelized Leeks and Caviar with Celery
Root, 306–307
Tataki's "Faux-Nagi," 186–187
temperatures, cooking, 13, 127
Tequila-Lime Marinade, 169
thermometer, digital, *12*, 13
Tom Yum Goong (Spicy Shrimp and Lemongrass
Soup), 84–85
Tomato Bread, 102
Tomato Vinaigrette, Charred-, 69
Tomato-Basil Salad, 260

Tomatoes, Fire-Roasted, with Wild Salmon
Chowder, 128
Tomatoes, Pickled, 274
Tomato-Espelette Butter, 51
tools, kitchen, *12*, 13–15
Torta with Pickled Jalapeños and Tomatoes,
Wahoo, 274–275
Tostones, Black Beans, and Tabasco Honey,
Mahi-Mahi with, 264–265
trout. *See* rainbow trout
truffle salt, 301
tuna. *See* albacore tuna
tweezers, fish, *12*, 14

U
unagi (freshwater eel), 187

V
vegetable oil, high-heat, 9
vermouth, as cooking wine, 9
videos, how-to, 8
vinaigrettes
Apple-Vanilla Vinaigrette, *222*, 223–224
Carrot Vinaigrette, *182*, 183
Charred-Tomato Vinaigrette, 69

W
wahoo (ono), 127, 267–277
general discussion, 268–269
Wahoo Torta with Pickled Jalapeños and
Tomatoes, 274–275
Wahoo with Coriander-and-Cardamom-
Spiced Coconut Sauce, *276*, 277
Wahoo with Grilled Pineapple and Poblano
Pepper Salsa, 272, *273*
Wahoo with Orange-Chile Caramel and
Blackened Broccolini, 271
See also fish, buying and handling
wild fish *versus* farmed fish, 19–21
wine, cooking, 9
wine pairings, 8
See also specific recipe
Wine-and-Balsamic Sauce, Red-, 213
wok-smoking fish at home, 163

conversions

VOLUME			LENGTH		WEIGHT	
UNITED STATES	METRIC	IMPERIAL	UNITED STATES	METRIC	AVOIRDUPOIS	METRIC
¼ tsp.	1.25 ml		⅛ in.	3 mm	¼ oz.	7 g
½ tsp.	2.5 ml		¼ in.	6 mm	½ oz.	15 g
1 tsp.	5 ml		½ in.	1.25 cm	1 oz.	30 g
½ Tbsp.	7.5 ml		1 in.	2.5 cm	2 oz.	60 g
1 Tbsp.	15 ml		1 ft.	30 cm	3 oz.	90 g
⅛ c.	30 ml	1 fl. oz.			4 oz.	115 g
¼ c.	60 ml	2 fl. oz.			5 oz.	150 g
⅓ c.	80 ml	2.5 fl. oz.			6 oz.	175 g
½ c.	125 ml	4 fl. oz.			7 oz.	200 g
1 c.	250 ml	8 fl. oz.			8 oz. (½ lb.)	225 g
2 c. (1 pt.)	500 ml	16 fl. oz.			9 oz.	250 g
1 qt.	1 l	32 fl. oz.			10 oz.	300 g

TEMPERATURE

OVEN MARK	FAHRENHEIT	CELSIUS	GAS	WEIGHT (cont.)	
				11 oz.	325 g
				12 oz.	350 g
Very cool	250–275	130–140	½–1	13 oz.	375 g
Cool	300	150	2	14 oz.	400 g
Warm	325	165	3	15 oz.	425 g
Moderate	350	175	4	16 oz. (1 lb.)	450 g
Moderately hot	375	190	5	1 ½ lb.	750 g
	400	200	6	2 lb.	900 g
Hot	425	220	7	2¼ lb.	1 kg
	450	230	8	3 lb.	1.4 kg
Very Hot	475	245	9	4 lb.	1.8 kg

Each book I've written with April Pogue (left) and Clare Barboza (right) has included our dogs. Clare's dog, Nina, was back home in Vermont when we snapped this candid of Izzy licking Clare's face. So we did what professionals do and badly photoshopped Nina into the photo so she didn't feel left out. Also pictured: Pippin, who refused on principle to face the camera.

about the author

When she's not squid jigging, fishing, or cavorting through the woods picking wild things for her next meal, **BECKY SELENGUT** is a private chef, author, humorist, and cooking teacher. A regular instructor for PCC Natural Markets and the Pantry, Selengut is also the author of three other books on food: *Shroom*, *Not One Shrine*, and *How to Taste*. In her spare time she cohosts a comedy podcast called *Look Inside This Book Club* where she reviews only the free Look Inside samples of outrageous romance novels. Selengut lives on Capitol Hill in Seattle with her wife, April, and their two dogs, Izzy and Pippin. In the near future, Selengut hopes to clone herself so she can find the time to do more of these fun things other people call "work." Visit her web site at BeckySelengut.com.

Sommelier **APRIL POGUE** is the general manager at Loulay Kitchen & Bar in Seattle, WA. Her career in hospitality spans nineteen years having worked in iconic restaurants such as the Fifth Floor in San Francisco, Spago Beverly Hills in Los Angeles, and Seattle's Cascadia, Yarrow Bay Grill, and Wild Ginger.

CLARE BARBOZA is a food photographer who divides her time between the Pacific Northwest and southern Vermont. Clare's passion lies in telling visual stories, particularly stories about how food goes from the farm to the kitchen to the table. Her clients range from publishers and packaging companies to chefs, farms, and restaurants.

Printed in China

Published by Sasquatch Books

22 21 20 19 18   9 8 7 6 5 4 3 2 1

Editor: Susan Roxborough | Production editor: Em Gale
Design: Anna Goldstein | Photography: Clare Barboza
Food styling: Becky Selengut | Copyeditor: Rachelle Longé McGhee

Library of Congress Cataloging-in-Publication Data

Names: Selengut, Becky, author.
Title: Good fish : 100 sustainable seafood recipes from the Pacific Coast /
   Becky Selengut.
Description: Seattle, WA : Sasquatch Books, [2018] | Includes bibliographical
   references and index.
Identifiers: LCCN 2017041101 | ISBN 9781632171078 (pbk. : alk. paper)
Subjects: LCSH: Cooking, American--Pacific Northwest style. | International
   cooking. | Cooking (Seafood) | LCGFT: Cookbooks.
Classification: LCC TX715.2.P32 S45 2018 | DDC 641.6/92--dc23
LC record available at https://lccn.loc.gov/2017041101

ISBN: 978-1-63217-107-8

Sasquatch Books
1904 Third Avenue, Suite 710 | Seattle, WA 98101
(206) 467-4300 | www.sasquatchbooks.com